Hoosier School Heist:
How Corporations and Theocrats Stole Democracy From Public Education

Doug Martin

D1479130

Brooks Publications
Indianapolis

Published in 2014 by
Brooks Publications
P.O. Box 441166
Indianapolis, IN 46244
http://hoosierschoolheist.com/

Cover design and painting by Theresa Rosado:
http://theresarosado.com/

Printed in the United States of America

First Edition

10 9 8 7 6 5 4 3 2 1

ISBN: 978-0-9820840-14

Library of Congress Control Number: 2013958180

CONTENTS

ACKNOWLEDGMENTS

This book would not exist without the help I received from so many individuals. First off, I would like to thank *NUVO*, the *Indianapolis Star*, and Terre Haute's *Tribune Star* for publishing my letters to the editors concerning the assault on Indiana public schools. Acknowledgment also needs to be given to *MyFiredoglake*, *Parents Across America.org*, Douglas and Sarah Storm's *Common Errant*, and Jim Horn's *Schools Matter* where my research first appeared. I would also like to thank publisher Matthew Brooks and Theresa Rosado, my book's illustrator who also helped me research New Horizons Youth Ministries.

So as to not leave out literally hundreds of parents, teachers, politicians, and activists I have spoken with personally during the time of writing this book, I have decided it best to keep individual names off the acknowledgment pages. To have received permission to mention them here would have taken several months. Everyone who has emailed me, phoned me, given me information and insight, read my research, did research for me, or helped me in any way, this book is for you.

This book is also for all public school teachers and specifically public school teachers Mark Wright, Sharon Kramer, and Marilyn Hawkins (and her husband Jerry) who all changed my life. If not for them (and Julia Wernz, Sarah Long, and Linda Lonneman, who helped me move to Indianapolis), I would probably be in prison or the graveyard today.

And finally to my brother, my father, to the force behind the universe, and to my wonderful mother, who continues to stress the importance of being a good person and telling the truth.

Legal Notice and Disclaimer

INTRODUCTION: MYTHS, MINIONS, MISINFORMATION, AND TORTURE

Sell a country! Why not sell the air, the great sea, as well as the earth? Did not the Great Spirit make them all for the use of his children?
Tecumseh, addressed to William Henry Harrison

The idea that American schools are now failing the nation is a Big Lie. And like all Big Lies, it has created a great deal of mischief and unhappiness for hard-working citizens and educators who deserved better from America's political leaders, industrialists, media figures, and others responsible for creating and spreading the Manufactured Crisis.
David C. Berliner and Bruce J. Biddle, *The Manufactured Crisis: Myths, Fraud, and the Attack on America's Public Schools*, 1995.

O N SEPTEMBER 21, 1976, ECONOMIST ORLANDO LETELIER, working for the Institute for Policy Studies, was dismembered and murdered by a remote-controlled bomb planted in the car he was driving in Washington, DC by hit-men the CIA allowed to slip into the country. Less than a month earlier in "The Chicago Boys in Chile,"[1] Letelier had condemned economist Milton Friedman for training Chilean dictator Augusto Pinochet's chief economists who helped Pinochet carry out the starving, torturing, and killing of civilians standing in the way of unregulated and out-of-control capitalism. In Chicago, Friedman had not only prepared foreign economists to initiate programs with brutal regimes in Chile, Uruguay, Brazil, and Argentina, but he had even flown to meet Pinochet after the US-aided coup overthrew the democratically elected Salvador Allende. During Pinochet's reign of terror, up to 150,000 people were tortured and thousands killed, as the Chicago-trained economists locked in place a free-market privatizing scheme of the public infrastructure which led to massive unemployment, disastrous poverty, and school vouchers.[2]

Today in Chile, where only 45 percent of high schoolers attend traditional public schools, the blood still pours as protestors rebel against Friedman's school vouchers that Pinochet first used to replace the Chilean public school system. In August 2011, 600,000 students, parents, teachers, and workers from eighty labor groups marched in the Chilean streets, demanding a true public and free education from K through college. Thousands were jailed, and one of them, a sixteen-year-old boy, was shot dead.[3]

Pinochet and Friedman's crimes against humanity are not whispered when so-called school choice gets discussed in America today, and the fact that school vouchers were first applied as a weapon of racial segregation even earlier in Virginia is never mentioned. In 1955, Friedman wrote "The Role of Government in Education,"[4] which first promoted school vouchers, and shortly after Virginia established the first modern US school voucher law. As a way to duck the 1954 *Brown v. Board of Education* Supreme Court ruling, Virginia's arrangement subsidized white kids' enrollment in private schools, away from black students. Other southern states followed with school vouchers for white children until vouchers were ruled unconstitutional, as they violated the equal protection clause of the Fourteenth Amendment.

Now the school voucher push is invading America, with Friedman's original goal of defunding public schools and transferring taxpayer money, without any accountability, into private hands. Even though, as Rachel Tabachnick notes, children in the longest running US voucher programs in Milwaukee and Cleveland perform well below their counterparts in the public schools,[5] voucher advocates don't believe in holding private schools answerable to the same flawed demands like standardized testing they shove at public schools, because vouchers are not about better educating kids. Academic progress is irrelevant to voucher supporters, for the goal is not to improve schools through competition, as they claim, but to completely dismantle traditional public schools altogether. In fact, those calling for school privatization don't want to hold anyone with profit motives accountable, as Florida has proven. There Jeb Bush's voucher program has shelled out millions of taxpayer dollars to kidnappers, burglars, and sociopaths running private schools for kids with special needs, where students are hoarded in classes above liquor stores and beaten and deprived in environments free from state intervention, in what *Miami New Times'* Gus Garcia-Roberts has referred to as "a perverse science experiment, using disabled school kids as lab rats and funded by nine figures in taxpayer cash."[6] With the largest school voucher program in the country, Indiana lawmakers also have opened up this "lab" for business, expanding vouchers for special education kids. As we will see in chapter 2, the racism behind school vouchers in the 1950s is still very much alive today, as is the desire for profit.

School vouchers wed the free-marketers, the theocracy-seeking Religious Right, the Catholics, and higher-income families. As they have succeeded in using vouchers to "get the government out of the business of building and owning public housing, operating job-training programs and day-care centers, collecting garbage, and running hospitals and clinics," corporatists and their mouthpieces like the libertarian Cato Institute's Joseph L. Bast and David Harmer "see vouchers as a major step toward the complete privatization of schooling....the *only* way to dismantle the current socialist regime."[7] Religious Right school leaders are thrilled to acquire public money to teach creationism in their schools, and Catholic school officials, having less funding because sex abuse lawsuits against the US church have sent people with their money running,[8] are eager for a taxpayer bailout for their private schools which pick the best students they can pull in. Low-income parents can't afford the tuition the voucher does not cover at non-religious private schools; well-off parents can. Vouchers delight the anti-government Religious Right, the Catholics, and the affluent parents sending their kids to elite private schools, but more importantly they drain money from public schools. It is no coincidence that this shortage of funding places these public schools in a bad position—with fewer teachers, aides, and resources—so for-profit education management companies can take them over with temporary teachers or justify starting charter schools by deeming the neighborhood schools as "failing."

Milton Friedman played a role in launching the profitable charter school movement in America, too. Ninety-three years old and on his deathbed, Friedman kicked off New Orleans' charter school groundswell after Hurricane Katrina. In a *Wall Street Journal* op-ed three months after the hurricane, Friedman wrote that it was the perfect time to demolish what was left of the New Orleans school system and turn its keys over to the well-to-do to make money.[9] Naomi Klein responds to Friedman's school privatization push in *Shock Doctrine: The Rise of Disaster Capitalism*:

> In sharp contrast to the glacial pace with which the levees were repaired and the electricity grid brought back online, the auctioning-off of New Orleans' school system took place with military speed and precision. Within 19 months, with most of the city's poor residents still in exile, New Orleans' public school system had been almost completely replaced by privately run charter schools.
>
> The Friedmanite American Enterprise Institute enthused that "Katrina accomplished in a day . . . what Louisiana school reformers couldn't do after years of trying." Public school teachers, meanwhile, were calling Friedman's plan "an educational land grab." I call these orchestrated raids on the public sphere in the wake of catastrophic events, combined with the treatment of disasters as exciting market opportunities, "disaster capitalism."[10]

Making money from disasters is a Wall Street specialty, and investors have jumped on the opportunity for school privatization. Besides generating tax-exempt bonds, stocks, and other shady financial gimmicks, school privatization allows big bank

CEOS, private equity firm honchos, and hedge fund managers to collect interest on loans to non-unionized charter schools which employ a temporary teacher workforce. The mega-wealthy subsidizing charter schools also receive new markets tax credits from the US Department of Treasury's Community Development Financial Institution Fund to write off their donations, dollar for dollar, on their taxes. As *New York Daily News'* Juan Gonzalez first noticed, by using the new markets tax credits, investors can double their money in no time. In an interview with *Democracy Now's* Amy Goodman, Gonzalez details how these schemes have worked in Albany, New York:

> The investors who put up the money to build the charter schools get to basically virtually double their money in seven years through a 39 percent tax credit from the federal government. In addition, this is a tax credit on money that they're lending, so they're collecting interest on the loans, as well as getting the 39 percent tax credit. They piggyback the tax credit on other kinds of federal tax credits, like historic preservation or job creation or Brownfields credits. The result is, you can put in $10 million and in seven years double your money.
>
> And the problem is that the charter schools end up paying in rents the debt service on these loans. And so, now a lot of the charter schools in Albany are straining paying their debt—their rent has gone up from $170,000 to $500,000 in a year, or huge increases in their rents, as they strain to pay off these loans, these construction loans. And the rents are eating up huge portions of their total cost. And, of course, the money is coming from the state.
>
> So, one of the big issues is that so many of these charter schools are not being audited. No one knows who are the people making these huge windfall profits as the investors. And often there are interlocking relationships between the charter school boards and the nonprofit groups that organize and syndicate the loans.[11]

Gonzalez is right. Unlike traditional public school boards, charter school boards are unelected, undemocratic, and cloaked in mystery. Their conflicts of interest enable schemes like high rent to waste public education money. Information in the charter school tax records is very limited. Moreover, when researchers have filed freedom of information act requests with charter schools, the CEOs and boards either completely disregarded the requests or only released select financial material about these schools. Hedge fund managers especially like this lack of transparency. Their inner workings on Wall Street, likewise, are almost impossible for the public to access.

Hedge fund managers working to eliminate veteran teachers from the schools have already been making money from these teachers' pensions. As Matt Taibbi notices in *Rolling Stone*, Paul Tudor Jones—a mega-rich charter school investor in New York City—"manages $15.7 million from the School Employees' Retirement System of Ohio." Jones' friend Dan Loeb already oversees money invested from a whole slew of various state employees' pensions in his hedge fund, including ones in Ohio. Loeb—who gifted former Indiana superintendent of schools Tony Bennett $25,000 for his reelection campaign—spoke at an event in April 2013 held by the Council of Institutional Investors (CII), "an umbrella group that represents the institutions who manage the retirement and benefit funds of public and corporate employees all over America—from bricklayers to Teamsters to teachers." The event's moderator was none other than Anne Sheehan, the director of corporate governance for the California State Teachers' Retirement System. It was obvious Loeb was courting the CII for a chance to "manage" its money. Both Loeb and Jones sit on the board of Students First New York, run by corporate school veteran Michelle Rhee, which is calling for states to end teachers' defined benefit pension funds around the country "in favor of defined contribution plans, where the benefits are not guaranteed." What is more, since Wall Street crashed the economy in 2008, many states, including Ohio where Loeb manages some of the Ohio Public Employees Retirement System's funds, are now advocating for or have passed laws for higher retirement ages for teachers and more contributions from workers, since the state governments either don't have the money to pay out for pensions or are lying about not having it. As Taibbi writes: "In other words, Loeb has been soliciting the retirement money of public workers, then turning right around and lobbying for those same workers to lose their benefits. He's essentially asking workers to pay for their own disenfranchisement." Hedge fund managers like Loeb want their hands on teachers' pensions (and more financial contributions from teachers) and to pocket what they don't pay out, at the same time, getting their "two-and-twenty cut, or whatever obscene percentage of their retirement monies" the managers get as a fee to manage the money.[12]

To legitimize the privatization of schools so hedge fund managers and wealthy investors could cash in, the government and billionaires first had to manufacture a crisis. This manufactured crisis is rooted in early twentieth century America when the business sector attempted to place Taylorism in the public schools to spit out students as interchangeable parts in factory-line production to better its bottom line. The recent school crisis myth has circulated since Sputnik and was carried over into the National Commission on Excellence in Education's 1983 hyperbolic *A Nation at Risk* report, followed by the 1989 Business Roundtable (which now sponsors Indiana's Education Roundtable) guidelines to bust teachers unions, deskill teachers, destroy students' critical thinking, and give companies cover for job outsourcing. As David C. Berliner and Bruce J. Biddle's *The Manufactured Crisis: Myths, Fraud, and the Attack on America's Public Schools* proves, cronies working for policymakers and corporatists today have merely updated the propaganda first used during the Reagan years, as they did for Bill Clinton's Goals 2000 and George W. Bush's No Child Left Behind, the latter which required all schools where 100 percent of students were not performing proficiently on standardized tests be restructured by 2014, priming them for privatization. Barack Obama is continuing the manufactured crisis by pressing for charter school expansion, using Recovery Act money to fund 700 charter schools,[13] and calling for teacher evaluations based on faulty test score measurements for states to qualify for Race to the Top funding. The manufactured crisis paints students as unprepared for future jobs and public schools as failing, all myths meant to evoke fear in the public to carry out the privatization agenda.[14]

One can't flick on a TV or open a newspaper without hearing the myth that public schools are not preparing students for the twenty-first century workforce. Despite constant rants about STEM (science, technology, engineering, and mathematics), America has too many trained scientists, as Harvard labor economist Richard Freeman and others have remarked.[15] Actually, one recent study suggests that America needs more plumbers and carpenters, not scientists.[16] Besides giving cover to companies who outsource jobs, the STEM hype ignores studies like Indiana University's Center for Evaluation and Education Policy's recent report, which shows that in math and science "Indiana eighth-graders outperformed most of the world and scored ahead of the U.S. average, continuing a trend for the state."[17] The lack of jobs for engineers in Indiana is the untold story. An August 2012 Indiana University Indiana Business Research Center report notes that since Wall Street collapsed the economy Indiana college graduates with engineering degrees now have one of the "highest probabilities of becoming unemployed," compared to students graduating with other degrees.[18] Peter Cappelli, director of Wharton's Center for Human Resources at the University of Pennsylvania, says US students are doing just fine; it's the companies' hiring practices that are at fault. Corporations do not want to take the time and money to train workers. In surveys, companies hardly ever mention job applicants lacking academic skills. According to Cappelli there is no skills gap in America.[19]

This workforce readiness meme is just one of many repeated constantly by Indiana newspapers and TV stations which advertise corporate school talking points, portray front group spokespeople as "experts," and seldom, if ever, question the profit motives and rigged research behind the corporate-sponsored statements that our schools are failing. Some reporters and editors are undoubtedly clueless, but many con the audience because their papers are owned by corporations. Some, like *Indianapolis Star's* Scott Elliott, lead organizations funded by many out to privatize public schools.

Fort Wayne's *Journal Gazette* thankfully is an exception to the rule of newspapers hyping the school privatizing agenda. In a *Journal Gazette* piece, Tracy Warner ridicules school privatization public relations campaigns by comparing schools and teachers to police departments and the police. With tongue in cheek, Warner writes that crime is up, so we should permit charter police departments to remove funding from local police stations because crime rate reflects how terrible Indiana police departments have become with their overpaid officers who only care about bloated pensions. Officers' salaries, Warner joshes, should be based on how many crimes occur in their neighborhoods. Indiana, Warner says, could even authorize universities like Ivy Tech to sponsor charter police departments.[20]

Warner's spoof would be funny if it didn't so brilliantly peg the school privatizers' absurd talking points, and one can expose a few more myths. First off, all legitimate studies confirm that charter schools either perform no better or worse than traditional public schools.[21] In fact, most Indiana schools (and those in other states) are not "failing." After examining twenty-three years of data, Dr. Vic Smith notes that Indiana schools are "currently performing at or near their historic high."[22] If charter schools were held to the same accountability standards as traditional public schools in Indiana and elsewhere, a good majority of them would be closed down. In Indiana, as we will witness in chapter 3, charter schools with dismal records are kept open (and their leaders able to lease or buy a closed-down traditional public school building for merely one dollar a year) because of political ties.

To sneak more politically connected for-profit charter schools into Indiana, in 2010 legislators cut $300 million annually from the public school budget and mandated tax caps to purposely ensure the destruction of public schools. After so-called school choice bills passed in 2011, public schools lost

$38 million to private schools in 2012 alone.[23] Today school corporations are forced to ask voters, who can't pay their own property taxes because they lost jobs in the Wall Street meltdown the hedge fund managers helped create, to vote on referendums to fund the schools. In recent years, voters have only approved new school construction projects in sixteen of the forty school districts that have asked for more money.[24] Thanks to state lawmakers, school districts needing cash to pay for programs and avoid laying off personnel must also ask for local tax referendums through special elections they sometimes have to fund themselves. Since the state controls the purse strings, Republican lawmakers have purposely bolted in place everything needed to start closing down Indiana schools and expanding for-profit charter schools.

The traditional public schools not measuring up in any shape, way, or form are in poverty-stricken areas where government money intentionally has been decreasing for years. Indiana's new "follow the student" funding formula, too, is set up to lead to a system where rich counties will win in the long run. Hammond schools, where 20 percent of households receive public assistance income, "will lose $2.3 million in state funding over the next two years." In Hamilton County where one in every three households brings in over $200,000 yearly, Carmel Clay Schools "will gain almost $1 million."[25] The minority and 342,172 poor kids in the Hoosier state are the victims.[26] In Indiana, close to 70 percent of charter school students are minorities, and over 72 percent of charter school students live in poverty.[27] As Matthew DiCarlo writes at the Shanker Institute's blog, the state gave "a little over half" of Indiana's poverty-stricken high schools "an F or D [grade], and "of the 125 elementary/middle schools that got an F" in 2012, "100 were in the highest poverty quartile."[28] These are the ones in threat of being taken over by the state and handed to for-profit companies operated by government officials' friends and campaign donors. This history of not funding schools which low-income kids attend is no coincidence. By not financing these poor schools appropriately, government officials have shaped the perfect disaster for the privileged class to profit from.

To kick off this school heist, Indiana locked in a place a confusing, Jeb Bush Florida-based system to grade its schools on test scores, so they can be deemed "failing" and given to privatizers. Standardized tests questions are geared toward upper-income level whites and discriminate against non-whites and poor students. These tests are not used at the expensive private schools (where teachers hold advanced degrees) those working to privatize the public schools attended. Creative kids, moreover, seldom ever do well on these tests. Standardized tests are weapons of mass misinformation. Hoosier scholar Phil Harris, Joan Harris, and Bruce M. Smith detail the misuse of standardized tests in their *The Myths of Standardized Tests: Why They Don't Tell You What You Think They Do*, a must-read condemnation of George W. Bush's No Child Left Behind, Obama's testing blueprint, and former Indiana school superintendent Tony Bennett's drive for testing "drill camps."[29] Indiana spends roughly $46 million on standardized testing and remediation yearly, instead of putting money into poorly funded schools and pre-school for all.[30]

Overusing standardized tests also has political advantages. Although a calamity for teachers and students, standardized tests aid corporate politicians like Mitch Daniels in less obvious ways. Counting on an uninformed public to vote them into office, politicians like how these tests stifle the development of critical thinking skills necessary in a truly democratic society. Many politicians have ties to the companies behind the testing, too. Pearson, the educational mega-corporation funding many a lawmaker, has made a killing off of standardized tests since No Child Left Behind became law, along with Libyan dictator Muammar Gaddafi who owned a $453 million stake in Pearson.[31] The McGraw-Hill family, owners of the testing mega-giant holding Indiana taxpayers hostage in a $95 million contract for ISTEP, are long-standing friends with the Bush family,[32] which is very active in promoting the corporate school model in the Hoosier state.

More importantly, in reference to this book's first chapter, standardized tests are designed to stress teachers since their jobs depend on their students passing. In this way, corporate school leaders either drive or fire well-qualified teachers out of the workforce. The more good teachers leave the public schools, the more the schools are set up for "failure." As traditional public schools are closed and more for-profit charter schools are opened, these qualified teachers can be replaced with deskilled, low-wage, temporary teachers. These temporary teachers, if they are able to bond at all with students they have nothing in common with, disappear for high-paying careers after only a few years, leaving kids who need constant emotional connections feeling used. The kids are being used. Instead of receiving highly qualified teachers, they get five-week boot camp recruits who, for rich people seeking to dismantle the teaching workforce for profit's sake, are as disposable as the school children. This is fine with Milton Friedman disciples like Mitch Daniels and Indiana Republican lawmakers who want the privatization of public schools at any cost. It is also what makes the Indianapolis Mind Trust and its pseudo-liberal supporters tick. ■

1.
KIDNAPPING KIDS' TEACHERS:
THE PRETEND-LIBERAL SAVIORS

Teacher quality has been found to be 20 times more important than any other factor, including poverty, in determining which kids succeed. Class size, by comparison, is virtually meaningless.
Mitch Daniels, mouthing manufactured lies, "Union Revamping Reform Effort, Says ISTA Chief Nate Schnellenberger," *Evansville Courier & Press,* **January 17, 2011**

Most of the times, their hands get tied by either the contract language or the statute language. We have to take a look at the process used, and the complexity of the process, to really remove poor principals and poor teachers.
Tony Bennett, "How Hard Is It to Fire a Teacher, Really?" *Indianapolis Business Journal,* **November 6, 2010**

W HEN FORMER NBC *TODAY* SHOW CO-HOST AND OBAMA stumper Jane Pauley walked on stage at the Indiana Repertory Theater in Indianapolis on June 3, 2010,[1] some in the audience understood what was behind the corporate reporter's supposed empathy for Indiana's school children, even though it may have eluded those there to see a celebrity. At this Mind Trust event for ousted Indianapolis Democratic mayor Bart Peterson, Pauley bragged about her son Ross, a California KIPP charter school teacher and past director at Boston's MATCH Corps Recruiting, a charter school outfit, tutor-training ground, and teacher residency program along the lines of the corporate-led Teach for America. Pauley talked about the wonderful things she heard in Washington elite circles about the school reform movement back in her hometown, Indianapolis, and just had to lend a hand.

As it did with entertainer John Legend, who spoke at Butler University later in 2010, the Mind Trust was using Pauley—a Mind Trust board member and donor—as its celebrity spokesperson to sell the 2011 dismantling of Indiana public schools with several million in its bank account. A day after 2011 opened, the Mind Trust announced it was hunting for more fellows to join its Education Entrepreneur Fellowship program. Each fellow would receive a $90,000 salary plus $20,000 more to unleash a school privatization project on Indiana. Full benefits would arrive with the package.[2] The Mind Trust claims it is about giving every Indianapolis child an excellent education, but its goal is to turn public schools into money-grabbing private enterprises.

The Mind Trust typifies America's counterfeit political Left. Mouthing the rhetoric of class warfare, civil rights, and female empowerment, the mock liberals at Education Sector, the Center for American Progress, and the New America Foundation, all supportive of the Mind Trust specifically or school privatization in general (and most bringing home six-figure salaries), attack teachers unions and public schools and connive to mount in place a school system based on corporate profit, one which disenfranchises the female teachers and minority and poor students they claim to be helping.

Started in 2006 with backing from the Richard M. Fairbanks Foundation,[3] the Mind Trust is the product of Bart Peterson, then the Indianapolis Democratic mayor who lost his reelection bid partially because of his corporate school agenda. Peterson's former Indy charter school director, David Harris, is currently paid by the wealthy 1 percent nearly $200,000 yearly to command the Mind Trust, which places him in the top 2 percent of earners nationwide.[4]

Peterson and Harris' crony school capitalism goes way back. In 2001, after a Democratic governor signed a law making Peterson the first US mayor to authorize charter schools, the duo have carried the company water in Indianapolis. School privatizers have been infesting Indiana, with Bart Peterson—deemed the "Peyton Manning of Charter Schools"[5]—and David Harris opening the way for private profit. In fact, Peterson's family business, the Precedent Companies, a real estate development and construction services firm headed by Bart before he became mayor, was paid over $664,000 to renovate Stonegate Early College High School, once named Lawrence Early College High School, under mayor Greg Ballard's watch.[6] The charter school was so financially in shambles that the school's unelected board—which included lieutenant governor Becky Skillman's educational point man Virgil Madden—not the mayor's office, eventually closed it.

Leaders of for-profit charter schools and bank tycoons also did extremely well under Mayor Peterson's watch. When the Annie E. Casey Foundation from Baltimore put up funding in Indianapolis for fifteen charter schools with then-Mayor Peterson in April 2005, the Local Initiatives Support Corporation (LISC), replete with Walmart and US Department of Education money, gave a financial guarantee so that JP Morgan Chase could lend up to $20 million to charter schools and profit from interest. But it was merely show and tell. The City of Indy, with taxpayer money, was really the first entity responsible for paying off the loans if the charter schools failed.[7] Today, the almost $2 billion strong Annie E. Casey Foundation, which bankrolls the Mind Trust, Oregon-based Stand for Children, and Teach for America, is run by UPS' former CEO Michael L. Eskew, a Vincennes-born Eli Lilly board member.

With Bart Peterson now drug giant Eli Lilly's senior vice president of corporate affairs and communication, the Mind Trust might as well be called a division of Eli Lilly. The Lilly Endowment, the Ruth Lilly Philanthropic Foundation, and the Eli Lilly and Company Foundation all subsidize the Mind

Trust. As a Lilly all-star like Mitch Daniels before him, Bart Peterson has stocked the Mind Trust board with several existing or former Lilly officials, including Alecia DeCoudreaux, general counsel at Lilly USA, former Mind Trust president Claire Fiddian-Green who now mans the state authorizing Indiana Charter School Board, and Anne Shane, the Lilly Endowment's community development and education consultant, a Tony Bennett campaign donor, and a Teach for America Indiana board chair.

The same deception and lack of ethics behind the Mind Trust's supposed concern for teachers and minority students have been Eli Lilly's trademarks regarding its drug consumers for years. While claiming to care about American seniors, Eli Lilly's illegal marketing of Zyprexa to nursing homes set state Medicaid programs in the red. According to Dr. David Graham in testimony before a DC congressional hearing, it also may have killed thousands of elderly people yearly. Even in patients taking legally marketed Zyprexa, the drug has caused a whole host of serious health problems that Lilly should have or did see coming. In 2009, Lilly agreed to pay a $1.4 billion settlement for dishonestly marketing Zyprexa,[8] but that same year the drugmaker bought out Monsanto's cow growth hormone that taints milk and causes cancer, dozens of studies show. It was a move Jeffrey Smith from the Institute for Responsible Technology calls the "perfect cancer profit cycle," since Lilly also makes drugs to treat the disease.[9] When Mitch Daniels was a Lilly high-roller, the drug company weathered some of its biggest corruption cases. The Center for the Public Integrity writes:

> In the decade that Daniels climbed the corporate ladder at Eli Lilly, the company was illegally marketing its leading osteoporosis drug, Evista, as well as its blockbuster antipsychotic, Zyprexa, putting tens of thousands of patients in harm's way. Lilly pleaded guilty to two criminal misdemeanors, paid more than $2.7 billion in fines and damages, settled more than 32,000 personal injury claims—and copped to one of the largest state consumer protection cases involving a drug company in U.S. history.[10]

But these fines are chump change compared to the billions Eli Lilly gets from county, city, state, and federal tax breaks, aided by the likes of the Bush family and Bart Peterson, money which could be used to fund traditional public schools. Using *The Nation's* Alexander Cockburn's research, psychologist Bruce Levine points out how then-vice president George H. W. Bush, a former Lilly board of directors member who failed to disclose his Lilly stock ownership, "sought special tax breaks from the IRS for Lilly and other pharmaceutical corporations that were manufacturing in Puerto Rico"[11] where one Lilly facility was later cited by the Food and Drug Administration for failing "to adequately investigate critical deviations" of its drug Humalog.[12] When Bart Peterson was mayor, Indianapolis gave $1.6 billion in tax breaks and incentives to Lilly in 2004, when the drug company promised to generate 9,500 jobs. After Lilly hired a few thousand workers, it decided those jobs were no longer needed and slashed many of them to boost its profit. Recently, Lilly moved $21 billion in untaxed profits abroad, while Indiana school buildings fall apart, art classes gets cancelled, and teachers are fired and replaced by temporary recruits.[13]

Lilly and the Mind Trust specialize in churning out these temporary teachers in Indiana with the goal of lowering standards from the top down, producing fewer credentialed educators and hiring those with few degrees. The plan, utilized by most corporate schoolers, calls for anchoring in place a temporary, low-paid, non-union, deskilled workforce to ultimately teach in an all-charter school educational system owned by private and for-profit companies. These teachers, most trained a mere five weeks, are already numerous in Indianapolis and other US cities. Often they arrive from Ivy League universities, share absolutely no life experience with their students, and after a few years leave for Wall Street or build their own for-profit charter schools and are replaced by another new batch of temporary teachers. Short-term teachers save defunded school districts and charter school management CEOS money, since they don't require much pension money or pay raises. Plans are already in place to fire professors at universities whose students' students don't do well on standardized tests then close down schools of education and replace them with corporate-sponsored teacher prep academies to mass-produce these interim teachers to enter our most vulnerable children's classrooms nationwide. In Indiana, a 2013 law promoted by Republican and American Legislative Exchange Council (ALEC) member Jim Banks requires the state Department of Education to evaluate schools of education based on their students' teacher licensure tests scores and the number of times these teachers took to pass these licensure tests.

To drive a wedge between qualified teachers already in the classroom, Lilly has given millions of dollars to academic opportunists at the University of Indianapolis' Center of Excellence in Leadership and Learning (CELL) to implement TAP (The System for Teacher and Student Advancement) in Indiana.[14] Built on the myth that teachers worship money as much as greedy CEOS do, TAP is a teaching accountability and merit-pay program operating in seventeen states. Supported by billionaire Eli Broad and the Chicago-based Joyce Foundation, the liberal-leaning nonprofit whose board of directors once included a young Barack Obama, TAP was launched in 1999 by the family foundation of convicted felon Michael Milken who served two years in prison in the early '90s after being charged with ninety-eight counts of racketeering and securities fraud.[15] TAP seeks to pit teacher against teacher, hold teachers' jobs and pay over their heads, and create very uncomfortable work environments. In 2011, instead of financing preschool and other proven educational programs, Indiana gave out $48 million of federal money to roll out TAP in forty-four schools.[16]

Although Lilly had given the Mind Trust $4 million since 2007[17] to recruit short-term teachers to Indianapolis, the Mind Trust's Grow What Works ceremony at the Indianapolis JW Marriott in May 2011 was important for showing off more national celebrities and its timing. Lilly PR people shot out a press release featuring Arne Duncan's praise for Lilly and the Mind Trust's "philanthropic investments" since America needed to start "growing what works as schools, as districts, as states, and as a country."[18] Known for privatizing Chicago's public schools, US Secretary of Education Duncan had given an address at corporate-led Teach for America's twentieth anniversary summit a few months earlier. Duncan would have fit right into the Mind Trust/Lilly event which starred Jane Pauley, governor Mitch Daniels, *New York Times*' corporate slack David Brooks, and Eli Lilly executives, held just days after Daniels, on April 20, 2011, signed the Republican-backed collective bargaining bill, wiping out all teacher negotiations on evaluation procedures, class size, and working conditions except salary and wage-related benefits. At the end of April, Daniels penned Senate Bill 1 into law, requiring that yearly teacher evaluations focus on student test scores and lessening the influence of teacher seniority in the new merit-pay system. Setting younger teachers against older ones who should be mentors, the law says the amount of degrees teachers earn shouldn't determine what they are paid. To take advantage of Daniels' anti-teacher bills, Lilly granted $2.5 million to the Mind Trust at the Grow What Works ceremony to set up an even more conducive environment in Indiana for the New Teacher Project and Teach for America.

IN NOVEMBER 2011, the Mind Trust landed another Lilly Endowment grant of $3.5 million for the New Teacher Project and Teach for America to train 350 more temporary teachers for Indianapolis.[19] The Mind Trust has passed $1.7 million to the New Teacher Project since 2006, when the group first arrived in Indiana.[20] The New Teacher Project is headquartered in Brooklyn and from 2011 to 2012 had over $62 million in revenue. Praised by pseudo-liberals like the *Washington Post's* Ezra Klein, in 2007 the New Teacher Project and the Mind Trust teamed with Catholic Marian University to form the In-

dianapolis Teaching Fellows program, which, according to the
New Teacher Project website, has trained 300 temporary teachers for Indianapolis and Northwest Indiana. Ariela Rozman,
the New Teacher Project's CEO, sits on the Mind Trust board.
From October 2011 to the end of September 2012, Rozman
made a hair short of $300,000 in total compensation to plant
short-term teachers across the country, even though she comes
from the consulting and pharmaceutical industries and has no
teaching experience.[21]

With branches in seventeen states and twenty-five cities, the
New Teacher Project has recruited or trained over 28,000 teaching fellows. Like Teach for America, the New Teacher Project
sends teaching troops into minority areas in urban cities where
privatization agents falsely maintain that traditional teachers
are lazy, that all black families desire charter schools, and that
minorities are incapable of running and bettering their own
classrooms. The New Teacher Project collects revenue from
contracts with states and budget-grieved school districts which
dodge colleges of education to hire teachers who won't stay
around long enough to cost too much money. It receives taxpayer money from the federal government's AmeriCorps,
which pays $5,000 of the $6,000 cost to train each of its new
teachers.[22]

The New Teacher Project was founded in 1997 by the
Oprah-hyped former DC school chancellor and Democrat
Michelle Rhee, who is quite snug in right-wing circles. Besides
donating money to Republican candidates, Rhee embraced
Scott Walker's Wisconsin union-busting and joined Florida's
Republican governor Rick Scott's educational transition team.
Rhee gets paid well to use Republican talking points to bash
unions and criticize teachers. One Kent State speaking engagement in 2011 got Rhee $35,000, a first-class flight, a VIP hotel
room, and her own luxury rent-a-car, tax free.[23] After telling
teachers at a statehouse rally that "teachers are all making too
much money,"[24] Mitch Daniels had Rhee pump his sweeping
anti-teacher bills when she spoke to religious and charter school

students who skipped school to join her and the governor at the statehouse Ed Reform Rocks Rally sponsored by the Indiana Chamber of Commerce and right-wing School Choice Indiana. When speaking to the *Indianapolis Star's* Scott Elliott before the rally, Rhee sold the corporate school model hook, line, and sinker. "The pressure charters put on DC public schools to change was an important one," Rhee said. "Charters are regulated. You just don't let anybody open a charter. You have to meet certain thresholds of quality, and we have to have an accountability system that says if you are not doing well by kids, we close you down."[25] Rhee's "You don't let anyone" is appropriate, given that charter school leaders with friends on the DC charter school authorizing board make out fabulously in the city's system of unaccountability.

In December 2008, *Washington Post* reporters David S. Fallis and April Witt unearthed severe cronyism at the city's charter school authorizing board beginning a few years before Rhee's rein and continuing until 2010. As a DC Public Charter School Board member and a United Bank employee, Thomas Nida funneled money to his employer, sometimes even approving to increase student enrollment and public funding to charter schools his bank was profiting from. Nida had been placed on the board in 2003, and out of "the $55 million United has lent since then to charters, their landlords or developers, Nida has been directly involved in loans worth at least $35 million, as loan officer or a bank representative." Furthermore, "United loans have paid for the purchase, refinancing or renovation of buildings used by at least 10 of the 60 schools that Nida regulates."

To justify this cozy arrangement, Nida maintained that his United Bank officemate Thomas McCracken handled the charter school loans and Nida was merely a "mentor as necessary." Nida told the *Washington Post* he did not receive any direct commissions himself on the bank loans but admitted the bank pays him a yearly bonus on how much loan business he brings to the company. The reporters proved Nida's statements were inaccurate. When United Bank loaned $11.6 million to Fred Ezra's Bethesda-based developing company in 2004 to turn two dilapidated warehouses into charter school-friendly buildings, "Nida was the loan officer, records show, and he acknowledged that he toured the buildings with the buyers on behalf of the bank." Nida also helped Ezra rent the buildings. Without disclosing his conflict of interest, Nida met with charter school officials wishing to rent out the warehouses. William E. Doar Jr. Public Charter School for the Performing Arts struck a deal to lease the top floor of one of the warehouses, hoping to use the entire warehouse for its school. Fallis and Witt write that after Nida and his board approved a higher student enrollment for the school, United Bank lent the school $1.6 million for renovations.

If one believes academic excellence is the temporary teacher and charter school movement's motive, as the Mind Trust and Lilly claim, nothing speaks clearer of corporate leaders' true intentions than Nida himself. Having written a banking primer on charter schools, Nida—as Fallis and Witt point out—swanked to other bankers that after twenty-five deals with charter schools "I've had no losses or even late payments. The loans give me my largest margins and they are the most profitable piece of my portfolio." His appointment to the DC Public Charter School Board was based on a recommendation from the executive branch of the Bush White House, after he published an article in 2002 praising the profits from taxpayer money that banks could net through charter schools. The DC charter board took Nida's lessons to heart. Other board members also cashed in on another $20 million in taxpayer money through various banking and other schemes. [26]

Rhee, supposedly watching over the city privatizers for three and a half years as D.C's school chief, didn't pay much attention to what the DC charter school board was up to because she was too busy attempting to conceal her own scandals. Just days before the Indy Ed Reform Rocks rally, *USA Today* revealed that high test scores in DC, which Rhee flaunted while the city's school chancellor, were fabrications. The paper's investigation showed that since 2008 over one hundred DC schools had extensive erasures on test scores. Rhee—who became school leader in 2007—had praised and given bonuses to teachers based on what was essentially a cheating scandal. At Crosby S. Noyes Education Campus from 2007 to 2008, "six classrooms out of the eight taking tests ...were flagged by Mc-Graw-Hill because of high wrong-to-right erasure rates. The pattern was repeated in the 2008-09 and 2009-10 school years, when 80% of Noyes classrooms were flagged by McGraw-Hill." *USA Today* reporters went on to state that "odds are better for winning the Powerball grand prize than having that many erasures by chance, according to statisticians." Actually, the state education superintendent had noticed problems and called on Rhee and other officials to investigate. Rhee and her officials did, hiring Caveon Consulting Services, a Utah company which admits that its investigators merely asked teachers if they were cheating and how they were trained to administer the tests.

Rhee's cheating scandal worsened in April 2013 when PBS Rhee supporter John Merrow was slipped a confidential memo claiming that widespread cheating on DC standardized tests could have involved nearly seventy schools and 191 teachers, even though Rhee, DC school officials, and the DC inspector general said the problem was limited to the Noyes school and the US Department of Education cleared several schools of cheating. Drafted by Fay "Sandy" Sanford, who Rhee enlisted to look into the cheating, the 2009 memo was sent to Rhee's accountability deputy and Merrow says Rhee was very much aware of it. In 2010, nonetheless, Rhee fired over 600 teachers (many of them black) and "241 of them in one day" for low test scores. After the Sanford memo surfaced, *USA Today*'s Greg Toppo found that "among the 96 schools flagged for wrong-to-right erasures [by *USA Today* analysts] were eight of the 10 campuses where Rhee handed out so-called TEAM awards 'to recognize, reward and retain high-performing

educators and support staff.'" Toppo figured that "Rhee
bestowed more than $1.5 million in bonuses based on increases
in 2007 and 2008 test scores." Rhee was never held accountable, even though she had set up the perfect environment for
cheating with her test-based teacher evaluation system where
teachers felt forced to break rules just to keep their jobs. [27]

When good teachers are fired like the ones in DC over test
scores, more money falls into the pockets of leaders at the New
Teacher Project and Teach for America. Teach for America
sells itself as the liberal savior of poor kids, but it has become
a union-busting, better-than-thou group with a poor track
record. Studies show that its new teachers perform much worse
than credentialed beginning teachers.[28] From the beginning,
the group took corporate money from Lilly and the likes of
Mobil and recently accepted a $49.5 million five-year grant
from the anti-union and right-wing Walmart Walton family.[29]
Teach for America's CEO's close to $400,000 pay in 2010
proves money motivates its leaders more than children.[30]

Teach for America was first recruited to Indianapolis by the
Mind Trust with Lilly Endowment money in 2007. The Mind
Trust's Grow What Works campaign has granted almost $5 mil-
lion to the group.[31] According to Teach for America's website,
"more than 10% of public schools in Marion County are run
by Teach for America alumni." In Indianapolis, Teach for
America has 260 alumni and 140 members. Among these, seventy are teachers, twelve are school heads, and fifteen are advocacy and policy wonks stacking the boards of charter schools
and government offices calling the tune on Hoosier education.

One Teach for America operative is Challenge Foundation
Academy Indy's principal, Charles Schlegel, who teaches at
Marian University's Academy for Teaching and Learning Leadership which houses the Turnaround Leadership Academy.
Ironically, as principal at Wayland Middle School in Massachusetts, Schlegel violated 2008 campaign laws when he sent
emails through his school address to parents, begging them to
support a local property tax increase to fund the schools.[32] Now

back in Indiana, Schlegel made $120,000 for running the libertarian charter school in the tax year ending in June 2011.[33] Mindy, Schlegel's wife, was the senior advisor for teacher quality at the Indiana Department of Education, where she helped rewrite the teacher and principal evaluation method. A Democrats for Education Reform member, she also sits on the board of the Indianapolis KIPP charter school with former Mind Trust member Claire Fiddian-Green. Mindy, too, is a former Teach for America member.

In April 2011, two Teach for America graduates attending Marian University's Academy for Teaching and Learning Leadership were featured in Mitch Daniels' Aiming Higher Political Action Committee's anti-teacher seniority TV ad. A Teach for America alumnus and Harshman Magnet Middle School teacher, Pam Heuer protested that although she raised her students' reading scores, she was laid off from the Indianapolis school district in 2009 because she was the last one hired. The school district rehired Heuer before the next school year started, but Daniels' ad producers didn't mind using Heuer for their mostly out-of-state-funded agenda.[34] Now a manager for Teach for America in Indianapolis, Heuer was invited to the Bill Gates-financed NBC *Education Nation*, a free promotion week for charter schools, school vouchers, and anti-seniority billionaires, where she elbowed with Arne Duncan and Michelle Rhee. Heuer has also made videos for Stand for Children, another Mind Trust and Joyce Foundation-funded anti-teacher seniority clique we will soon meet. The Hollywood anti-public school fantasy *Waiting for Superman* director Davis Guggenheim touted Heuer as one of the top ten teachers in America.[35] Another Teach for America Marian University leadership student and Harshman Magnet Middle School teacher used in an Aiming Higher TV ad is Lanier Echols from Florida. Echols—who now is a coordinator for the Indiana Public Charter Schools Association—emotionally testified before the Indiana House Education Committee to support merit-pay based on student testing, saying she feared older teachers might bump her out of a job.[36]

At the Turnaround Leadership Academy, Teach for America, the New Teacher Project, Lilly, right-wing think tanks, and Marian University train the corporate leaders who will hire these temporary teachers to replace veterans when the state turns over their schools to for-profit companies. When first starting the Turnaround Leadership Academy, Marian University consulted with Rob Smith, Lilly Foundation's president and local Teach for America board member, Teach for America's Jason Kloth, who now is Indianapolis' deputy mayor of education, and the Christian Right Kerns Family Foundation which paid the Sagamore Institute to help align Marian and Notre Dame's principal training programs with the Indiana Department of Education's MBA-based guidelines.[37] Now managing school voucher money for parents, the Sagamore Institute is a conservative pseudo-research group whose founding chairman was Indiana senator Dan Coats. For the MBA-shaped training program, the hundreds of millions of dollars-strong, liberal-promoted Teach for America seems fine with Marian using content from the Center for Catholic Stewardship for its academy curriculum and had no problem being a part of the Christian Right-funded program. In order to work with twenty-two so-called failing schools, Marian's Turnaround Leadership Academy used a $500,000 grant from the Indiana Department of Education in 2010 which was rewarded because of political connections. Marian University president Daniel Elsener, a Tony Bennett campaign donor, former leader of Daniels and Bennett's mega-donor Christel DeHaan's family foundation, current board member of School Choice Indiana, and Indiana State Board of Education member, was Tony Bennett's wife's boss when she worked for Teach for America at the campus, and "the contract proposal cites Marian's partnership with Teach for America as an example of prior leadership in the area of school turnaround programs."[38] To pump out corporate school leaders to manage public schools like businesses, Marian now also teams with the George W. Bush Institute's Alliance to Reform Education Leadership and hired Steve Farr, from Teach for America's national office, to its faculty.

The New Teacher Project's national leadership, likewise, chastises traditional teachers. It includes David Keeling, co-author of the Center for American Progress and US Chamber of Commerce-touted *The Widget Effect: Our National Failure to Acknowledge and Act on Differences in Teacher Effectiveness.* Released in 2009 as an excuse for Arne Duncan and Barack Obama's Race to the Top initiative to target veteran teachers and tie teacher evaluations to student test scores, the New Teacher Project's *Widget Effect* was funded by college-dropout Bill Gates, the Joyce Foundation, and the Walmart family. In the report, Keeling and others "found that [in] evaluation systems with two ratings, 'satisfactory' and 'unsatisfactory,' 99 percent of teachers earned a satisfactory. In evaluation systems with more than two ratings, 94 percent of teachers received one of the top two ratings and less than one percent were rated unsatisfactory."[39] Even though, as education professor and historian Diane Ravitch has pointed out, the study carefully selected school districts to spread "false assumptions" that "teacher evaluation is universally broken,"[40] it was used as "evidence" for Gates to launch the Measures of Effective Teaching program (MET). MET includes eavesdropping on teachers with video cameras, student surveys, and test data, and currently has thousands of educators participating in urban class settings across the US, even though scholars like Rutgers' Bruce Baker have detailed the flaws of using MET to grade teachers.[41]

The New Teacher Project wreaked havoc in Tennessee in 2010. Overseeing the New Teacher Project's "business line," Victoria Van Cleef—a board member of the Tennessee State Board of Education's teacher certification advisory council— took $90 million from the Bill & Melinda Gates Foundation and road tripped to Memphis, where the New Teacher Project took charge of the complete hiring of teachers. Things did not go well. After Tennessee passed a law to replace principals in schools which had shown no gain in so-called achievement for two years, a typical corporate move to create chaos and job dissatisfaction, hundreds of teachers, nervous over the ditching of their principals, applied for transfers to teach at other schools. As school started, 125 classes were without teachers and 569 vacancies were still not filled in Memphis' school system.[42] Theresa Laperche dropped out of the New Teacher Project in Tennessee because she felt the group's inadequate training for teachers was making kids suffer. Laperche told Diane Ravitch that "the Teaching Fellows Program doesn't care one bit about closing the achievement gap but in fact victimizes our low income minority students to achieve their own agenda which is enrollment in the TNTP academy and to fill their own pockets with outlandish salaries."[43]

THE MIND TRUST spin-off Teach Plus also flashes the "closing the achievement gap" card, instructing its young novices to question the abilities of older, more experienced teachers. The Mind Trust's David Harris and the Joyce Foundation's John Luczak staff the Teach Plus board and both groups heavily fund Teach Plus. Teach Plus was started by Mind Trust education entrepreneur fellow Celine Coggins. Coggins made $140,000 in total compensation from October 2010 to September 2011, and the group's president, Monique Burns Thompson, reeled in over $175,000, which is not bad for a relatively new corporate outfit.[44] Teach Plus also has $4 million from the Gates Foundation to infiltrate six cities over three years, adding to its offices in Chicago, Los Angeles, Memphis, and Boston.[45] In 2010, after Massachusetts's Democratic governor signed a new law to let districts sack half of the teachers at their lowest-performing schools, Teach Plus rushed in to place its own instructors in a quarter of staffing positions at three "turnaround schools."[46] Besides lobbying for the law requiring teachers' evaluations be based primarily on how well their students do on the state ISTEP test, Teach Plus' *The Domino Effect* asserted that once Indiana closes down low-performing schools, apathetic senior teachers at those schools will replace younger ones at other public schools in the district, and this must be stopped at all cost.[47] Teach Plus distributed this policy propaganda to give ammo to win jobs at schools in Indiana.

Like Teach for America and the New Teacher Project, Teach Plus' self-serving agenda involves playing politics, and Teach Plus superstar James Larson has excelled at it. As an inexperienced teacher, Larson went to work at the Charles A. Tindley Accelerated School, and his political connections at Tindley, the Mind Trust, and Teach Plus secured him an appearance on Jane Pauley's former network, NBC, and later a job with Tony Bennett. On NBC's *Education Nation* website, Larson writes that in the public schools "too many teachers are simply allowed to close their doors when the bell rings. Too many administrators close their doors, too."[48] Larson graduated in 2005 from DePauw and started at Tindley in 2008, so he's not seen much, if anything, of how teachers and administrators do business in Indiana public schools.

The Tindley charter school is well-hooked into the Indiana school privatization movement. Partnering with the Greater Indianapolis Chamber of Commerce, Tindley gets funding from the Bart Peterson-connected Challenge Foundation and loans from Peterson's friend Gene Zink, who leads the gentrification project in the Avondale Meadows neighborhood in Indianapolis where Tindley is located.[49] Tindley took $250,000 from the Walton family in 2011 and received startup money from the Bill Gates and Lilly-funded Center of Excellence in Leadership and Learning (CELL) at the University of Indianapolis. When Bill Gates' so-called "researcher" visited Tindley, then-Mayor Peterson's office wrote that Gates' representative found everything working. After witnessing the school's female-male classroom segregation, Gates' operative "noted that she had never seen so many female students who were unafraid to participate, debate, discuss, and question openly in a math class."[50] Tindley's audits from the Indiana State Board of Accounts covering July 2009 to June 2011 tell a different narrative of Tindley's leadership. Auditors say school officials raked up $16,504.09 in credit card charges for mostly meals and travel that were not documented by receipts or "approved" by any legitimate policy and were charging whatever they fancied for textbooks while making errors in and not completely verifying portions of the school lunch program.[51]

When Tony Bennett hired James Larson to direct the Indiana Department of Education's Office of School Improvement and Turnaround on June 8, 2011, he ignored Larson's inexperience and Tindley's financials and focused instead on the rookie teacher's political clout. Shortly after hiring Larson, Bennett and the Indiana Department of Education offered the Mind Trust over $680,000 to arrange a plan so that turnaround for-profit companies would not have to give back schools to a school board that would send the schools back into "failure."[52]

By school board "failure," the IDOE and the Mind Trust mean publically elected officials who won't sign the school privatization pledge outlined in the Mind Trust's "Opportunity Plan." The Mind Trust enlisted longtime corporate shill Bryan Hassel to craft its "Opportunity Plan" for IDOE, which calls for replacing local control of the Indianapolis Public Schools with a mayor's cherry-picked board to rubberstamp more charter schools who will employ temporary teachers.[53] In fact, the "Opportunity Plan" has a lot in common with the Center for American Progress' blueprint to eliminate democratically elected school boards nationwide. A Wall Street Democrat and pro-Afghan war think tank financed with liberal George Soros' money, the Center for American Progress is fronted by John Podesta, Bill Clinton's chief of staff whose sister-in-law, Heather, once lobbied for for-profit Edison Schools.[54] Recently, the Center for American Progress and the right-wing Fordham Foundation's Michael Petrilli cooked up a three-year design that makes the John Birch Society's attempts to plant anti-communist, anti-civil rights operatives on school boards in the 1960s seem tame. Completely ignoring the crony capitalism behind the school privatization movement, Petrilli notes in "One Size Fits Most" that the 14,000 US school boards damage education because there's "too much opportunity for nepotism and cronyism."[55] Focusing on national Common Core standards and eliminating local school boards, Petrilli says, will allow educators to be more productive. Not surprisingly, Petrilli says that corporate-led charters and digital schools should be permitted to "opt out of the Common Core framework entirely, and to proffer their own evidence of educational achievement."[56]

When Caitlin Hannon, Teach Plus Indy's network coordinator, used lumps of corporate money to win an Indianapolis Public Schools board seat in November 2012, the Mind Trust didn't have to worry about officially getting its anti-democratic proposal into place. Grassroots education activist John Harris Loflin discovered that Hannon was one of three winning candidates purchased by mostly wealthy, out-of-state donors. For her race, Hannon received $57,437 from funders like Greg Penner, Walmart's Carrie Walton Penner's husband, and Indiana's Al Hubbard. Emails show that Hubbard helped a group of Indiana businessmen and operatives recruit Betsy DeVos and Jeb Bush's school privatization plan to Indiana before even lawmakers had caught wind.[57] A Tony Bennett campaign donor and now Indiana Education Roundtable representative, Hubbard worked for George Bush Sr. and Jr. and directs the largest real estate company in the world, Simon Property Group, that helps run dozens of public schools in its shopping malls so students can incorporate consuming into their course loads. Another Hannon donor was Alan Fournier, a New Jersey Republican hedge fund manager who helped Michelle Rhee assist governor Chris Christie's school privatization plan. Fournier is just one American hedge funder manager out of many who are planning to steal our schools for profit. Stand for Children, based in Portland, Oregon, is a front group lending them a hand.

IN 2010 AND 2011, Stand for Children, Republican hedge

fund managers, and private equity giants bought out Illinois lawmakers and hired lobbyists to pass anti-teacher seniority bills. Caught red-handed on tape at the June 28, 2011 Aspen Institute's Ideas Festival, Stand for Children's leader Jonah Edelman gloated about how the media never caught on in 2010 when he purchased six Democrats and three Republicans for $610,000 in campaign donations and tiptoed home with a $200,000 paycheck to head Stand for Children that year. A PhD in politics holder, Rhodes Scholar, and son of African-American Children's Defense Fund leader Marian Wright Edelman, Jonah Edelman was extremely proud of buying Democrat and Illinois House Speaker Michael Madigan after the teachers unions threatened to disown the representative for supporting a teacher-unfriendly pension reform bill. In the passage below from his Aspen talk, Edelman speaks first of Advance Illinois, a front group led by the former mayors' son and brother Bill Daley before he joined Obama's White House, then details how Madigan, after the election, paid the rich investors back by pitching teachers under the bus:

> After the election, Advance Illinois and Stand had drafted a very bold proposal we called Performance Counts. It tied tenure and lay-offs to performance. It let principals hire who they choose. It stream-lined dismissal of ineffective tenured teachers substantially, from 2+ years and $200,000 in legal fees, on average, to three to four months, with very little likelihood of legal recourse, and, most importantly, we called for the reform of collective bargaining throughout the state. Essentially, proposing that school boards would be able to de-cide any disputed issue at impasse. So a very, very bold proposal for Illinois, and one that six months earlier would have been unthink-able, undiscussable.
>
> And after the election, I went back to Madigan and I con-firmed, I reviewed the proposal, and I confirmed his support, and he was supportive. The next day he created an education reform com-mittee and his political director called to ask for our suggestions for who should be on it. And so in Aurora, Illinois, in December, out of nowhere there were hearings on our proposal.
>
> In addition we hired eleven lobbyists, including the four best insiders and seven of the best minority lobbyists, preventing the

unions from hiring them. We enlisted a statewide public affairs firm. We had tens of thousands of supporters. And with Jim's, and many others stepping up, Paula and Steve, thank you, we raised $3 million for our political action committee between the election and the end of the year. That's more money than either of the unions have in their political action committees.

And so essentially what we did in a very short period of time was shift the balance of power. I can tell you there was a palpable sense of concern if not shock on the part of the teachers' unions in Illinois that Speaker Madigan had changed allegiance, and that we had clear political capability to potentially jam this proposal down their throats, the same way the pension reform had been jammed down their throats six months earlier. In fact, the pension reform was called Senate Bill 1946 and the unions took to talking to each other about it like, "we're not going to allow ourselves to be 1946ed again," using it as a verb.[58]

Although Edelman later apologized for his statements after the media responded because of a backlash from public school advocates who had reposted online the then-deleted speech video, the damage had been done. Even the corporate school shill the *Chicago Tribune* said Stand for Children's leader had violated "a cardinal rule of Statehouse power plays—what happens under the dome stays under the dome."[59] The group's true motives had finally been exposed to a wider audience in Illinois and in its own Oregon backyard. Richard Sanders, Oregon Education Association's executive director, told Corey Paul of *Willamette Week* (who attempted to justify Stand's Oregon work) the following: "You have to realize in a short period they raised $3.5 million [in Illinois]. That's as good as an example as you'll see anywhere of the role that the corporate interests want to play in reorganization of the education system."[60] *Portland Tribune's* Jennifer Anderson asked if Oregonians should trust a group the Gates Foundation gave $3.5 million to and the Walton Foundation another $1.3 million in 2010 alone. *Rethinking Schools'* Bill Bigelow, a former Oregon public school teacher, answered when he called Stand a bullying organization. "Now that Edelman has gone public in his Aspen Institute talk, he's free to rename his organization 'Stand Against Teachers,'" Bigelow stated.[61] In the *Black Commentator*, Reverend Robin Hood lambasted Stand for its ties to rich people then narrated how Edelman's group attempted to buy off Chicago clergy members. Stand was anti-union, Hood said, and the community needed living-wage jobs. Hood said: "Most of these parents have been arguing about how we don't have books in school. Those are not the things Stand for Children were talking about. They were talking about taking power from teachers."[62]

That was the hedge fund plan. To open the way for the wealthy to loan money to new charter schools that use taxpayers' money to pay back the loan with interest, the hedge fund managers and private equity titans who gave almost $1.7 million to Stand for Children before and after the election included James Schine Crown, president of the public and private securities and real estate investment company Henry Crown and Company. James Schine Crown, in fact, was the one who introduced Edelman at the Aspen festival, after calling the Chicago and Illinois schools "awful" but praising Teach for America for stepping in to clean up the mess. As Aspen Institute's billionaire trustee who inherited most of his wealth, Crown celebrated Arne Duncan's "Chicago Miracle" just two years earlier. Then, when the time was ripe to hand over more schools to private companies and break the unions, the Aspen Institute declared Chicago schools in immediate crisis and said students would suffer if politicians didn't pass anti-seniority teacher bills and other laws detrimental to public education.[63]

And pass laws the Illinois government did, with a helping hand from Obama's prior chief of staff, investment banker, and Chicago mayor Rahm Emanuel, who Edelman says accelerated Stand for Children's anti-teacher agenda "behind the scenes."[64] Emanuel appeared with Edelman, Dan Montgomery, the Illinois Federation of Teachers' president, and a marching band at Pat Quinn's June 2011 signing of the law which bases teachers' evaluations on student performance, rolls back seniority rights, makes it harder for teachers to strike, and opens the schoolhouse for Teach for America, the New Teacher Project, and Teach Plus.[65]

With Stand for Children's school privatization buddies in the windy city, it was a done deal. Arne Duncan had hired Jonah's brother Joshua Edelman to be the CEO of Chicago's Office of New Schools even though Joshua had had no experience in education whatsoever. As a school privatization operative, Joshua Edelman "was responsible for the closing of more public schools in Chicago than any executive in the 150-year history of public education in Chicago."[66] Joshua also oversaw ninety-two charter schools and the creation of new ones under Mayor Daley's Renaissance 2010 and was paid $135,000 in 2007 for his role in Chicago, as *Substance News* editor George Schmidt notes.[67] The $300,000 gift Stand for Children took from Penny Pritzker and her anti-union Hyatt Hotel-owning family, after Emanuel picked her for his Chicago school board, also didn't hurt.[68] Penny Pritzker is a former high-ranking official from Superior Bank, which the feds closed down after depositors got shafted. Superior Bank kicked off the subprime loan crisis which eventually collapsed the market in 2008.[69] Pritzker is a tax dodger who donates to the campaigns of both parties. She was Obama's campaign finance chair and is now his commerce secretary.

THE MIND TRUST had a similar scheme in mind, when it paid Stand for Children $242,300 to match the Joyce Foundation's $150,000 to import the anti-teacher seniority outfit to Indiana.[70] Stand for Children quickly set up shop using the Indiana Public Charter Schools Association's address and bought "two high-priced Statehouse lobbyists and a ton of positive publicity courtesy of *Indianapolis Star* columnist Matthew Tully"[71] to lobby for Senate Bill 1, which now, as a passed law, makes it easier to fire veteran teachers since annual teacher evaluations are based on student performance. Stand for Children also devoted a little over $24,000 to the campaigns of Democrats Mary Ann Sullivan and Justin Moed and Republicans David Frizzell, then national chairman of the right-wing bill-writing American Legislative Exchange Council, Tony Bennett, and Brian Bosma.

Since the Indiana environment was conducive to a corporate overhaul of education, Stand's Hoosier leader, M. Karega Rausch, didn't need to pull off anything as drastic as Edelman had in Illinois, but thanks to Brian Bosma, Rausch—a former teacher, educational psychologist, and Indianapolis' past charter schools director—landed a spot on the new Indiana charter school authorizing board in September 2011, which put another Mind Trust broker in a position of power. Around this time, Indy Republican mayor Greg Ballard announced his five-point sweetheart deal with the Mind Trust to use the $2 million the city landed from selling its Indianapolis Water Company as startup funds to entice more charter schools by giving the non-profit corporate-selected boards running the schools even more generous tax breaks.[72] A few weeks earlier, Rausch had spoken at the Mind Trust's Grow What Works dinner at the Indiana Landmarks Center, where Stand for Children, Teach Plus, Teach for America, and the New Teacher Project were given more Mind Trust funding from the $100,000 Indiana University Health had donated to the event.[73] Rausch had been both Bart Peterson and Greg Ballard's Indianapolis charter school office leader since 2007. Breakfasting with Matt Tully in April, Rausch said the voices of parents, teachers, and students "are too often drowned out by the special interests," by which he meant the teachers unions.[74]

IN MASSACHUSHETTS, STAND for Children found a hero in Bain Capital. A private equity firm, Bain Capital was launched by Mitt Romney with millions of dollars in startup money from rich Latin Americans who funded the right-wing death squads responsible for killing most of the 35,000 civilians who died in El Salvador during a civil war in the early 1980s that threatened the ruling oligarchy.[75] Using tactics similar to school turnaround management companies, Bain Capital buys out distressed companies, loads them with debt, and slashes the workforce in order to profit. In 2006, Bain took over drug and alcohol treatment franchise CRC Health Group, charged $20 million in management fees, piled the company with massive debt, and bought out a tough-love treatment center for youth, the Aspen Education Group, with a history of lawsuits against it and allegations of fraud, abuse, and questionable deaths. Instead of making the Aspen center's problems better, Bain—to help the bottom line—created similar conditions at CRC's Camp Recovery in Scotts Valley, California, tripling the price of admittance, handpicking a new director to destroy the drive for a workers union, and cutting staff, all of which made conditions at the treatment center downright dangerous. Meanwhile, after Bain and CRC Health Group's Aspen takeover, six more teenagers died at the center.[76]

In the name of caring for children, another firm where Mitt Romney used to work is sure to inspire Stand for Children and is already making money by slashing teachers' jobs and privatizing education. With seventy-five global offices and past employees like superstar John Legend and hedge fund Democrats for Education Reform's manager Whitney Tilson, the Boston Consulting Group is restructuring school districts in Cleveland, the state of Illinois, and Florida (where it has been funded by college-dropout Bill Gates). Known for working with the US Postal Service on its five-year business plan to close rural post offices, lay off workers, and move the mail one step closer to complete privatization, the Boston Consulting Group was hired by the unelected School Reform Commission in Philadelphia to shrink the school district's central office, use test scores to fire teachers, lay off nurses and psychologists for special needs students, shut down sixty-four schools in five years, mass-produce charter schools, launch networks of schools managed by outside groups, and outsource "2,500 blue-collar, union jobs...to the lowest bidder."[77] Applauded by Michelle Rhee, Tom Corbett, the governor, had purposely devised the financial crisis when he slashed from the education budget for two years straight.

This slash and burn approach to America has impressed Stand for Children so much that the group invited Bain Capital members to sit on its board and exhausted $1 million from Bain in Massachusetts to press for a ballot initiative to judge teachers by test scores, opening the way for more Teach for America types.[78] Stand for Children's support for blended-learning for the Boston district's Race to the Top application had in mind the goal of school privatization, but government money could aid Bain Capital, too, which owns a good chunk of Skillsoft, an online learning corporation and education software provider. Blended-learning schools typically hire three or four teachers per school who teach half-time, while low-paid workers (in what Douglas Storm calls "the digital nursery") monitor kids supposedly doing online school work. This funnels more money into the bank accounts of the schools' CEOs.

Aided by Bill Gates' financing, the Mind Trust, like Stand for Children, expects friends to make a bundle from blended-learning. After the state charter school board approved Phalen Leadership Academies, the Mind Trust granted the blended-learning group $1 million in late June 2012 from its charter school incubator fund to help Martin Earl Phalen, an Obama education campaign advisor and Mind Trust education entrepreneur fellow, open ten blended-learning centers in Indy.[79] Blended-learning is a major component of college-dropout Bill Gates' vast school privatization agenda. A month after the Gates Foundation gave the Mind Trust's nationwide CEE-Trust $500,000 in October 2011, the Mind Trust's Patrick Herrel pointed out in a webinar on November 4th with the Gates Foundation that online learning charter schools built on Gates' Next Generation model would be perfect for the Mind Trust, which wanted "charter schools that are sustainable on public dollars, and next gen may be the only way to do that."[80]

Although dependent on Bill Gates' money, the Mind Trust is just a small fish in the richest man in the world's desire to expand online learning and establish a temporary teacher workforce for charter schools. Besides funding the Mind Trust's CEE-Trust, the Bill & Melinda Gates Foundation has handed millions to Teach for America alone. In 2010, the year before the major Indiana corporate school bills passed, the Gates Foundation gave Stand for Children over $3.4 million. In 2011, Gates handed the New Teacher Project $6.5 million, and in 2012 Gates donated a little more than $5 million to Teach Plus. A funder to Mitch Daniels' Education Roundtable, the Gates Foundation from 2008 to 2010 gave over $73 million to charter schools, just part of the $1 billion the group pumped out for corporate school projects in those three years.[81]

To have the power to dismantle the US public school system, Gates hides money overseas and pays his foreign workers pennies. In 2011, Microsoft "stashed over $60 billion in offshore tax haven countries to avoid paying income taxes" of $19.4 billion.[82] Gates would like to see the teacher workforce in America look more like China's workforce, where Microsoft pays young people sixty-five cents an hour to work in factories with prison-like conditions.[83] Gates publicizes his call to have increased class sizes and fewer and less educated teachers with less furlough school days, but his newest Big Brother plot is to force students to wear galvanic skin response bracelets to measure teachers' "ineffectiveness" by the sweat responses kids have to them in the classroom. If the biosensors kids wear report too much anxiety or inattentiveness, this will be "evidence" teachers are not doing their jobs. Adapted from the new trend in neuromarketing to measure consumers' responses to products, Gates' Big Brother project is sure to help replace qualified teachers with more temporary recruits.

ALTHOUGH STAND FOR Children's hedge fund managers are Republicans, some New York City billionaires use the cover of the Democratic Party to purchase school privatization. Knowing there's money to be made investing in charter schools with short-term teachers, hedge fund managers have their own front group. The Democrats for Education Reform (DFER) cheer for teacher merit-pay based on student test scores and coerce state Democrats nationwide to wreck the lives of teachers and school kids. They pile money into charter schools, court US mayors, and buy out school boards.

Even though DFER only opened its Indiana branch in early 2011, it has lurked in the shadows for some time and is still behind the scenes. DFER adopted Bart Peterson as a corporate son in 2007, rewarding him, a prior Evan Bayh aide, its Education Warrior Award at a New York City hedge fund party in Central Park.[84] In its "Education Transition Memo" to president-elect Obama, who attended DFER parties as a senator, the hedge fund group asked the president to select the past Indy mayor to be the assistant secretary for elementary and secondary education, saying that "Peterson's appointment would send a clear signal that urban school improvement is a key priority of an Obama Administration."[85] On January 24, 2012, DFER declared Democratic candidate for Indiana governor John Gregg its monthly national school reformer and began floating money to his campaign through a Democratic Party-affiliated website. Knowing he had no chance at winning, DFER, for good gesture, gave Gregg a small $1,000 gift but claimed on its website that the candidate had been laboring over its "Ticket to Teach" merit-pay map which targets colleges of education and further breaks Indiana educators, slighting the many teachers who had provided hard-working dollars to Gregg's campaign. To the Mind Trust's delight, in November 2012 DFER funded Teach Plus' Caitlin Hannon's successful Indianapolis Public Schools board campaign.

Larry Grau heads DFER Indiana. As the senior education policy advisor to Indiana Democratic governor Frank O'Bannon from 1998-2002, Grau helped implement the now business-loaded and Bill Gates-funded Indiana Education Roundtable and worked on a charter school bill for Indiana. Endorsing Christian Right corporatist school vouchers, Grau also holds a place on the board of School Choice Indiana. Days after Grau surfaced at an Evansville League of Women Voters' Q & A with Indianapolis corporate Democrat Mary Ann Sullivan,[86] DFER's hedge fund boss Whitney Tilson blogged an email he received from Grau. In the email, Grau refers to the "angry mob-mentality" of teachers protesting at the statehouse after the Indiana House passed the 2011 charter school expansion bill, which Sullivan, funded by DFER, co-authored and was the only Democrat to vote "yes"on. Grau calls Sullivan "courageous" for not backing down when booed upon the House floor, even as her fellow Indiana House Democrats were packing for Illinois to picket the Republican assault on teachers and other workers. Grau also says, in the Tilson email, that "Dems will be left with the teacher unions and some of the other groups that have historically fought any change in the education system, while the Republicans are taking a victory lap for what they did to free the many students who have been neglected in the current system and are lingering in poor performing schools, with ineffective teachers."[87]

Grau's comparison of Democrats to Republicans is telling. To con people into accepting school choice for hedge fund managers to siphon public money, Whitney Tilson and DFER playact as old-time Democrats, when, in fact, Walmart's John Walton and the Republican Party inspired DFER's formation.[88] Toward the end of 2008, Tilson divulged this to his email admirers:

> Even if you like McCain's education reform proposals better, you still want Obama to be President because only a Democrat can bring about the needed reforms. It's like only Nixon could have gone to China and only Clinton could have reformed welfare. It's the whole idea behind Democrats for Education Reform: it has to be an inside job! As long as it's Republicans pushing for reform, the unions can continue to make this a Republican vs. Democrat issue.[89]

One DFER "inside job" was the 2010 coup to lift the New York City charter school cap. To pass the charter school expansion bill, DFER packed Harlem candidate Basil Smikle's campaign chest. As researcher Ken Libby discovered, Smikle had secured $159,065.20 in donations, mostly from corporate school endorsers and real estate moguls eager to make money providing buildings to non-unionized and temporary teacher-filled charter schools.[90] Although Smikle and two other school privatization supporters lost their election bids, the charter school cap was lifted, thanks in big part to DFER. DFER and its affiliated anti-union Education Reform Now (which subsidizes the Mind Trust) sponsored TV ads, radio announcements, and op-eds, and the media quickly fell in line. Leonie Haimson writes, between March 1 and May 29, 2010 (the date legislators voted to lift the charter school cap) the newspapers didn't even pretend to be fair and balanced, when "99 percent of the editorials, opinion columns and opeds praised charter schools and/or explicitly supported raising the cap."[91] Joe Williams, paid $218,565 (and another $46,764 in other compensation) from Education Reform Now in 2010,[92] told the *Daily News,* where he was once a reporter, that the new "legislation introduced by the Senate leadership will position New York to earn $700 million in Race to the Top funding by increasing the cap on charter schools."[93]

As a former news reporter and now school corporatist, Joe Williams has had his say about how journalists report the privatization of our schools, helping write the Joyce Foundation-funded primer for reporters at the Hechinger Institute on Education and the Media at Columbia University's Teachers College, whose *Report* stories sneak into major newspapers across the country and whose advisory board enlists many school privatizers including DFER's Liam Kerr.[94] Besides the Joyce and Gates foundations (both of which also fund NPR's corporate school promotions, as does the Walton family), the Indianapolis-based STEM-promoting Lumina Foundation finances the Hechinger Institute's educational coverage which repeats corporate school memes concerning teacher performance and training, among other things, and publishes writings from the likes of Stand for Children's Jonah Edelman. Alumni of the Teacher's College—which was once prized for its teacher training—have been up in arms about the college's recent corporate direction.

The DFER has also depended on Mind Trust board member, former Bill Clinton education advisor, and Renaissance man of school privatization Andy Rotherham to spin tales to advance the billionaires' hidden agenda. Once DFER's director, Rotherham praised Peterson back when Peterson was mayor and now spends his free time writing for *TIME* magazine and charging subscribers $499 monthly to read his *Education Insider*. Rotherham, who believes Marine Corps standards could improve the teaching profession, made just short of $300,000 in total compensation between September 2010 and September 2011 at the Walton and Gates-funded Bellwether Education Partners.[95] For years, Rotherham has carried the water for college-dropout Bill Gates to drown public school teachers. In 2007, Rotherham's Education Sector published the Joyce Foundation-funded *Frozen Assets: Rethinking Teacher Contracts Could Free Billions for School Reform*. In this report, Marguerite Roza, now senior data and economic advisor for the Gates Foundation, shows that corporate schoolers could win $77 billion of annual public school funding if more students were herded into classes and teachers were stopped from getting advanced degrees and therefore higher paychecks. Calling for Teach for America-like recruits, she stresses that "money spent on seniority-based raises and generous health plans for more veteran teachers might be better used for raising minimum salaries to recruit younger educators who meet high teaching standards."[96] Professor Philip E. Kovacs and others point out it is deceptive, to say the least, to call the $600,000 Gates-gifted Education Sector an "unbiased" research institute, as Rotherham does, when right-wingers like Frederick Hess from the American Enterprise Institute known for corporate school propaganda fill its ranks.[97]

But Rotherham, Williams, and DFER's assertion that so-called school reform is for the children completely falls flat when one learns that deception and unethical behavior are pre-requisites for being a hedge fund manager. As Wall Street investigator Les Leopold notes, much of the hedge funders' money "comes from what normal people call cheating—some of it legal, some of it borderline, and much of it criminal." Since hedge fund managers "profit from illegal insider tips, high frequency trading, rumor-mongering, front-running trades, special tax loopholes and even by creating financial products that are designed to fail so that they can collect the insurance," the billionaires "have their hands in our pockets 24/7," Leopold says. This "hands in our pockets" approach brings results. On average, hedge fund managers make $843,000 per hour. The same year DFER was hurling New York educators under the bus, "the top 25 hedge fund chiefs made as much as 685,000 teachers who educate 13 million children."[98]

While teachers are laid off and classes overflow with kids, hedge fund managers are making money from the same banks loaning to charter schools employing temporary teachers. DFER's Whitney Tilson—who helped found Teach for America—owns thousands of stocks in JP Morgan Chase. JP Morgan Chase is not celebrated for its overly ethical behavior. After the housing collapse when investors and the US taxpayers lost $40 billion bailing out the banks, JP Morgan Chase paid a small fine of $154 million for not telling investors that it fashioned a mortgage-securities deal for hedge fund Magnetar to bet against to make even more money.[99] Besides profiting from loans to Indiana charter schools, JP Morgan has set aside $325 million to loan to charter schools nationwide, at the same time taking advantage of new markets tax credits.[100] As Economic Policy Institute's distinguished fellow Jeff Faux points out, JP Morgan's chief finance officer reported that "75% of the net increase in corporate profits between 2000 and 2007—before the financial crash—was a result of cuts in workers' wages and benefits."[101] No wonder the banks and hedge fund managers seek a temporary teacher workforce to fill charter school classrooms across the country. Faux writes that "having been rescued from the consequences of its own folly by the Bush/Obama bailouts with its de-regulated privileges intact, Wall Street is once more on the prowl for the new 'big thing'— a new source of potential profits upon which to build the next lucrative asset bubble."[102] With the too-big-to-fail immoral activity of the big banks and hedge funds now history, the next "big thing" is creating a profitable charter school with temporary teachers on every corner in Indiana and beyond. When charter schools start crumbling under their own debt, the hedge fund managers, banks, and other wealthy backers who put up the loans will be "rescued" with taxpayer money, as they were during the housing crisis. While the wealthy get paid back with interest, kids will lose their schools like their parents lost their houses because of a system rigged against them.

Plain and simple, hedge fund managers and the pretend-liberals could care less. Setting out to fire more qualified teachers and decimate the links teachers have to the community, the Mind Trust and people who dare call themselves liberal want stacked boards to call the shots and all democratic principles erased. By tying teacher evaluations to test scores, the sham liberal crowd—stuffed with Lilly, Bill Gates, and Walmart money—is bent on an educational arrangement where temporary teachers are paid less and kids are merely trained for low-paid jobs. Led by the rich for the rich, the educational future they seek is an America where all classes are deprived of true educational choice but the wealthy. The pseudo-liberals want taxpayer money for their pseudo-public charter schools to fatten their own bank accounts. For some within the Religious Right, it is time to close down the public schools altogether. ■

2.
THE FREE-MARKET JESUS
IN THE CLASSROOM

I would like to think that, yes, Jesus would destroy the
public education temple and save the children from despair
and a hopeless future. And he would smash a temple that has
been perverted to meet the needs of the administrators,
teachers, school board members, unions, bureaucrats and
contractors.
Kyle Olson, "Jesus Isn't in Michigan," March 17,
2011, *BigGovernment.com*

I imagine every Christian would agree that we need to
remove the humanism from the public schools. There is only
one way to accomplish this: to abolish the public schools.
Robert Thoburn, *The Children Trap*

T HE RELIGIOUS RIGHT'S DESIRE TO ELIMINATE PUBLIC SCHOOLS
reaches back to the 1800s but recently surfaced in force in the
1980s when its leaders, after decades of preaching biblical capitalism in churches and lashing out at the so-called satanic and
socialist public schools—were able to finally wed their God
with free-market advocates to seek a common goal. The Religious Right believes that the Bible and Jesus demand the
destruction of everything from social welfare programs for the
poor to collective bargaining rights for teachers. Some on the
free-market side, no doubt, also believe that God is the
Capitalist Upstairs who is recruiting an army of angels to fight
off poor people and lazy public workers, but many are merely
writing propaganda favoring school vouchers and contributing
to the Religious Right's attacks on public schools because they

make money from those out to completely privatize education. Although Christians who hate the public schools have combined forces with the Friedmanites, what to do with public schools is still hotly contested in Religious Right circles. Many believe the schools should be infiltrated with Christian organizations like the Good News Club, active in thousands of schools across America with eight Hoosier branches through the Child Evangelism Fellowship of Indiana. Others think Christians should homeschool their children, if they cannot afford to send them to private schools. Homeschooling in Indiana depletes the public schools of financing and furthermore gives tax breaks to Christian parents who keep their kids at home. The Religious Right supports charter schools, too, because schools run by private companies weaken traditional public school funding and pave the way for religious outfits to open charter schools and teach Bible principles with tax money.

Christian Right leaders who aspire to wipe out public schools entirely are the most dangerous. They want total school dismantling to accomplish one or two things: to set up a system where taxpayers end up funding nothing but Christian schooling in America as the country becomes a complete theocracy; or to put in place a privatized school structure where parents foot the bill, no taxpayer money is used, and in the words of Independence Hall Tea Party president Teri Adams, Americans have "private schools only, eventually returning responsibility for payment to parents and private charities."[1] The latter would leave the majority of kids in America without any schooling whatsoever. This, according to many, is the ultimate goal of the Bradley Foundation. Michigan's DeVos family from Amway also contributes.

With Bradley and DeVos operatives already in Indiana, the Republicans funded by many of the groups detailed below, and Mitch Daniels as governor, the Hoosier state, in 2011, was the perfect target for school privatization. Having founded the Catholic Oaks Academy private school and taken Eli Lilly into greater profit, Mitch Daniels has always liked the biblical capitalism behind school vouchers. Not only did they funnel money to private Christian schools, vouchers also siphoned money from public schools and readied them for so-called "failings," making them suitable for privatization. Daniels—a Tabernacle Presbyterian Church elder—was fit for the job of combining the corporatist with the Christian. He signed into law the biggest school voucher bill in US history, where more than half of Indiana school children are eligible to attend private schools. He left copies of his racist and poor-bashing friend Charles Murray's book *Real Education*, at one point, for Indiana Education Roundtable members to read.[2] Millionaire Daniels had moved in all the right circles. Daniels, in 2013, won the $250,000 prize from the Bradley Foundation. He was also once a Bradley Foundation board member and supported the group's strategy for years, as we shall see in this book's last chapter. For now, let's examine how the Bradley Foundation has been on the forefront of school privatization from the movement's inception.

HAVING GROWN OUT of the New World Order-paranoid John Birch Society formed in Indianapolis in the late 1950s, the Milwaukee-based Harry and Lynde Bradley Foundation (better known as just the Bradley Foundation) is behind many anti-public education troops acting in Indiana and elsewhere which use school vouchers as a smoke scene for the real agenda, the complete privatization of public schools. Now headed by Wisconsin governor Scott Walker's campaign co-chair Michael Grebe, the Bradley Foundation has given $31.3 million to school privatization groups since 2001. Since 2006, Bradley has handed the anti-teachers union Center for Union Facts $1.8 million. To expand charter schools, Bradley contributed $3 million to the Charter School Growth Fund in 2010 alone. The Bradley Foundation also finances Teach for America, the school voucher Washington Scholarship Fund, and the George W. Bush Institute's Education Leadership Initiative, which backs Marian University's school turnaround academy in Indiana. Bradley similarly subsidizes the Hoover Institution's Koret Task Force on K-12 Education, the State Policy Network, Harvard University, and the Thomas B. Fordham Institute, many of them prizing online learning schools. Bradley delivered $50,000 to Jeb Bush's Foundation for Excellence in Education, a group which bad-mouths public schools and is also active in Indiana. In 2010 alone, as the buildup to school privatization in Indiana intensified, Bradley supplied $20,000 to the Alliance for School Choice, which paid School Choice Indiana to support corporate school bills. [3]

High school dropouts, the Bradley brothers, Harry and Lynde, were the wealthy owners of the Milwaukee-based Allen-Bradley Company, the electronics and radio manufacturer known for its sexism, worker discrimination, and racism, traits prevalent in corporate school leaders. Although employing females since 1918, Allen-Bradley did not give equal pay to women until a federal judge intervened in 1966. Allen-Bradley had railed against a union workshop, until a seventy-six-day strike in 1970 led to the company finally agreeing to let union dues be taken from payroll deduction. In fact, Allen-Bradley was one of the last companies in Milwaukee to racially integrate, and then only because of public outrage and pressure from lawyers. As A Job Is a Right Campaign's Phil Wilayto notes, by "1968, when the company's workforce had grown to more than 7,000, Allen-Bradley employed only 32 Blacks and 14 Latinos."[4]

Not surprisingly, Bradley has funded many racist anti-affirmative action initiatives across America. Besides giving millions to the deceptively named American Civil Rights Institute, the National Association of Scholars, and other anti-affirmative action factions, Bradley subsidized the Center for Individual Rights which won the 1996 *Hopwood v. the State of Texas* case against racial diversity at the University of Texas, until the Supreme Court ruled against it. Bradley was also behind the Pacific Legal Foundation's work for then-California governor Pete Wilson, when he fought several state employment statues supporting affirmative action. Clint Bolick, from the Koch brothers and Bradley-funded Institute for Justice which successfully fought the Indiana school voucher lawsuit, drafted a national bill to end all affirmative action programs across the country.[5]

To convince legislators that poverty was the result of blacks being genetically lazy and stupid and not of low wages and no work, the Bradley Foundation hired Charles Murray—one of Mitch Daniels' friends—to write junk science the media passed off as scholarship. Murray's first book attacking the poor was *In Losing Ground*, where he stated that the government should stop providing money to single mothers and eliminate food stamps and subsidized housing, since, as Wilayto remarks, "plant shutdowns and layoffs, periodic cycles of recession and depression, or racial and gender discrimination,"[6] Murray maintained, had nothing to do with poverty. Poverty was the fault of the poor. This propaganda would not only demolish welfare but lead to the privatization of government housing in Milwaukee, which went hand in hand with the privatization of the public schools. Although the Bradley Foundation had been paying Murray $90,000 yearly, after his infamous *The Bell Curve* was released, his salary jumped to $163,000. With co-author Richard Hernstein, Murray, in *The Bell Curve*, suggests the best way to treat the problem of poverty and mothers out of wedlock was to stop all social welfare and set up, as Phil Wilayto notes, a "work-centered program of coercion and behavioral modification."[7]

The Bell Curve evoked a dark time in American history when the eugenics movement crossed country borders and eventually led to the Holocaust. *The Bell Curve*, in fact, "relied heavily on studies financed by the Pioneer Fund, a neo-Nazi organization that promoted eugenicist research."[8] *The Bell Curve* was not advocating death chambers or sterilization, but it intended to make the lives of the poor extremely uncomfortable and the wealthy richer. It was quickly denounced by the American Psychological Association. As famed evolutionary theorist and paleontologist Stephen Jay Gould exposed in his sharp blow to *The Bell Curve*, Murray's one-dimensional take on intelligence was merely pseudo-science used to oppress the poor and minorities. Calling *The Bell Curve* "one of the best examples in recent times of right-wing ideology dishonestly presented as objective science," sociology professors Brett Clark and Richard York write:

> As Gould explains with razor sharpness, Herrnstein and Murray accept without thoughtful reflection that IQ tests measure a singular, one-dimensional intelligence that is highly heritable and largely immutable, although the balance of existing evidence does not support this view. They then march ahead, with this dubious presumption unquestioned, to argue that IQ is a key factor determining where individuals end up in society, that it therefore varies across social classes due strictly to merit driven stratification, that blacks are typically on the lower rungs of society because they have on average lower IQs than whites and other races, and that all of these "facts" taken together indicate that social programs aimed at improving the lot of the poor are a waste of effort, since the poor occupy their social position due to their inherently inferior intellects. All of these dubious claims are supposedly established by a highly selective reading of existing evidence, where findings suggesting interpretations counter to their own—e.g., IQ is influenced by social position, therefore lower IQs among the underprivileged are the effect, not the cause, of inequality—are ignored; by wild speculation in the absence of appropriate evidence; and by reifying IQ in the same unthinking manner as their biological determinist predecessors.[9]

With Charles Murray's IQ propaganda set in place in 1994, the Bradley experiment was good to go. In *The Feeding Trough*, Phil Wilayto notes the following. With Eli Lilly's J. Clayburn La Force as a board member, the Bradley Foundation unleashed its racist experiment on Wisconsin. First, they funded a bogus study accusing Illinois residents of getting Wisconsin's welfare checks. Then, along with the Annie E. Casey Foundation, Bradley handed the Indianapolis-based Hudson Institute money to camp in Wisconsin for two years to develop Wisconsin Works or W-2, a welfare program eventually passed by both Republicans and Democrats in 1996. For the W-2 plan, the Hudson Institute hired Charles Murray himself as consultant. The think tank was thriving from Eli Lilly money and the success of Mitch Daniels, the Institute's CEO who had left a few years earlier for his Lilly job. Hudson's board, at the time, included Dan Quayle, the former US vice president from Indiana. The group also employed Charles E. Finn Jr., the father figure of the corporate school movement behind Edison Schools' beginning and funder of Tony Bennett's failed 2012 superintendent campaign.

The Bradley Foundation believes that taxes—especially corporate ones—should not be used for any social programs and that privatization gives the deserving rich their fair shake. The W-2 program proved this. As Phil Wilayto comments, Bradley and its politicians had the rights of corporations like McDonalds in mind when it "overhauled" the social welfare program. Instead of creating "decent, union-wage jobs or guaranteed income for all," Bradley's W-2 trapped the disabled, people with mental problems, and women (many of them black and Latina and with infants) into "a life of low-wage, dead-end jobs, many of them at temp agencies."[10] Since there weren't many opportunities in poor Milwaukee for "workfare," mothers were removed from W-2, lost all forms of income, and the state came in and took away their kids. After merely three months, the government gave some of these kids up for adoption. But in this servitude system, "privately operated W-2 agencies have made huge profits, while local businesses and 'non-profits' have found free labor for their enterprises."[11]

W-2 was a direct attack on Milwaukee's black and Latino communities, a continuation of Bradley-supported school vouchers started in 1990. As Wilayto writes, both W-2 and school vouchers went under the guise of offering upward mobility to minorities, but the truth is "the major role of both programs has been to further undermine the principle that the people are 'entitled' to anything from their government, while expanding the opportunities for the privatization of public services."[12]

A 2005 investigative report by the *Milwaukee Journal Sentinel's* Alan J. Borsuk and Sarah Carr gives us a glimpse into what society can expect from private schools that are not held accountable to open door meetings, can hire unqualified teachers, discriminate against people who hold different lifestyle and religious beliefs, and refuse to release any information to the public whose money supports them. Although ten schools the *Journal Sentinel* reporters visited "appeared to lack the ability, resources, knowledge or will to offer children even a mediocre education,"[13] the mugging of taxpayers' pockets was a high priority on the private and mostly religious schools' agenda. At the Mandella School of Science and Math, for example, the CEO "over-reported students and used state dollars to buy two Mercedes-Benz automobiles."[14] A convicted rapist cashed in by founding Alex's Academics of Excellence, which "continued to enroll students even after facing two evictions, allegations of drug use by staff on school grounds, and an investigation by the district attorney."[15] The reporters discovered the voucher program was better at financially bailing out Catholic schools than giving minorities a better education. That year, 2005, the Milwaukee school voucher program shifted $83 million of public money into private hands.[16]

Bradley's Michael Joyce was the architect of Milwaukee's school voucher movement. One of the leaders of the Reagan Revolution, Joyce understood that, if enough cities and states ultimately gave out school vouchers, public money eventually would be used to pay for upper-middle class and rich families to send their privileged kids to private institutions, financially draining the public schools and setting them up for privatization. It was probably Joyce's idea in 2000 to establish the all African-American front group the Black Alliance for Educational Options to sell school privatization nationwide. In 2000, Bradley and the Walton Walmart family did just that, with operatives from Indiana playing a major role.

BEFORE THE NATIONAL Press Club at the Washington, DC Mayflower Hotel and a live August 24, 2000 C-SPAN audience, the Black Alliance for Educational Options (BAEO) broadcasted its formation just in time for the new school year. Although it claimed to be committed to empowering low-income parents and opening up options for minority students left in an "educational wasteland," it was obvious by those bankrolling and leading the BAEO that school privatization was its motive. Although now BAEO has funding from the Democrats for Education Reform, Bill Gates, and the Dick and Betsy DeVos Family Foundation to sponsor its "symposiums," when the front group started it was headquartered in Milwaukee and completely owned by the Bradley Foundation, Walmart, and Mitch Daniels and Milton Friedman's Friedman Foundation.

Spun out of conferences at Marquette University's Institute for the Transformation of Learning, Howard Fuller lead BAEO to misinform the African-American community about voucher and charter schools. Fuller beamed on the national radar in 1987, when he tried to establish a totally black school district in Wisconsin. When he later became superintendent of the Milwaukee Public Schools, the state passed a bill to exempt him from certain requirements, since Fuller didn't have the essential "three years of pre-collegiate teaching experience" the job required.[17] In 1999, Texas governor George W. Bush selected Fuller for his Hudson Institute-led education policy advisory board. Fuller's wife, Deborah McGriff, when BAEO started, was president at Edison Teacher Colleges and had worked for Edison Schools since 1993, owning $3 million in Edison stocks in 1999.[18]

BAEO first helped Edison move into Indiana. Reverend and former Democratic US Rep. Floyd Flake, as Edison Schools' president and BAEO representative, headlined the July 2001 Education Reform and the Black Community: Understanding Your Options event, sponsored by the Indy BAEO, the Black Chamber of Commerce, the Indiana Black Expo, the Light of the Christian Church, the Urban Christian Schools Coalition, and the *Indianapolis Recorder*.[19] Having spent $140,000 that year on lobbying,[20] Edison was wishing for an Indiana miracle. In April 2001, Edison lost the bid to seize five New York City public schools after parents voted against the for-profit company.[21] The month before Flake's Indy speech, the San Francisco Board of Education severed its ties to Edison for "discriminating against black students, urging special-education students to apply elsewhere and threatening teachers."[22] By August, Edison was taking heat in Philadelphia for Flake's Washington connection to former congressman Tom Ridge, who was now Pennsylvania's governor.[23] Flake and Edison were able to dupe Indianapolis. In a no-bid contract with Perry Township, Edison stamped its name on the Jeremiah Gray-Edison Elementary School and the Rosa Parks-Edison Elementary School in 2002 and 2003, both still managed by Edison. As *NUVO's* Jack Miller noticed, the Lilly Foundation supplied a $4.6 million grant to Perry Township to pay for Edison's services at a 17 percent higher cost per student than other district schools. In 2004, Tony Bennett and Mitch Daniels' mega- millionaire donor Christel DeHaan hired Edison for $3 million to run her Christel House Academy in Indianapolis, a charter school at the time with low test scores, a high rate of teacher firings, and no union.[24]

While the Reverend Flake was busy selling Edison in Indianapolis, he was hired in 2002 to be president of Ohio's Wilberforce University, where he quickly planned his cash-in. A Methodist, Flake tapped his past congressional chief of staff and Edison Schools employee Marshall Mitchell to be vice president of institutional advancement at America's oldest private black college where 90 percent of the money comes from taxpayers. After cutting professors' retirement funding or salaries by 10 percent and slicing the number of majors the school offered by two-thirds, Flake awarded Mitchell a pay raise of $64,000 in 2005 to add to his $76,000 salary and gave other crony administrators higher salaries, too. By 2008, Flake had a $340,100 compensation package, even though he only flew in on an airplane to work one day a week. Flake said he was working forty hours a week at a nonprofit out of his house, but the college also insisted he worked forty hours at the school each week. Sliding "around the campus in a new $54,000 Cadillac Escalade,"[25] Flake doubled his salary to $204,998 and bought a $190,000 condo while "his expense account shot up to $39,300—almost exactly what would be needed to put a 20 percent down payment on the condo."[26] Flake even handed *Princeton Review* $1,180,998 in federal money by forcing the university to use the company's online high school classes, which were too low-level for college students. At this point, Flake—who was pulling in almost $300,000 yearly from his Greater Allen AME Cathedral nonprofit and a music enterprise and "likely $23,000 from his congressman pension"—sat on the *Princeton Review's* advisory committee and was privy to stock options in the company.[27]

Edison's coup in Indianapolis couldn't have been achieved without Jacqueline Joyner (Jackie) Cissell, who first welcomed Flake into the city. Jackie Cissell was a founding BAEO member and helped with BAEO Indiana. A business school graduate of Christian Indiana Wesleyan University, at the time of BAEO's creation Cissell held a position promoting school vouchers and charter schools at the Walton family-funded Greater Educational Opportunities Foundation (GEO Foundation). As *Black Commentator's* Glen Ford determined, Cissell's GEO Foundation paycheck was coming from the Bradley Foundation and the Indianapolis-based school choice Friedman Foundation.[28] Besides providing BAEO with $1.3 million over three years in 2003 for a media campaign to peddle school vouchers and charter schools,[29] the Bush administration's Department of Education gave GEO $2.1 million in No Child Left Behind promotional money.[30] One of GEO's targeted cities for No Child Left Behind was Gary, Indiana, where Kevin Teasley opened GEO's 21st Century Charter School in 2005. The other was Denver, an hour away from where the company unveiled its Pikes Peak Prep charter school, also in 2005.[31]

Even though the BAEO supposedly held meetings attended by its founder Howard Fuller and then-US secretary of education Rod Paige to plug the charter school, the backlash in Gary erupted in May 2006 when parents at GEO's 21st Century Charter School boycotted the school because there was no nurse, teachers were teaching basic math in upper-level courses, and two teachers were suspended for a week for hitting students with drumsticks and touching them inappropriately. Even worse, the week after the boycott, a teacher's aide was arrested for choking a twelve-year-old student with a trash bag in February of that year in a social studies class until the boy turned red and couldn't breathe.[32] More recently, the Indiana State Board of Accounts cited the Gary school for sloppy financial record keeping and poor management.[33] In early April 2011, when Jackie Cissell tailed Tony Bennett to market school vouchers on the pastor Raymond Dix Jr.'s WLTH *Higher Ground* radio show, she was still praising the 21st Century Charter School, despite its problems.

In Colorado, GEO was up to similar monkey business at its Pikes Peak Prep School. In a June 30, 2009 audit, John Cutler & Associates note that the school was required to pay GEO 100 percent of all the $1,604,230 in state and federal funds for students enrolled, and the school didn't have enough money to fulfill its contract and still owned GEO $349,159. In October 2010, the Colorado Department of Education stressed that the school had a $551,659 deficit fund balance and didn't include an analysis of management statements in its reports to the department.[34] Since the school also pays GEO an administrative fee (as schools often do to private management companies), this heightens the school's financial troubles. *World Law Direct* claims that in June 2010 the school and the GEO Foundation were further investigated for creating a hostile work environment, wrongfully terminating staff, and misusing funds.[35]

Both Cissell and GEO's CEO Kevin Teasley have contacts within the Christian Right and school voucher crowd. A year after BAEO's formation, Cissell was circling with powerful black men who were supporting the corporate-controlled theocracy some rich white men wanted for America, beginning her career with Black America's Political Action Committee (BAMPAC). BAMPAC is the anti-abortion, pro-school prayer, pro-social security privatization, and pro-school voucher political action committee which Alan Keyes—Ronald Reagan's US ambassador to the United Nations Economic and Social Council—established in the early '90s to pipe money to Republican candidates. Keyes co-founded BAMPAC with Alvin Williams, a George H. W. Bush presidential transition team member who, in 2005, grabbed a seat on BAEO's board.

Kevin Teasley—whose taxpayer-supported paycheck reached $200,000 in the 2011-2012 tax year[36]—is a former Reagan Office of Public Liaison official who has crusaded for school vouchers in several states. While at the Reason Foundation in California, Teasley worked alongside the Excellence Through Choice-in-Education League (EXCEL), underwritten and/or supported by Indiana's own Dan Quayle, William Bennett, and Milton Friedman, a group which then-California's state school superintendent Bill Honig said was wanting to use taxpayer money to breed "cult schools" that could end up becoming "David Duke Academies."[37] Despite Teasley and EXCEL's efforts, the school voucher measure on the November 1992 California ballot did not pass. In Wisconsin, Teasley and John Walton, the son of Sam Walton, Walmart's founder, steered the American Education Reform Council (whose lobbying branch was the American Education Reform Foundation). Bankrolled by the Walton family and the Bradley Foundation, the American Education Reform Council campaigned for turn-of-the-century vouchers in Colorado and other states. As People for the American Way notes in *Community Voice or Captive of the Right?: A Closer Look at the Black Alliance for Educational Options*, in 1997 Teasley—then American Education Reform Foundation's president—and Hoosier J. Patrick Rooney (whose Indiana CHOICE voucher group

once employed Jackie Cissell) were investigated by the Wisconsin election board for conspiring with Mark Block, campaign manager for the reelection of Wisconsin Supreme Court justice Jon Wilcox. Wilcox was pro-voucher, so it was essential to reelect him to continue the Bradley Foundation's Milwaukee voucher scheme. Although Teasley, Rooney, and the American Education Reform Foundation did not violate election law, according to officials, Teasley supposedly raised over $10,000 for Wilcox's campaign after he wrote letters to voucher backers. Wilcox won, but he and Mark Block (who now directs Wisconsin's Koch-funded Americans for Prosperity branch) were both fined for illegally coordinating a get-out-the-vote effort.
38

GEO's 21st Century Charter School board members also epitomize the loose ethics of those involved in the school privatization movement. Besides financing Teasley's GEO, the Bush Administration lent Nina Rees to the school choice outfit. Now a GEO board member, Rees was Dick Cheney's former domestic policy adviser and helped the Bush Administration implement No Child Left Behind, even though she holds no degree in education. She now is the government relations policy person in DC for Knowledge Universe, a global education corporation with 3,700 education locations, 40,000 teachers, and a network of online schools and colleges, according to its website. Knowledge Universe is chaired by Mike Milken, the TAP teacher merit-pay promoter who served two years in prison in the early '90s. Rollin M. Dick is also onboard the GEO Foundation. A donor to Mitch Daniels, Tony Bennett, Indiana Republican Brian Bosma, and the Mind Trust, Dick was chief financial official for the insurance investor Conseco when it nosedived into bankruptcy after an aggressive acquisition plan and the $95 million price tag to stamp its name on Conseco Fieldhouse, the Indianapolis Pacers' stadium. As a result of the upheaval, Dick and Conseco CEO Steven C. Hilbert both resigned in 2000. In 2004, the Securities and Exchange Commission sued Dick and Conseco's James Adams for $5.6 million.[39]

Jackie Cissell must have felt comfortable working with Teasley's crew, since, as the community relations liaison with the Indiana Family and Social Services Administration, she later pushed for the same low standards represented at the GEO Foundation. In 2007, Cissell—a past minority affairs consultant liaison for the Indianapolis Power and Light Company—encouraged Chaplain Michael Latham, a former Fort Wayne NAACP leader, to apply for the position of state chaplain. As the *New York Times* mentioned at the time, chaplains can legally work with the police, military, and fire agencies where employees are heavily stressed, but there is no need for a chaplain program in the Indiana Family and Social Services Administration, an office essentially responsible for aiding the poor. Besides, Latham holds no degrees and does not have the credentials to work in Indiana nursing homes, hospitals, or psychiatric units. He did, however, deliver the benediction for Governor Daniels' Allen County inaugural event in 2004.

After being hired, Latham was to be paid $60,000 yearly as the highest paid chaplain in Indiana to recruit chaplains to oversee services for the Indiana Family and Social Services Administration, but he disappeared from the office for months on end, leading employees to believe the program had been cancelled. By late September 2007, the Indiana Family and Social Services Administration ditched Latham from its payroll and ended the program, after the Wisconsin-based Freedom from Religion Foundation filed a May 2007 lawsuit.[40]

Cissell went on to work for the Indiana Department of Education's Office of School Improvement and Turnaround, which hands schools over to private companies.

ALTHOUGH CISSELL IS a Republican, Kevin P. Chavous calls himself a Democrat, even though he spends a good deal of time marketing Christian Right causes. A founding Black Alliance for Educational Options board member and the author of several corporate school-promoting books, Chavous is the Indianapolis-born African-American lawyer who helped form Democrats for Education Reform and still chairs its board of directors. Chavous began his anti-public school career as a DC councilman in Ward Seven, where, as the education committee chief, he offered the city to the school choice industry. In 2008, Chavous joined Barack Obama's policy committee but later placed a full-page ad in the *New York Times*, condemning the president for his anti-voucher stance after Barack failed to endorse the District of Columbia Opportunity Scholarship, which was recently reauthorized by Duncan and Obama to deliver millions of more in taxpayer money. In fact, Chavous helped start the District of Columbia Opportunity Scholarship in 2004 with Rod Paige, Anthony Williams, and Bradley operative Clint Bolick, who then was president of the DeVos family's Alliance for School Choice.

Besides selling school vouchers, Chavous effectively carries out the Bradley Foundation's ploy to drive a wedge between blacks, Democrats, and teachers unions and to pit blacks against blacks. Chavous—who held a 2011 private screening for the corporate school film *Waiting for Superman* at the Indiana statehouse—used the recent lawsuit over school closings in New York City to spin more Bradley propaganda. In a June 3rd, 2011, *Washington Post* editorial, Chavous knocked the NAACP for filing a lawsuit with the United Federation of Teachers to stop twenty public schools in NYC from closing and charter schools from sharing space with public schools. Thousands of anti-NAACP black parents took to the streets to protest, motivated by deceptive articles like Chavous' attacking the lawsuit. In his misleading piece, Chavous reminisced how he rode on his mother's shoulders in Indianapolis in the 1960s, while attending an NAACP demonstration against racist Alabama governor George Wallace who was visiting Butler University. Chavous remembers "carrying a sign that I pointed in Wallace's face" because Wallace and other white men didn't want him to get an education. His mother was proud of Chavous becoming a card-carrying NAACP member. Now, according to Chavous, "the NAACP has become the protector of the status quo it once fought."[41]

During the NYC battle, which the NAACP and union lost, 100 Black Men's David Brand had no apprehensions assaulting the NAACP, either. In comments he emailed to hedge fund manager and Democrats for Education Reform's Whitney Tilson on June 8th, Brand insults unions, teachers, custodians, and the NAACP, saying: "The reason why our schools are cleaner is because—DUH!—we clean them as opposed to relying on corrupt custodial unions. New books and smartboards don't educate kids. Good non-UFT teachers do." According to Brand, the NAACP "becomes the source of income for most of its leaders today. They are easily bought."[42]

With its own charter schools in at least six major cities, the 100 Black Men group fully understands what it means to be "easily bought." In Las Vegas, charter-chain Imagine Schools used then-100 Black Men vice president Shaundell Newsome's Newsome Marketing Enterprises to recruit students for the Imagine 100 Academy of Excellence when the school opened in 2006. When 100 Black Men of Las Vegas agreed to sponsor the school, its mentors were seen often when the school year started, but parents say the mentors quickly disappeared.[43] According to the *New York Times*' Stephanie Strom, the school went through three principals in four years, most of them fired after complaining there was no money to hire a nurse and to buy textbooks. The school was paying Imagine $3.6 million a year for rent.[44] A September 11, 2009 *Las Vegas Sun* article pointed out that parents protested and passed out fliers to passengers in cars after one of these firings, but Imagine controlled the purse strings.[45] Authorities cited the school for lax accounting, breaking state law in having a deficit owned to Imagine, and not offering competitive bidding in handing over the school to Imagine's CEO Dennis Bakke, a Mitch Daniels acquaintance.[46] Las Vegas' TV station Action 13 reported on March 11, 2010, roughly a month in a half before the *New York Times*' article, that an arsonist was setting fires at the elementary school and at least four of them had gone unreported, according to a parent who spoke with the TV station. Administrators agreed to mount more security cameras inside the building, but the North Las Vegas Fire Department investigated and parents pulled their children from the school the following year. Action 13 noted that "for two days, Imagine regional vice-president Vickie Frazier-Williams has ignored Action News' repeated requests for comment."[47] In early September 2010, one special education teacher set the school's copier room on fire and was arrested for felony arson.[48] As early as 2008, another parent told *Las Vegas Sun* reporter Emily Richmond she waited in her daughter's unsupervised first grade classroom but no teacher ever arrived. After several adults dropping off their kids joined her, the parent went to the office and was told that maybe the teacher was out of town.[49] The 100 Academy of Excellence in Las Vegas is still managed by Imagine Schools. The current board chair is Sylvia Allen, vice president of the 100 Black Women of Las Vegas.

Chavous' Black Alliance for Educational Options has also run into trouble with its charter schools. With college-dropout Bill Gates' money, BAEO founded the New Media Technology charter school in Philadelphia, where its board chair pled guilty to twenty-eight counts of wire fraud, theft, and conspiracy in federal court in 2012.[50] Pennsylvania lawmakers have purposely imposed an austerity crisis on the public school system, so that more schools can fall into private hands, despite the fact that in 2011 nineteen Philadelphia charter schools were investigated for massive fraud and corruption. The BAEO has been behind this Philadelphia school privatization plan from the beginning, with Chavous' cousin Dawn a key player. A board president at the Oprah-funded Mastery Charter Schools, Dawn is on the board of Boys' Latin Philadelphia Charter School and handles the Students First PAC. Recently, her Students First PAC received $1.1 million from the Indiana-registered American Federation for Children PAC, one group which schemed to get the Indiana 2011 anti-public school bills passed and similar bills across the country.[51]

Kevin Chavous himself has profited from and holds high positions in the American Federation for Children and its sister the Alliance for School Choice, two front groups headed by Betsy DeVos of Michigan's DeVos family. A former Michigan Republican chairwoman, Betsy DeVos is treasurer for the Bradley Foundation-funded, Christian Right, free-market Action Institute. Like the Bradley Foundation, the DeVos family devotes a good deal of money to Christian Right causes. Bankrolling the likes of the Family Research Council and Focus on the Family, the DeVos family supports the biblical capitalism goal to cut social services to the poor. Erik Prince, Betsy DeVos' brother, owned Blackwater, the private security and Christian-based militia which swindled money from taxpayers during the Iraqi War on Terror when several of its guards were arrested for murder. Richard and Helen DeVos, Betsy' in-laws who once owned their own island, have given over a million dollars to the anti-affirmative action Donors Trust. Betsy's husband Dick—who ran for governor of Michigan a few years back—is heir to the multi-billion dollar Amway Corporation, the home products business.

Dick DeVos, in a 2002 Heritage Foundation speech, outlined how school privatizers must buy out and threaten state legislators, establish front groups like the American Federation for Children, and mask the corporate and theocratic movement as grassroots, all the while keeping it hush-hush from the public:

> And so while those of us on the national level can give support, we need to encourage the development of these organizations on a state-by-state basis, in order to be able to offer a political consequence, for opposition, and political reward, for support of, education reform issues.
>
> That has got to be the battle. It will not be as visible. And, in fact, to the extent that we on the right, those of us on the conservative side of the aisle, appropriate education choice as our idea, we need to be a little bit cautious about doing that, because we have here an issue that cuts in a very interesting way across our community and can cut, properly communicated, properly constructed, can cut across

a lot of historic boundaries, be they partisan, ethnic, or otherwise. And so we've got a wonderful issue that can work for Americans. But to the extent that it is appropriated or viewed as only a conservative idea it will risk not getting a clear and a fair hearing in the court of public opinion. So we do need to be cautious about that. We need to be cautious about talking too much about these activities.[52]

This is the plan the DeVos family carried out in Indiana. Using heavy funding from thirteen donors which included Betsy DeVos, Walmart's Alice and Jim Walton, Pennsylvania hedge fund managers, two leaders of charter schools in Indiana (John Bryan and J.C. Huizenga, who we will meet later), and Jeb Bush friend John Kirtley, the American Federation for Children's Indiana-registered PAC in 2010 funneled over $4.6 million into the Hoosier state (through the Hoosiers for Economic Growth PAC) and six other states using the Terre Haute office mailbox address of Christian Right lawyer James Bopp Jr., the man behind the Citizens United case which gave rights to corporations to fund campaign super-PACs without publically disclosing their donors.[53] In 2010, the American Federation for Children gave various Indiana corporate school front groups $375,000 to attempt to swing eighty-five primary and general elections, using millionaire Fred Klipsch, School Choice Indiana, and Hoosiers for Economic Growth to elect a super-majority of Republicans to the Senate and take total control of the House to pass anti-public education laws in 2011.[54] For his part in doing the Catholics good, Klipsch was handed the 2012 Catholic's Career Achievement Award at an Archdiocese of Indianapolis ceremony with Tony Bennett which raised money from corporations who benefit from a 50 percent state tax credit for donations to the Educational CHOICE Charitable Trust.[55]

American Federation for Children originally operated under the name All Children Matter. In Indiana, All Children Matter gave Republicans $700,000 over the last few years and $250,000 to Mitch Daniel's Aiming Higher PAC in 2011. To spread its message in 2009, All Children Matter's Iowa branch used Faulkner Strategies, the right-wing PR firm Tony Bennett hired to do holiday campaign cards which recently employed newly retired Indiana State Board of Education member Jo Blacketor.[56] All Children Matter has violated campaign rules in several states. Besides being fined for not registering its Virginia PAC in Wisconsin, All Children Matter has yet to pay a $5.2 million fine in Ohio, as the Associated Press noted in a March 29, 2011 story, for illegally directing "$870,000 in contributions from its Virginia political action committee to its Ohio affiliate" which "violated a $10,000 cap on what Ohio-based political-action committees could accept from any single entity."[57]

With vast amounts of money, the DeVos family is speed-dialing the agenda of school privatization. While discussing school voucher and segregation schemes, Rachel Tabachnick sums up what is behind the DeVos and right-wing push for private school scholarships:

> Whatever they may say about giving poor students a leg up, their real priority is nothing short of the total dismantling of our public educational institutions, and they've admitted as much. Cato Institute founder Ed Crane and other conservative think tank leaders have signed the Public Proclamation to Separate School and State, which reads in part that signing on, "Announces to the world your commitment to end involvement by local, state, and federal government from education.[58]

David D. Friedman, Milton's son who sits on the Friedman Foundation board, has signed the Public Proclamation to Separate School and State.

The secret "activities" Dick DeVos spoke of at the Heritage Foundation event are meant to sucker parents, kids, taxpayers, and teachers. If teachers are confused about why schools are closing and being turned over to private management companies where all democratic rights are lost, they should know that wealthy funders like Amway and their junk science sell-outs have designed the corporate and theocratic school movement to intentionally confuse the masses.

Kevin Chavous is paid well to confuse the masses for the DeVos family. When Chavous joined the board of Alliance for School Choice in 2010, the DeVos squad provided Chavous' SNR Denton law firm $102,000 for consulting services. Chavous made $50,000 when he was selected to be the group's "secretary" in 2011. In 2010, while Chavous was onboard the American Federation for Children, the group passed SNR Denton $117,000. In 2011, Chavous was paid an additional $50,000 to be American Federation for Children's "secretary."[59]

The American Federation for Children has nearly the same directors as the Alliance for School Choice. Besides Chavous, these include Pennsylvania hedge fund manager Joel Greenberg, hedge funder and Democrat for Education Reform's Boykin Curry, Walmart's Carrie Walton Penner, and Florida money-man and Jeb Bush friend John F. Kirtley, who bought out both Florida Republicans and Democrats while running the DeVos school voucher outfits in that state. In 2010, Greenberg handed the American Federation for Children Action Fund in Indiana $434,000—Kirtley $80,000.[60]

A big Black Alliance for Educational Options donor, the Alliance for School Choice has patrons with bottomless pockets. The Walton family has given the front group millions, alongside money from the Kern Family Foundation and the Charles G. Koch Foundation, run by the Koch brothers, the billionaire oil, gas, and land firm titans. The Bradley Foundation dished out $20,000 to Alliance for School Choice in 2011, the same year it gave the Black Alliance for Educational Options $115,000.[61]

This is the mob Kevin Chavous hobnobs with, and when he returned to Indiana to join Mitch Daniels at the 21st annual Dr. King Indiana Holiday Celebration at the statehouse on January 12, 2012, he laid it on thick. While protests over the right-to-work anti-labor bill were erupting in other statehouse locations, Chavous didn't mention that Martin Luther King Jr. was killed while standing up for the rights of workers. Chavous gave no word that his son and BAEO's Washington bureau chief Kevin B. Chavous had been arrested just days before for allegedly soliciting an undercover police officer for sex on K Street in DC.[62] And he spoke not about the Klu Klux Klan's recent announcement that it supported racially segregated charter schools, which most are. After local radio personality Abdul Hakim-Shabazz admired Chavous for his Louisiana school voucher work, Chavous leaned into the microphone and said hello to BAEO's Jackie Cissell in attendance. Then hired-gun Kevin Chavous, to hundreds of school children at the MLK event, said this: "See, I don't sleep, because I know there are children who will wake up tomorrow and go to a bad school. That bothers me. And if it doesn't bother all of us, then it ain't right."[63]

ANOTHER MICHIGAN FRONT group with DeVos family ties snaking around Indiana is right-to-work champion Kyle Olson's Education Action Group (EAG). EAG has shot videos, circulated its "Hoosier Report Card" to thousands, and bashed the Indiana Democrats for their walkout to Illinois to slow down anti-worker legislation. EAG oversees *ISTA Exposed*, a website condemning the Indiana State Teachers Association.

At the end of 2010, after squandering over a million dollars, EAG still had a fund balance of $381,000 to spin anti-teacher and anti-public school tales.[64] That year, the Indianapolis-based Friedman Foundation gave EAG $65,000.[65] EAG received $115,000 in Bradley Foundation money for its new Wisconsin shop in 2011.[66] Katherine Stewart, in *The Good News Club: The Christian Right's Stealth Assault on America's Children*, traces EAG's funding to the Gleason Family Foundation, a DeVos Alliance for School Choice donor.[67] Although EAG refuses to release the names of its corporate suppliers, the two-man group emerged from the 2000 Michigan school voucher initiative mastered by the DeVos family, which also was behind

Michigan governor Rick Snyder's right-to-work law.

Critics of EAG suspect Michigan's right-wing Mackinac Center for Public Policy is involved.[68] Kyle's brother Ryan was employed at Mackinac until 2008. Mackinac receives money from the Bradley Foundation, the DeVos and Walton families, and the Charles G. Koch Charitable Foundation and Claude R. Lambe Charitable Foundation.

The Lambe Foundation is just one of many foundations run by the Koch brothers, and it subsidizes the Ayn Rand Institute's "educational program" where free-market operatives dupe teachers with the yearly Ayn Rand essay contests, a series of monetary awards handed out to school kids who wish to go to college and hopefully join an Ayn Rand club. Each fall through spring, teachers, both in Indiana and across the US, pass out guidelines to students in their high school English courses to apply. The students write essays (like "How Reading Ayn Rand Novels Has Affected My Life") on Rand's *Atlas Shrugged* and other books, and winners—often Hoosiers—are announced in the Rand Institute-affiliated free-market *Objective Standard*, alongside articles demanding all American public schools be turned over to private hands.

Based in Irvine, California, the Rand Institute never mentions school privatization when it courts trusting teachers with pure deception to pass on free-market orthodoxy on steroids. The group offers free sets of Rand books for high schools, encouraging their adoption on many teachers' blogs and websites. Teachers who sway students to submit to the Rand essay contests obtain "nice gifts from us as well," the Randians note. This tactic generates a winning situation for the free-marketers. Educators see these free books as a godsend, since due to budget cuts they can't stock their classrooms with many books at all, if they don't forfeit their own money, which many do. Besides showing that Rand has become God for Tea Party Republicans like Paul Ryan who pursue free-market government programs that steal from the poor and middle class to provide for the rich, David Johnson points out that "Rand wrote that the serial killer was an 'ideal man,' a superior form of human because he didn't let society impose their morals on him. He didn't worry about what others thought and just did as he pleased."[69] Rand's pseudo-intellectualism stresses that every individual should break laws, steal, and even kill to fulfill his or her individual needs. With this plundering mentality, corporations seeking to privatize education classify teachers as mere impediments to CEO gain. Rand hated that taxes were used for public schools. Yet politicians, universities, school corporations, and Indiana newspapers praise Hoosier students who have won these awards. The students have no idea they are victims in a ploy to spread a message which places private profit over the needs of a free society.

Whereas Randians promote free-market ideology in the classroom, Education Action Group's Kyle Olson wants more of it in children's bedrooms. A frequent *Glenn Beck Program* guest and author of the anti-public school rant *Indoctrination*, Olson says that *Click, Clack, Moo, Cows That Type* is unacceptable as a children's bedtime story because subversive cows weave tales of good workers unions and greedy capitalists.[70] Kids, according to crony capitalists, must be indoctrinated with books teaching the "morals" of robbing from the poor, making money off of slave laborers, and destroying everyone and everything in sight to reach "the top." The *Johnny Profit* bedtime story fits this scenario. Unlike Moses, Johnny Profit (who physically resembles the old prophet) leads the town into slavery, paying his workers only with new shovels.[71] *Forbes Magazine's* Steve Forbes wrote a blurb for the book. As a leader of the DeVos and Bradley Foundation-funded Freedom Works, a Tea Party outfit, Forbes petitioned against Indiana teachers' collective bargaining rights.

Teachers' collective bargaining rights and anti-union spin take up the majority of Kyle Olson's film *Kids Aren't Cars*.[72] Released on February 1st, 2011, Olson's movie was touted far and wide by school privatizers. In the *Nevada News & Views*, Olson said: "Our public school system, under union domination for the past four decades, is designed to benefit adults at the expense of children."[73] As an example of this benefit to adults, the *Nevada News & Views* offered a snippet of Michigan as it's represented in the movie:

> In one film, an executive director of a literacy clinic in Detroit—where high school graduates go to learn how to read—compares the actions of the pro-union school board to the Ku Klux Klan. "If they were sitting up there in Klan robes," she says, "we would be marching and screaming." [Eight of the nine school board members are black.][74]

Olson's opinion of unions is quite slanted and racist as it represents Detroit. Unions helped guarantee blacks jobs in the teaching field, not to mention the Detroit auto factories, which ushered in a class of black professionals safeguarded by seniority and immune to the discrimination they encountered in the anti-union south. This job guarantee looks to end now, with Michigan governor Rick Snyder's emergency management program sweeping Detroit and his attacks on unions.

In another *Kids Aren't Cars* episode, Tony Bennett, anti-union since his grad school days, appears in front of the American flag in one scene and ignores his own research. Since the former Indiana school boss constantly knocked unions in his scripted media appearances, it is not well known that Tony Bennett's EdD dissertation proved that teachers unions in Indiana were not stopping school administrators from firing "bad teachers" at all. In "The Effects of Just Cause Contract Language on Teacher Dismissals in Indiana Between 1999-2004," the former principal and basketball coach discovered in 2005 that Hoosier school corporations "have not encountered measurable resistance by teachers' unions against their recommendations to dismiss teachers" and that "just cause contract language has not presented insurmountable hurdles for school corporations as they work to improve teachers' performance and behavior."[75] Although Bennett found that administrators were not in any way handcuffed from holding teachers to high standards, this didn't stop him from bashing unions in Olson's movie or telling the *South Bend Tribune's* Kim Kilbride in 2011 that "we find numerous, not single, but numerous clauses in collective-bargaining agreements that really are obstructions to school corporations."[76]

IN JANUARY 2011, when Kyle Olson was directing National School Choice Week, the multi-million dollars strong Milton Friedman Foundation for Educational Choice—an Indianapolis nonprofit propaganda mill, lobbying group, and corporate school funder founded by Milton Friedman, Mitch Daniels, and a few others—was ballyhooing its just released "Indiana K-12 & School Choice Survey." Funded by the Walton family, the Bradley Foundation, the Koch brothers, and other wealthy donors, the Friedman Foundation's message was predictable: Hoosier parents overwhelmingly favor getting their kids into non-union charter schools and school voucher institutions and "are unsatisfied with the current public education system."[77]

But despite the media hype, the phone survey results were skewed and actually bad news for the corporate school movement. Even though low-income minority kids are most affected by so-called school choice, 91 percent of the people interviewed across Indiana were white people. Responders, in fact, were adamantly against online learning outfits, with 51 percent saying they "opposed" them. Only 10 percent of Hoosiers interviewed across the state said they "would like to send their child to a charter school," and a mere 17 percent rated Indiana schools as "poor" in their role educating children. Only 32 percent surveyed even knew what a school voucher was, so those answering voucher questions were doing so without prior serious thought. Finally, only 36 percent of Hoosiers surveyed had kids attending K-12 schools. In one county, this dipped to just 28 percent. The people interviewed for Friedman's sham survey didn't even have a need to select so-called school choice—more proof that this is not about parents but profit.

Friedman's tweaking of the survey data is not surprising, since professors at the National Education Policy Center have proven how the Friedman Foundation is good at using faux research to say what it wants it to say. While reviewing the Friedman Foundation's Greg Forster's "Win-Win Solution" study, for example, Christopher Lubienski, a University of Illinois professor, notes how Forster's report was not blind peer reviewed, makes assertions not backed up by evidence, and cherry-picks a majority of studies done and supported by pro-voucher groups. Only two of the seventeen studies Forster examined were published in independently reviewed scholarly journals; the rest were circulated by school choice advocates. After detailing for twenty pages how Forster's study is scholarly worthless, Lubienski states that Forster's "logic is similar to that of market fundamentalists who, in the face of a global economic crisis widely considered to be caused by deregulated markets, are arguing that the remedy is further deregulation and more markets."[78]

Robert Enlow, who hyped the Indiana study, has been with Friedman since it was founded in 1996, but he only took the group's reins in 2009 when ex-Eli Lilly official and former Indiana Democratic chairman Gordon St. Angelo stepped down after twelve years and a $781,601 paycheck from Friedman for 2008 through 2010.[79] Enlow made almost $200,000 from Friedman in 2010.[80]

A point man at the right-wing Bradley-funded Sagamore Institute in Indiana, Robert Enlow once chaired the Education Task Force at the American Legislative Exchange Council (ALEC). ALEC has written and/or promoted most of the anti-public school laws which have made their way throughout the country and the Hoosier state, where close to thirty Indiana lawmakers are ALEC members.[81] Since ALEC wants to put bankers, hedge funders, and other corporatists who took part in the US home ownership collapse now in charge of our schools, it is little surprise that past ALEC affiliates are well represented at Friedman and in Indiana government, with

Hoosier lawmaker David Frizzell in 2010 and 2011 operating as ALEC's national chairman.

In 2010, Enlow championed school vouchers before the Pennsylvania Senate, a state where the Black Alliance for Educational Options' connections with ALEC go way back. At ALEC's 2005 School Choice Academy in Philadelphia, BAEO's Virginia Walden Ford—now a Friedman Foundation board member—and Howard Fuller keynoted their addresses to fifty-two legislators from twenty-four states, among them then-Wisconsin Republican lawmaker and now DeVos family operative Scott Jensen, who the following year was found "guilty of misusing state workers and public resources to run Assembly Republican campaigns"[82] in the 2002 legislative caucus scandal but did no jail time. Alliance for School Choice president Clint Bolick also attended, where his Institute for Justice donated copies of Ford's *Voices, Choices and Second Chances: How to Win the Battle to Bring Opportunity Scholarships to Your State* to all attendees.[83] Moreover, when the Arizona Scholarships for Pupils with Disabilities Program and the Displaced Pupil's Grant Program, both school vouchers schemes, were challenged in the Arizona Supreme Court, superintendent of the schools Tom Horne's defenders were the Alliance for School Choice, BAEO, the Friedman Foundation, ALEC, and the Bradley Foundation-funded Institute for Justice.[84]

Chris Atkins, Friedman's senior fiscal analyst, has worked for ALEC, the Institute for Justice, and Mitch Daniels. As ALEC's past tax and fiscal policy director and a former summer intern for the Institute for Justice's Human Action Network, Atkins does not want to spend more money to eliminate inequality in the public schools. In 2007, while working for the Koch and Eli Lilly-affiliated Tax Foundation, Atkins released *Appropriation by Litigation: Estimating the Cost of Judicial Mandates for State and Local Education Spending* at yet another Philadelphia ALEC meeting. The report claimed that lawsuits forcing states to pay adequate funding to inadequately funded school districts have led only to higher tax rates. Atkins commented that "lawsuits may be able to build schools, but they haven't proven effective at teaching kids."[85] Thanks to anti-taxers like Atkins and the Tax Foundation, taxpayers and public schools lose millions of dollars each year because of tax breaks given to billionaires who fund nonprofits like the Friedman Foundation. Atkin's betterment to public education[86] has been limited to directing Mitch Daniels' Office of Management and Budget, where he was part of the team which put in place anti-public school property tax caps to sap funding from the schools and give out tax breaks for people who own mansions.

One of these mega-rich people is Fort Wayne-born Overstock.com's Patrick Byrne, who commands the Friedman Foundation board and like four other Friedman officials was a major Mitch Daniels and Tony Bennett donor. Since 2007, Byrne has given a total of $601,500 to Mitch Daniels, Tony Bennett, and the Hoosiers for Economic Growth PAC to fund anti-public school legislators. In Utah in 2008, Byrne and his mother and father contributed three-quarters of the $4 million the pro-voucher movement blew while unsuccessfully attempting to pass school choice legislation in the state.[87]

Scott Enright, Friedman's secretary, is vice president at Emmis Communications, the radio, digital, and publishing company conducting business in Indiana, Los Angeles, St. Louis, New York, Austin, and Bulgaria. Emmis owns ESPN 1070 The Fan, Country 97.1 Hank FM, WIBC 93.1 FM, and Soft Rock B105.7 in Indianapolis, each with market revenue of $75 million, according to the company's website. Emmis' Terre Haute stations include Hi-99 Radio and 105.5 The River, each worth revenue of $7.1 million. Emmis also owns the 45,000 circulating *Indianapolis Monthly* and Network Indiana. Network Indiana feeds news programming to stations across the state and has revenue of $1.5 million. Emmis received $118,750 from Friedman to "educate the public" on school vouchers, crafting, among other things, the "Why Not? Indiana" ads that appeared online and littered Hoosier newspapers.[88] Since the company has a member aboard the school voucher lobbying Friedman Foundation, Emmis has a pure conflict of interest and is clearly deceiving its readers and listeners.

Friedman also endorses charter schools. Friedman's vice president of programs and state relations is Republican Leslie Hiner, the board chair at Irvington Community Charter School, where she sits alongside former Black Alliance for Educational Option's Barato Britt, Eli Lilly's John Williams, and Jennifer Suzanne Thuma, a previous Daniels legislative director and education coordinator to the Indiana General Assembly from 2009 to 2010. Hiner, who made close to $160,000 for her work with Friedman in 2011, is former chief of staff to the Indiana House and previous attorney to the state senate.[89] Friedman Foundation's Jeffery William Reed (an alumnus of the Charles G. Koch Charitable Foundation's Koch Associate Program and a past Education Task Force director for ALEC) is working to open Nexus Academy of Indianapolis by Better Blended Learning for Indiana.

But vouchers, counterfeit research, and charter schools tell only half of the Friedman story. It also offers an enormous amount of money to those pursuing total school privatization. The Friedman Foundation, in 2010 alone, gave $30,000 to the Black Alliance for Educational Options and $65,000 to School Choice Indiana. Elsewhere, Friedman threw out $14,500 to the Tea Party's Americans for Prosperity, $15,000 to the New Jersey hedge fund-supported Excellent Education for Everyone (E3), headed by Black Alliance for Educational Options' Darrell Bradford and founded by now-Newark, New Jersey mayor Cory Booker, who was an original Black Alliance for Educational Options board member. Friedman also handed $25,000 to Jeb Bush's Foundation for Excellence in Education and money to other school privatization advocates in several states, including the pro-voucher Institute for Justice, School Choice Wisconsin, and Education Writers Association, led by the *Indianapolis Star's* Scott Elliott.[90]

If Elliott lacks a quotation, he merely needs to dial Friedman's national media relations office, where reporters can request comments and statements on any given subject from the "experts." Or merely visit one of the events sponsored by Friedman's Speakers Bureau, made up of past legislators, charter school operators, and lobbyists, including Kevin P. Chavous.

WHILE PURDUE SOCIETY of Non-Theists president Jen McCreight and Reba Wooden, the executive director of Center for Inquiry Indiana, were waiting at the Indianapolis airport on their flight to a DC rally, a woman from the Christian Focus on the Family's Indiana Family Institute interrupted their conversation and asked Wooden if her secular humanist Center for Inquiry Indy would help the Indiana Family Institute rewrite and pass the bill to teach creationism in the schools. For the Indiana Family Institute, the bill wasn't extreme enough. The Indiana Family Institute's representative recalled testifying over some of the same bills in Indiana as Wooden but forgot they were always on opposing sides. The scene got slightly awkward when Wooden mentioned her center was opposed to teaching creationism in the public schools. Jen McCreight told the Indiana Family Institute woman that maybe she was confusing the Center for Inquiry with the Discovery Institute, a DC and Washington state group which could assist her with the bill.[91] But the Intelligent Design-promoting Discovery Institute had, ironically, already blasted Indiana's creationism law, stating that, unlike the intelligent design theory, it contained no science.[92]

Dennis Kruse, the auctioneer and Senate Education Committee head who first introduced the creationism bill, is an advisor to the Indiana Family Institute and is tied to right-wing religious organizations like the American Family Association of DeKalb County, Right to Life, and Advance America. Kruse's bill attempted to convert science classrooms across the state into the Creation Museum in Petersburg, Kentucky, where dinosaurs and Sarah Palins roam Eden hand in hand and schools receiving state vouchers like Anderson's Liberty Christian School visit on field trips and teach a free-market Jesus in the classroom.[93] Close to 120 students at Liberty Christian receive state voucher money,[94] while Anderson schools recently lost 1000 students, $6 million, and 200 teachers, one-third of its teacher force.[95]

Before the bill passed in the Senate, Democrat Vi Simpson was able to amend the bill to include the teaching of Buddhism, Islam, and Scientology to the science class curriculum. The *Village Voice's* Tony Ortega asked Simpson if Kruse was stupid for approving her amendment to add other religions, since he was being "punked." Simpson laughed as she told Ortega: "Well, he supported my amendment. I can't imagine that we were on the same page, but he came up to me afterwards and he said, 'Now that we supported your amendment, are you going to support the bill?' No, I don't think so."[96] By including Islam and Scientology in a Christian state like Indiana, it was Simpson's hope that the bill would be so unattractive to school boards that they would ignore it, and the bill died.

This bill sought to fashion public schools in the image of right-wing Christian schools in Indiana which promote creationism and paint Jesus as a Milton Friedman-type capitalist. Many voucher schools like Liberty Christian, as Zack Kopplin and Steve Hinnefeld have noted, use A Beka and Bob Jones texts which vilify liberals, plug free-market inequality in the manner of Charles Murray, lie about global warming, and forget or don't know that Jesus fought against the Roman oppression of the poor. Hinnefeld, in his research, unearthed some disturbing examples, including these below from the teacher guide to *United States History in Christian Perspective: Heritage of Freedom*, an A Beka 11th-grade book:

> *FDR and the New Deal:* "New Deal socialism is but a halfway house to Communism; what Communists seek by violent revolution, socialists seek by legislation, regulation, and taxation ... The effects of the New Deal can be seen today in the Social Security system, Medicare, various welfare programs, and the numerous federal

regulatory agencies in operation today. Many Americans depend on the government for their daily needs and all suffer from excessive government regulation in one way or another."

LBJ and the Great Society: "Higher taxes drained money from individuals and business to fund programs that destroyed the work ethic among the poor while eroding the self-sufficiency of the American family."[97]

These textbooks, as professor Frances Paterson and Rachel Tabachnick observe, also compare gay people to child molesters and rapists and display hatred toward Hindus, Native Americans, Buddhists, and even Roman Catholics and non-evangelical Protestants.[98] Tabachnick also points out the texts' prejudice against African Americans, writing that "concerning slavery in America, a Bob Jones high school text states, 'To help them endure the difficulties of slavery, God gave Christian slaves the ability to combine the African heritage of song with the dignity of Christian praise. Through the Negro spiritual, the slaves developed the patience to wait on the Lord and discovered that the truest freedom is from the bondage of sin.'"[99]

One Christian Right organization profiting from education in Indiana doesn't seem to be using any textbooks at all, but this didn't alarm the Indiana Department of Education. When the Indiana Department of Education was told that True Beginning Ministries Biblical Learning Center was selling fake diplomas, the IDOE said the state could do nothing about it. The IDOE, in a statement to the press, hoped "that consumers would do their research to ensure the entity they plan to study with is indeed accredited and approved by the state."[100] By blaming the "consumers," Tony Bennett's IDOE perceived a Christian group stealing people's money as merely a free-market consequence, business as usual.

True Beginning handed out diplomas to people who paid twenty-five to fifty dollars and passed a short test with questions like "Have you ever heard of a poem?" and "What language do you speak?" When one student paid and aced the test, the Christian school awarded her a diploma and a transcript falsely claiming she completed 153 credit hours of classes with a 3.61 grade point average. True Beginning told the Indy Channel it had given out 1,000 diplomas and had a wonderful track record but wouldn't give any evidence to prove it wasn't a complete scam.

When the Indy Channel's Rafael Sanchez tried to interview True Beginning's owners Crystal and Lee Hill Jr. at their home, things got weird and the couple threatened to call the police on the reporter. Crystal Hill even said that Sanchez was going against God's plans for asking questions about True Beginning: "You are the one that is wrong. God is going to judge you," Mrs. Hill said.[101]

ESCUELA CARIBE IN the Dominican Republic gives us a clue on what can go wrong when extreme right-wing and Milton Friedman-inspired Christians educate children. With a long history of alleged abuse and help from Indiana taxpayers, Christian reform school Escuela Caribe was founded in the 1970s by Gordon Blossom, a former student of Floyd Starr's Starr Commonwealth boarding school in Michigan. Under Blossom, his son Tim, Charles Redwine, and other leaders, New Horizons Youth Ministries (NHYM) operated Escuela Caribe and other schools in Michigan as part of the "tough-love" teen rehabilitation movement. Inspired by Starr and profit, Gordon Blossom wooed Michigan officials, and in 1973, in fact, addressed a George Romney-attended gathering to honor Floyd Starr's work with juvenile delinquents, as Keith Fennimore details in his 1988 book *Faith Made Visible: The History of Floyd Starr and His School*.[102] George Romney is Mitt Romney's father. How close to George Romney Pastor Blossom was is unknown, but many past teenagers once held in the NHYM schools believe Gordon Blossom's political clout may have had something to do with why alleged abuses went unheeded. Mitt Romney is well-entrenched with those profiting from the troubled-teen industry. *Mother Jones'* Kathryn Joyce noted that "key fundraisers for Mitt Romney's 2008 and

2012 campaigns hail from Utah's teen-home sector."[103] Romney's Utah finance committee co-chair Robert Lichfield even came under fire for running troubled-teen boarding schools rife with allegations of physical and sexual abuse.[104]

When Michigan stripped Gordon Blossom's licenses after media exposure over his boarding schools' harsh practices, he packed up his tough-love school for the Hoosier state, operating, besides Escuela Caribe in the Dominican Republic, a school in Canada and one in Marion, Indiana. Even though the state was paying NHYM, not much instruction occurred at the schools, and students did most of the work on their own, alumni say. Not only did the Blossoms acquire some of their students from court orders, they also fooled parents, some spending upwards of $40,000 for services and losing their homes in the process of sending their kids off to NHYM's various compounds.[105]

In 2010, NHYM boarding school survivors started posting horror stories on the website *The Truth about New Horizons Youth Ministries* and talking to those who would listen. According to one source, male students at the boarding schools had been "slammed into walls and floors," and "female students were given 'swats' by a thick leather strap called Mr. Brown, leaving bruises and sometimes bloody marks, the very same practices that led Michigan judges to revoke NHYM's license to practice." Then there was the Quiet Room, where students, locked in complete isolation in a Pepto-Bismol-pink and "small concrete cell without lighting or furniture," were stripped down, had their hair chopped off, and forced to "sleep on the concrete floor and scrub the cement for hours on end."[106] One past student, in an unheeded letter to state lawmakers protesting a new company's recent takeover of the reform school, wrote that in the 1980s she and a "group of female students were forced by staff to scrub a naked student with harsh bristle brushes in a bathroom because staff suspected that this girl had stolen money," when, in fact, one of the laundry employees, a Dominican woman, had. One Marion, Indiana, boarding school survivor writes that after she attempted suicide, the leaders beat her, forced her to do hundreds of push-ups, and called her a whore for "fucking her brother" because she told her brother she loved him in letters she sent to him when he was in the Dominican Republic compound. For this, several men beat her brother. The beating got so bad that in order to make it stop, her brother lied that he had had intercourse with his sister.[107] Under the Blossom family operation, there were alleged incidents of sexual misconduct, statutory rape, forced exercise to the point of vomiting, beatings, chaining girls to beds, and severe brainwashing at the boarding schools.[108] One former staffer was arrested for fondling a girl in 1994 at the group's Marion facility.[109]

In late 2011, when Fort Wayne-based Lifeline Youth & Family Services took over the NHYM schools, formed the non-profit Crosswinds, and renamed Escuela Caribe the Caribbean Mountain Academy, many saw this as damage control. Julia Scheeres' *Jesus Land*, a 2005 memoir describing her abuse at the hands of NHYM staff, was a *New York Times* best-seller.[110] There is more bad publicity to come, when Kate Logan's *Kidnapped for Christ* movie debuts soon. Shot at Escuela Caribe in the summer of 2006, the movie documents the conversion therapy practiced at the school. One scene shows several men waking a homosexual teenager named David, dragging him by his belt, driving him to an airplane, and flying him to the Dominican Republic boarding school to "de-gay" him.[111] While attempting to turn gay people straight, Escuela Caribe officials practiced a pseudo-science (if even that) the American Psychological Association and leading medical organizations deem harmful.

A faith-based company, Lifeline Youth & Family Services has retained some of the same staff or staff trained by former NHYM employees appearing in the movie and has refused to acknowledge NHYM had its license revoked by the state of Indiana in 2010. In a June 2011 letter sent to an alumnus in response to child abuse allegations at the school, Department of

Child Services' director James Payne (who later resigned after it was revealed he interfered with a DCS case involving his own grandchildren) said that although DCS revoked the school's license and would no longer be sending kids to the school with taxpayer money, "New Horizons Youth Ministries is a private, religious, non-profit organization therefore they can continue to operate without our licensure."[112] In other words, if parents want to pay NHYM to mistreat their kids, DCS doesn't care. Yet, instead of publically coming out and declaring the past alleged child abuse at the schools as despicable and saying he would clean up the mess and fire everyone who worked at the old schools, Mark Terrell, Lifeline's CEO who started the new Crosswinds company, has chosen to conceal it.

When former students started an online petition in mid-July 2012 to close down the new version of the school run by Lifeline's Crosswinds, a former Escuela Caribe student told me "the continuation of the same staff as trained by NHYM and from as late as 2005 indicates that the takeover was merely a fancy legal way of trying to dissociate from all the bad publicity." In fact, it appears hardly any of the current school leaders were hired after Lifeline took over, even though the group, on its website, deceptively said in the distant past that counselor Grant Anderson has worked at Crosswinds since 2010, when the company didn't even exist.[113] Crosswinds' new director is Scott Taylor.[114] Before moving to the Dominican Republic, Taylor worked at the Summit Church in Arkansas,[115] where lead pastor Bill Elliff is well associated with the Fellowship Bible Church (which gave $10,000 to support the state's 2004 marriage amendment)[116] and its former pastor Robert Lewis. Both Elliff and Lewis teach at the Downline Ministries, along with a few others from the Fellowship Bible Church. Robert Lewis published a book with the anti-gay Focus on the Family press and appeared on Focus on the Family's broadcast hyping his Men's Fraternity.[117] Two other current Caribbean Mountain Academy staffers, Rachel and Jon Sawyer, are carryovers from the NHYM school. Both also once worked at Heartlight Ministries' teen residential treatment center in Texas,[118] a program that HEAL, a leading watchdog group, calls a "money-making cult" which controls the families of kids in its boarding school and uses mail censorship to possibly conceal abuse. Heartlight's program charges $5,000 a month and allows children to attend public school, if they earn the right. HEAL also attacks how Heartlight forces kids, under certain circumstances, to sleep in the same room as staff. HEAL says "parents should also investigate whether or not the program is violating child labor laws."[119] Under an odd picture of kids at Caribbean Mountain Academy blindfolded with purple and pink cloth, Rachel Sawyer, who has worked at Escuela Caribe with her husband since 2005 and has never reported any abuse to authorities, on her blog writes: "Um –WOW! Nine of our students came to know Christ as their personal SAVIOR last week. In addition, many powerful, wonderful, exciting things are happening within this ministry at this time. Never have I seen more movement amidst such utter brokenness."[120]

Teen-brokenness brings in money, and Lifeline—to help its bottom line—is continuing the NHYM tactic of recruiting youth missionaries to work at the boarding school. Hordes of missionaries are still descending upon Caribbean Mountain Academy. In January 2012, a twenty-one-year-old missionary named Matt wrote:

> I want to share a couple of specific things with my supporters and the churches and groups which have made mission trips or are planning to make trips this year. First, thanks so much for your support through gifts, prayers and friendships. I could not have made it all these years without your support and encouragement. Second, know that Caribbean Mountain Academy is still committed to working with mission teams and ministry outreach. As I prepare to leave the ministry, I have been training and supporting our chaplain and his wife, Scott and Meleah Taylor, to take over the community outreach and mission team's ministry.[121]

In 2011, volunteers from the Sagemont Church in Texas arrived to spread "love."[122] Sagemont's pastor Stuart Rothberg, too, describes how gays are lepers and deserve conversion therapy.[123] Besides being famous for its 170-foot tall cross, the Sagemont Church is where Andrea Yates (a friend of Yates noted) attended a homeschool support group with her children, all of whom she later drowned in a Texas bathtub.[124]

Lifeline Youth & Family Services, the reform school's new leader, is also politically entrenched in Indiana.[125] In fact, Mike Pence recently appointed Lifeline's CEO Mark Terrell to the Allen Superior Court Judicial Nominating Commission, a panel that selects the judges that may decide what kids and how many to send to Lifeline's boarding schools or its detention center, the Pierceton Wood Academy. Since Terrell draws his paycheck from these kids, it is an obvious conflict of interest.

Terrell says Lifeline's Crosswinds doesn't perform conversion therapy like NHYM did in 2006 when *Kidnapped for Christ* was filmed, but his connections to the anti-gay movement are not reassuring. In 2002 and 2003, Republican Mark Souder, the former congressman from Indiana, invited Terrell to testify on behalf of George W. Bush's Bradley Foundation-lobbied faith-based initiatives program. In a session filled with questions about pornography, homosexuality, and wife beating, all popular topics for the Religious Right and boarding school leaders, Terrell stated that, in terms of the "community service" Lifeline does,

> All of the facilitators that go in are Christians. It is amazing, the results that are happening. That is not by accident. That is truly a belief that is ordained by God that that has happened.
> What would it do with the donors? We raise a significant amount of our budget outside of the contracts that we get with probation, welfare, and Department of Corrections. They give to us because they know that we are a faith-based organization and that we are hiring Christians. We are hiring people with faith. They are going to make a difference.[126]

In the December 2001 *American Prospect*, troubled-teen industry expert Maia Szalavitz condemned Souder and Bush's faith-based initiative, exposing the president's history of ignoring deaths and abuses in religious extremists-run camps and boarding schools across the country. Szalavitz writes that

> in 1997, after Texas regulators had tried to shut down a Christian rehabilitation program called Teen Challenge because its staff failed to meet educational requirements, then-Governor Bush responded by scuttling all the state's training and safety regulations for such facilities. And in a speech two years later, Bush praised the fact that at Teen Challenge, "'if you don't work, you don't eat.'" Now that he's ensconced in the White House, Bush intends to deregulate Teen Challenge-type programs nationwide.[127]

During the faith-based testimony, Souder seemed to enjoy one Illinois faith-based panel member's statement that the reason his group became active in Indiana is because there is no regulation.

In 2004, Souder called conversion therapist Mike Haley and several other Focus on the Family adherents to the faith-based committee meetings. In response, Americans United for the Separation of Church and State's executive director Barry W. Lynn said the "so-called 'ex-gay' groups are nothing more than covers for fundamentalist indoctrination programs. They don't deserve one dime of taxpayer support. It would be outrageous if the Bush administration and Rep. Souder are seriously considering giving public funds to this sort of program."[128] Haley—who has recently accepted that he is gay—spoke at Bethel College in Indiana on September 28, 2009; Maggie Troyer, whose husband Rich Troyer was then managing Lifeline's Center for Responsible Thinking, spoke there, too, a few days later. The Center for Responsible Thinking offers classes at Pierceton Woods Academy and in parent/student meetings throughout Indiana. The Troyers later sold their home, rented an RV, and started travelling to motorcycle races across the US to turn people onto Christ.[129]

Souder, who opposed the Keeping All Students Safe Act in 2010, is also friendly with the faith-based Crossing Educational

Center, which runs its own schools and whose staff works with Lifeline's Pierceton Woods Academy. In 2008, Souder awarded Crossing's founder and director Robert Staley the Appleseed Award[130] and picked one of Crossing's students to be his Washington aide,[131] before the Fort Wayne lawmaker resigned because of adultery. Formed by Solid Rock Ministries, Crossing's schools are for high school dropouts, kids kicked out of alternative schools, and others with behavioral problems. The group, with fourteen facilities, has contracts with twenty Indiana school districts. It also runs the Fresh Start program for those released from prison. Crossing lists Republican Carlin Yoder—who introduced the Indiana gay-marriage ban and the pro-American amendment to the Indiana voucher bill—as its director in 2010 tax records.[132]

In his 2002 statement before Souder's panel, Mark Terrell mentions how Lifeline's Center for Responsible Thinking's Thinking Errors curriculum is based on Samuel Yochelson's 1970s inmate research with a heavy dose of Bible study thrown in.[133] Yochelson and Stanton Samenow's "Thinking Errors" theory is extreme, based on the belief that criminals, sex offenders, and drug users choose to be criminals, sex offenders, and drug users and that social factors, environment, bad parenting, and brain disorders play absolutely no part in how people turn out. Samenow, in his 1998 *Straight Talk about Criminals,* even claims sex offenders lie about having been sexually abused themselves.[134] With neuroscience completely revamping psychology and criminologists finally playing catch-up, Yochelson and Samenow's one-size-fits-all criminal personality theory is antiquated, to say the least. Since Lifeline bases its "therapy" for young drug offenders, sexual offenders, or just troubled youth on bad past theories, this is a problem. When Yochelson died, his research partner Stanton Samenow became a conferee for Ronald Reagan's White House Conference on a Drug-Free America, part of the anti-drug Just Say No crusade. One goal of the Just Say No program was to funnel taxpayer money to "tough-love" reform schools.[135]

Yochelson and Samenow's criminal personality books are highly favored by religious leaders, chaplains, and even the Indiana government. At a September 2009 meeting of IARCC: An Association of Children and Family Services in Indy which also included the Indiana Department of Child Services' director James Payne, Charles Redwine, who worked at New Horizons Youth Ministries for years, gave a presentation concerning Samenow's writings, among others, and even cites them in his 2002 ministry doctoral dissertation on so-called "pastoral counseling."[136] While praising Yochelson and Samenow's theories, one federal prison chaplain said prison ministers "should preach and teach with the Bible in one hand and *The Criminal Personality* in the other."[137] The Indiana Department of Correction still teaches former prisoners lessons from Samenow's book in its Juvenile PLUS faith-based program.[138] The Indiana Department of Child Services has even used a "Thinking Errors Worksheet" to train new caseworkers, although it is not known whether it is specifically adopted from Samenow and Yochelson or just repeating their terminology.[139]

The Indiana Department of Child Services has been in hot water lately for failing to remove children from abusive homes, many of them ending up dead. From 2006 to 2010, 198 children died from abuse and neglect in Indiana. A WTHR TV investigation found that "in a one-year period, DCS hired 511 new case managers. Twenty-one transferred to other positions during that same time, while 280 simply quit. It created a loss of 18.1 percent agency-wide, roughly the same loss as the previous year at 18.7 percent."[140] In 2010, however, the DCS returned $103 million to the state's general fund, announcing the money wasn't needed.[141] That same year, a Gibson County DCS official was convicted for keeping a teenager in a Vincennes shelter for thirty months without a court order and lying about it.[142] In March 2012, Indiana University's forensic pediatrician Antoinette Laskey resigned from her DCS role, saying DCS's death-numbers it releases each year were misleading. In fact, a recent study ranks Indiana as one of the leading states for high infant mortality.[143] In May 2012, DCS took fire when Morgan County judge Matthew Hanson, in a statement, wrote that it appears "DCS is simply waiting around until the child commits such egregious or dangerous acts that the (juvenile delinquency) system has no choice but to file charges against a child with a mental disease/defect, and then the DCS can simply ignore any pleas thereafter to aid such a child."[144] Also, in May, when the DCS said its caseworkers could not release confidential information on abuse and neglect cases to the courts, Allen Superior Court's Fran Gull called DCS's behavior "absurd."[145]

A large number of degree-holders from Indiana faith-based colleges like Grace College (which now sponsors the Smith Academy for Excellence charter school in Fort Wayne) and Indiana Wesleyan are employed by DCS, and some DCS people have worked for Lifeline, too.[146] With contracts in sixty Indiana counties, Lifeline Youth & Family Services actually plays a major role in DCS, offering home-based services, residential care for kids removed from their families, and court testimony, the latter a conflict of interest since Lifeline representatives help determine which kids are removed from homes and could easily ship these kids to the group's compounds in the Dominican Republican and Canada (where it just reopened the old NHYM school).

Lifeline holds a lot of power and taxpayer money for a group hiring many of its counselors from Indiana Christian Right colleges who have been indoctrinated with "biblical truths." Admitting that Lifeline only hires Christians, Mark Terrell, in 2010, was paid $158,457 with an additional $18,774 in other compensation. That same year, Lifeline raked in over $11.5 million in welfare fees, almost $266,000 of school money, and only $545,000 from grants, gifts, and other contributions and $48,527 from private fees (not the "significant" amount Terrell told the Souder hearing members). Besides the Department of Child Services, Lifeline holds contracts with the Department of Education and the Department of Correction, so taxpayers are footing the bill.[147]

Indiana politicians have yet to do anything about Escuela Caribe now hiding under its new name Caribbean Mountain Academy. Although ABC's Nightline is considering filming an episode which will include the school, the school has existed for way too long. Speaking at the US Senate hearings in January 1979, one month after Hoosier Jim Jones committed his Jonestown massacre where almost 300 kids died, the National Coalition for Children's Justice's Kenneth Wooden reminded lawmakers he had warned them about Jones' dangerous child care facilities, and they refused to listen. Wooden, at this hearing, pointed fingers directly at NHYM's Escuela Caribe boarding school as one of several putting children's lives at risk. Having visited Escuela Caribe in 1974, Wooden wanted to know, since years earlier he had reported his New Horizons Youth Ministries findings to the State Department, why nothing had been done to close down the boarding school and why Gordon Blossom was raking in $8,360 of taxpayer money per child to abuse these kids.[148]

After thirty-three years, nothing may have changed. Lifeline has never been accused of abusing kids. Nonetheless, Lifeline's Pierceton center must get more than a brief positive review by Indiana's faith-based office, which it has lately, and all of its out-of-country reform schools need closed now. Hoosiers and former boarding school students also have a right to know whether Lifeline intends to use our tax money to ship more kids to the compounds in Canada and the Dominican Republic, where US laws don't matter; or if it plans to open schools in Indiana where laws are either written to profit adults at the expense of children or don't matter at all, if you know the right people. ■

3.
TRAIN WRECK: THE INDIANA GOVERNMENT-CORPORATE SCHOOL COMPLEX

My friends, listen closely. A freight train of change is coming in our state.
Mitch Daniels, 2004 Indiana Republican Convention Speech

Second, local neighborhood charters started by parents, teachers, and community members with exciting new ideas for public education have now been overshadowed by large, multistate charter chains. Like a McDonald's franchise, these charter chains are often the opposite of locally-grown and community administered.
Cynthia Liu, "#OccupyBigEd," K12 News Network

W HEN TONY BENNETT REFUSED TO RELEASE the names of Edison Learning and four other potential takeover operators bidding for schools the state "failed" because of low test scores,[1] he was attempting to hush how Indiana government officials were moving taxpayer money to the bloated bank accounts of friends and out-of-state campaign donors. Selling short our most vulnerable kids, these rampant under-the-table deals have given charter school leaders free rein with their unelected school boards to whittle away democracy and steal public-owned property. Not only did Edison Learning win the takeover gig without any public input, it was handed, up front, $850,000 in taxpayer money for merely acquiring Roosevelt Career and Technical Academy in Gary. Boasting of serving

450,000 students across the globe, Edison has a history of unethical behavior and political contacts Bennett and Mitch Daniels concealed from Indiana taxpayers.

Public outrage has haunted Edison. As Gerald Bracey details in *What You Should Know about the War against America's Public Schools*, despite the Philadelphia NAACP, parents, and educators protesting Edison in 2001, Pennsylvania governor Mark Schweiker went against the wishes of mayor John Street and Chaka Fattah, a US representative, and turned over twenty schools to Edison.[2] Edison, then led by Black Alliance for Educational Option's Floyd Flake, had earlier received $2.7 million from then-governor Tim Ridge to declare Philadelphia schools a disaster so the company could move in and help itself to public money.[3] Lawsuits followed. Eventually, in 2002, the US Securities and Exchange Commission cited Edison for faulty accounting techniques, and US school districts quickly severed ties to the company. Unfortunately, it wasn't until 2008 that Philly was able to set in place a plan to rid itself of Edison Learning, after a twelve-year-old boy was raped in an Edison school and the company claimed in court that it is not responsible for student safety, yet quickly settled the lawsuit against it brought by the boy's family.[4]

Edison's low-income students in other cities are not safe from attacks and the threat of child labor either. Edison's Renaissance Academy of Pittsburgh Alternative of Hope was closed for not doing sufficient background checks on employees;[5] in St. Louis, nineteen students were hospitalized after Edison's security force randomly pepper-sprayed a crowd of students witnessing a hallway fight;[6] and Edison's 2007 E2 Design Sketch called for student child labor to benefit the company's bottom line. Chris Whittle, Edison's founder, boasted to Colorado school principals that 600 unpaid students could do the work of seventy-five salaried workers, so the more custodians and lunch workers Edison axed, the better.[7] It is unclear if Edison ever implemented this child labor agenda, but parents groups across the country were rightfully infuriated.

Security and child labor issues aside, Edison specializes in putting schools in debt. To profit even more, Edison leaves schools with enormous deficits, as it did with several in Louisiana over the last few years. The Linear Leadership Academy in Shreveport was in the red over $300,000 until the Martin Luther King Neighborhood Association dissolved its contract with Edison.[8] In 2011, New Orleans' Intercultural Charter School said Edison's high management fee put the school in the hole for $300,000, as well.[9] Citing poor management, Capitol High School in Baton Rouge canned Edison in 2011.[10] Thanks to five years of bad audits due to Edison's poor management, the Andrew Wilson Charter School in New Orleans in March 2013 was still sorting through the financial rumble, even though the school had severed its contract with Edison in 2011.[11] Edison has pulled its operations out of Louisiana entirely, with big bucks in its pocket.

Journalist and activist Caroline Grannan remarks that Edison Learning was so unsuccessful at running schools, despite its grandiose promises, that the company's "name is no longer mentioned when 'school reform' supporters talk about solutions for public education." Class Size Matters' Leonie Haimson echoes this sentiment. "Given the consistently poor results of its schools elsewhere in the country, it is astonishing that Edison Learning has been selected to operate schools in Indiana," Haimson says. "The only plausible explanation is that the company was selected not on the basis of its record, but because of its political connections."

Edison's political connections first fall on Mitch Daniels' potential White House running mate Jeb Bush. In 2003, as *The Nation's* David Moberg noted, Jeb Bush bailed out Edison when the then-Florida governor bought out its failing stock with teachers' retirement funding, sticking state pensioners to this day with a $182 million investment in a corporation out to destroy public education and teachers and workers unions.[12] Edison's Chris Whittle, Kenneth Saltman observes, "came out of the deal with about $21 million dollars, a 42 percent raise, a loan of $1.68 million, and eligibility for a bonus of 245 percent of his base salary."[13] As Jim Horn noticed, Edison's then-president and now New Jersey's education commissioner, Chris Cerf, was named as one of the beneficiaries in the buyout.[14] Chris Megerian recently writes that from 1999 to 2001 New Jersey governor Chris Christie lobbied for a firm representing Edison Schools in the state, when Cerf was Edison's general counsel.[15] Cerf is now a member of Jeb Bush's Chiefs for Change, a state school superintendents and privatization group which Tony Bennett chairs.

Another Bush family insider profiting from Indiana charter schools is J.C. Huizenga, whose National Heritage Academies education management company governs Indianapolis' Andrew J. Brown Academy. A board member of the Mackinac Center for Public Policy mentioned in the previous chapter, J.C. Huizenga is the cousin of billionaire Blockbuster founder, former Miami Dolphin's owner, and past Swisher Hygiene board member with Jeb Bush, H. Wayne Huizenga. J.C. Huizenga was one of the huge George W. Bush Pioneer donors in 2000 that Bush campaign officials tried to conceal,[16] and he makes an exorbitant amount of taxpayer money from charging his schools excessive rent. Huizenga has given nearly $200,000 to Indiana Republican candidates, some of which went to Tony Bennett and Mitch Daniels, and $30,000 to the DeVos family's American Federation for Children.[17] The Fort Wayne *Journal Gazette* quoted from Andrew J. Brown's state audit, which stated that National Heritage Academies "would not provide us access to their records . . . to present the financial information for the operation of the school corporation in the same fashion as other school corporations"—then ruthlessly accessed Huizenga's company:

> The 2011 audit for the Andrew J. Brown Academy cited concerns with oversight of the school's management contract with NHA, financial reporting, federal grants, cash receipts and more. It also noted there were no records to support enrollment claims made by the charter school on its September count date, which is used to de-

termine tuition support provided by taxpayers. [18]

It is no wonder National Heritage Academies was hiding its documents from state auditors. The company is good at pulling off rent schemes to grab taxpayer money. In Brooklyn, National Heritage Academies subleases its buildings to charter school boards "at as much as 1,000 percent markup."[19] In 2005, National Heritage Academies was pulling in $200 million from taxpayers.[20] An ALEC member,[21] National Heritage Academies profits from seventy-four different US locations and taught creationism alongside Darwin in its schools until the Michigan ACLU sued in 1998 alleging "that mothers held weekly prayer meetings at one Grand Rapids school, and a teacher read from the Bible in class."[22]

Indy Mayor Ballard has ignored Huizenga's lack of transparency, leasing rip-offs, and Christian schooling. In 2010, while granting the school its first full seven-year charter renewal, the mayor's office announced that Andrew J. Brown Academy "has received Indiana's highest school rating, Exemplary, every year it has been in operation; has consistently ended each year with a balanced budget; and leadership among the governing board and school administrators has been strong and stable over time."[23] Ballard didn't mind that only 45.7 percent of Brown's students passed the 2009 math and English tests.

But Edison Learning and National Heritage Academies are not the only for-profit charter school companies in the Bush family clan who have set up shop in Indiana. Bush crony Jonathan Hage's Florida-based Charter Schools USA (CS USA) was handpicked by Bennett and Daniels to seize three poverty-stricken and so-called "failing schools" in Indianapolis. Like Daniels who followed George H.W. Bush to Eli Lilly, Jonathan Hage is a longtime Bush family friend. Hage wrote speeches for George H. W. Bush's 1992 presidential campaign and was an educational talking head for the 2004 Bush and Cheney National Steering Committee. A former defense agent for the Heritage Foundation and past research head for Jeb Bush's Foundation for Florida's Future, Hage helped develop Liberty City Charter School, the first charter in Florida. Sponsored by Jeb and Miami Urban League's T. Willard Fair, Liberty City Charter School closed in 2008 with $1 million of debt.[24] In *A New Lease on Learning: Florida's First Charter School,* Bush and Fair co-wrote that the school would "focus much more on character and discipline then [*sic*] most public schools," with discussion and games based on "honesty and integrity."[25] But as Paul Moore remarks, Bush and Fair were less than honest themselves. Opening with fanfare from MSNBC and CNN, Liberty City Charter School was the perfect photo-op for Bush who was trying to win black voters after he said during his 1994 failed gubernatorial campaign that he would do "probably nothing" to help African Americans in Florida.[26]

CS USA's Jonathan Hage admits he knows nothing about education and credits Jeb Bush for helping him expand his private charter school company. Starting with a $5,000 loan, Hage ended up with millions of state dollars when Jeb was governor, and his group now has thirty-three schools in Florida. In 2001, Hage earned close to $40 million, most of it from taxpayers.[27] At Jeb Bush's Foundation for Excellence in Education's DC summit, while Tony Bennett sat on the "Top Gun Teachers" board with Teach for America and Troops for Teachers participants, Hage—the former Green Beret—paneled "The War on Charter Schools: Combating the Emerging Threats to Public School Choice." Although the summit was merely another example of how the charter school movement is led by those untrained in academics and purposely established to profit investors, many with criminal backgrounds, its messaging was appropriate since the Bush family knows a lot about profiting from war and bogus school reform slogans and programs like the International Education Arms Race and No Child Left Behind.

Cases of the Bush family and cronies cashing in on so-called school reform are numerous. Neil Bush—after scamming taxpayers out of close to $1 billion during the savings and loan scandal in the 1980s—fattened his wallet with No Child Left Behind money while his brother was president by starting Ignite! Learning. A "curriculum on wheels," Ignite! Learning was partly owned by the Bush family and backed by Saudi Prince Alwaleed Bin Talal, shady Russian billionaire Boris Berezovsky, and Michael Milken, the former junk bond guru and jailbird now behind the TAP teacher merit-pay system. As Bill Berkowitz notes, in an act of fake philanthropy Neil's mom, former First Lady Barbara Bush, "agreed to make a contribution to a Hurricane Katrina relief foundation for those victims that had relocated to Texas" but "stipulated that her donation had to be used by local schools to acquire Ignite products."[28] George H.W. Bush has played his private sector role, too. After George H.W. marketed its defense, energy, and security industries, the Carlyle Group, a private equity war-profiting firm, branched out into the for-profit education business, planting its corporate members on charter school boards in DC and investing in SchoolNet, the data-driven software company Pearson recently acquired. Pearson has made a killing off of grading standardized tests since No Child Left Behind. Now Sandy Kress, who hawked Bush's school privatization scheme in Washington, is a lobbyist for Pearson. Since Charter Schools USA and Edison Learning will be transforming Indiana's "takeover schools" into standardized testing factories, Pearson will profit, as will heirs to Libyan dictator Muammar Gaddafi's $453 million stake in Pearson.[29] Pearson enjoys this. That is why it dished out the funding for Tony Bennett's inaugural "State of Education" speech that was broadcasted on radio and TV stations across Indiana. A mere weeks before the speech, as Karen Francisco detected, "Indiana awarded NCS Pearson a $224,720 contract to rewrite the state's teacher standards" to line up with new academic guidelines.[30] In June 2011, Bennett's education department signed a six-year contract with Pearson Education to deliver textbooks to Indiana schools. CTB McGraw-Hill, the Indiana ISTEP+ test contractor, is also

eager for more money.[31] While George W. was president, his
own US Department of Education's inspector general "accused
the agency of improperly favoring at least five publishers, including The McGraw-Hill Companies,"[32] whose family has
been tight with the Bushes since the 1930s.[33] A Tony Bennett
campaign donor, CTB McGraw-Hill used pizza delivery boys
and hair stylists to grade Jeb Bush's Florida Comprehensive
Assessment Test for students.[34] Now Jeb is marketing Send-
Hub, a communications program he partially owns, to school
districts around the country.

When Tony Bennett and Mitch Daniels recruited Charter
Schools USA, it was merely another favor to Jeb Bush who has
sold the anti-public school agenda in Indiana since speaking at
the 2009 Bill Gates and Fordham Foundation-sponsored Indiana Education Roundtable. Thanks to Jeb, CS USA, with forty-
eight schools in five states, operates mostly in Florida. The
for-profit school management company has "no experience in
turning around low performing schools," says one longtime
public school teacher and advocate, "and has focused on elementary charters," not high schools, as the Indiana takeover
plan calls for. In fact, National Education Policy Center scholars have found that only 37 percent of CS USA-managed
schools in 2009 met adequate yearly progress. Given CS
USA's poor track record, Hage needs Jeb Bush and Mitch
Daniels to keep the money flowing.[35]

CS USA slides money to the right politicians. The day after
CS USA was awarded the Indiana gig, the company began a
race with several Florida for-profit charter schools to buy out
the Miami-Dade School Board, donating $500 to District Five's
Diaz de la Portilla. It was an obvious ploy to erect more
schools and pull off a money grab in the county.[36] Frank Attkisson, Jeb Bush's buddy, has also aided and abetted CS USA.
While sitting on the Florida House Education Innovation Committee, then-Representative Attkisson was a member of the
Hillsborough Charter Foundation, the puppet nonprofit
Jonathan Hage and CS USA erected. As *St. Petersburg Times*'

Kent Fischer explains, Attkisson and Hage also sat "on two state charter school committees."[37] Amazingly, in December 2003 the *Orlando Sentinel* reported that while Attkisson was state representative he earned $80,000 as a CS USA consultant until he was downsized out of a job.[38] Attkisson directed Jeb Bush's charter school authorizing board, the Florida Schools of Excellence Commission, after endorsing its formation while a representative. To approve charters that local school boards denied, Attkisson was paid $140,000 yearly, before Florida's First District Court of Appeals declared the commission unconstitutional in late 2008.[39]

From the end of August to the end of September 2012, CS USA's takeover of Howe High School in Indy was going about as well as its Florida operations at Bonita Springs Charter School. A few years back, among 911 calls on parents and teacher layoffs, the principal at Bonita Springs Charter School accepted $5,000 from the Parent Teacher Organization to pay for her son's funeral but also supposedly threatened to close the school's PTO down and have the school "absorb the organization's funds."[40] The PTO head wrote that CS USA desired to "put all of these 'wrongs' in a tidy little box, wrap it up with a pretty little ribbon and move on."[41] In Indiana, Howe High parents eventually protested in the parking lot, since special education students didn't have enough staff, students didn't have textbooks and weren't being offered Advanced Placement courses, and school security was in shambles. One mother claimed her daughter didn't have a permanent teacher for six weeks and that half a dozen teachers had quit. A football game brawl was also reported, and the hallways were filled with students fighting each other.[42]

By this time, the state had agreed to pay over $30 million to CS USA, Edison Learning, and Ed Power, the third company picked to flip so-called "failing" schools in Indiana, regardless of how many students enrolled in their charter schools for the year. The contracts, also, did not limit how much of this money the companies could put into their own bank accounts for their CEOs.[43]

CS USA's new Indy schools are just the beginning. Hage told the *Indianapolis Business Journal* that CS USA has a twenty-year commitment to Indianapolis.[44] More Indiana teachers will suffer, as they did when IPS laid off ninety-four because of the money it lost from the four schools taken over by the state, while CS USA hired Teach for America recruits to fill classrooms.[45]

Florida students, teachers, and community members were not in good company, either, when Bennett packed up and moved to the corrupt Sunshine state, where even vice president Joe Biden's brother Frank, despite owing $32,500 in unpaid income taxes, is making a nice living running charter schools.[46] Charter Schools USA's for-profit charter school development company Red Apple Development gave Bennett $10,000 in campaign donations, but it wasn't enough to get him reelected in Indiana. Bennett and Jeb Bush couldn't conceal Hage's campaign funding from the public, and news broke that Jeb held a lofty San Francisco fundraiser for Bennett in October 2011 (a little over a month from when CS USA and Edison Learning were picked to come to Indiana) as payback for all the superintendent's favors to Bush friends.[47] But they did a great job hiding their emails.

ON A FRIDAY afternoon just days before the 2012 state superintendent election, Indiana's public access counselor Joseph B. Hoage—without notifying the media—quietly voiced his opinion on the Indiana Department of Education failing to release Freedom of Information Act documents that could shed light on the crony capitalism behind Tony Bennett and Jeb Bush's Indiana school privatization plan.[48]

The debacle began on February 16th, 2012, when the Washington, DC nonprofit In the Public Interest requested private emails and other files from Tony Bennett which the Indiana Department of Education wouldn't release. When the IDOE refused to cooperative, In the Public Interest (ITPI) filed a formal complaint with Hoage's office on October 3th, 2012. In part, this complaint reads:

> In this request, the Indiana Department of Education has yet to produce documents despite acknowledgement of the request and the beginning of the review of responsive records on March 15, 2012. Even after In the Public Interest limited the scope of the request in August 2012—a limitation within the records the Department claimed it had begun collecting over six months ago—the Department has yet to produce documents. This failure to produce in such a long period of time is unreasonable. *See Opinion of the Public Access Counselor 08-FC-162* (finding unreasonableness for a public records request dated January 2008 when the complaint was filed June 27, 2008 despite the public records request being "more involved than is standard").[49]

IDOE officials claimed the original request was not specific enough to take immediate action, but this was not true. In part, this earliest demand asks for emails, faxes, and other written communications starting on January 1, 2010 between Bennett, Jeb Bush, Bush cronies, and Joel Klein of Rupert Murdoch's Wireless Generation, a for-profit outfit which funded Bennett's campaign and received $1.6 million from Indiana in 2008 to assess K-2 reading and math students for two years.[50] The request also seeks all communications and records of Bennett's expenses paid for by Bush organizations the Foundation for Excellence in Education and the Foundation for Florida's Future. Funded by the Gates, Broad, Bradley, DeVos, Robertson, and Walmart foundations, Bush's Foundation for Excellence in Education promotes charter schools and virtual learning and markets the fake parent trigger law allowing corporate charter schools to send paid operatives into communities to trick parents into signing forms to close their public schools and hand them over to for-profit companies. As the *Journal Gazette's* Karen Francisco notes, the Foundation for Excellence in Education bankrolled Bennett's visit to DC on November 15, 2011 to see Arne Duncan and chairman of the US House Education Committee John Kline.[51]

Documents Maine released to In the Public Interest may

give us an idea on what Bennett's emails contain. In September 2012, *Portland Press Herald*'s Colin Woodard detailed over 1,000 Freedom of Information Act (FOIA) documents on how Jeb Bush and online learning lobbyist Patricia Levesque first arranged a deal with Maine's educational commissioner Steven Bowen and governor Paul LePage to let Bush's Foundation for Excellence in Education execute Digital Learning Now! to drastically expand virtual schools in the state. In fact, staffers at Bush's foundation even drafted policy that would give millions of dollars to online learning corporations in Maine, while ALEC wrote the laws. Although in Maine many of Bush's online learning agenda was not put into place after outrage over the backdoor dealings, online learning outfits Connections Academy and K12 Inc. spent a lot of money on lobbying for the virtual schools bill, K12 even donating $19,000 to the Republican Governors Association Maine PAC funding LePage's election campaign.[52]

K12 Inc. is a "$708.4 million-a-year business serving more than 100,000 students a year in 32 states, including more than 2,000 school districts as well as charter schools."[53] Only one in four students entering K12's online schools graduate. Because of this for-profit corporation, 10,000 teachers lost jobs in 2012.[54] Known for having Arizona student essays graded by people in India[55] and for counting 120 students "for state reimbursement whose enrollment could not be verified or who did not meet Colorado residency requirements,"[56] K12 and other online learning establishments, as University of Colorado Boulder School of Education's Alex Molnar has noted, are "fundamentally trying to do to public education what the banks did with home mortgages."[57] K12 is currently being sued by shareholders for "making false statements to investors about students' poor performance on standardized tests."[58]

Kristin Rawls sums up K12's connections to the Christian Right in a recent *AlterNet* article:

> K12 got off its feet under the leadership of Bill Bennett, the frequent

CNN commentator and conservative Christian who once offered this crime reduction platform on his radio show: "[Y]ou could abort every black baby in this country, and your crime rate would go down." Bennett had to resign from the company over this comment, but it's not clear that his influence has waned. K12 notoriously treats creationism as legitimate science and the Bible as a useful history book. Other educators report racist language and glorification of the Confederacy—again, in a curriculum designed for school proliferation in inner cities.

Rawls also mentions a 2011 report showing that K12 has been spending millions of taxpayer dollars on advertising and "marketing to the Christian homeschooling crowd."[59] To profit from the homeschool movement, online learning outfits fund lawmakers across the country. *Washington Post* reporters have determined that K12 from 2004 to 2010 gave almost $500,000 to legislators across America.[60] Both K12 and Connections Academy subsidize Jeb Bush's Foundation for Excellence in Education, and Connections Academy's Mickey Revenaugh, as Lee Fang writes, co-chairs ALEC's "education policy-writing department," where the Virtual Public Schools Act sent to Maine and other US lawmakers debuted.[61]

In Indiana, online learning corporations are doing just fine, thanks to their campaign donations. In the Hoosier state, K12 manages three Hoosier Academies, two of which have received an "F" grade and one a "D." It also operates Indiana blended-learning schools. Now owned by Pearson, Connections Academy owns one Indiana school. K12 and Connections Academy have flooded campaign money to Indiana Republicans and Tony Bennett. Karen Francisco pegs the K12 donations to Indiana officials Brian Bosma, Teresa Lubbers, Dennis Kruse, and Mitch Daniels at $50,000, as they connived to privatize Indiana schools.[62] K12 gave Bennett $2,000 in 2008 and $5,000 more a few years later. Connections Academy has handed $19,900 to mostly Indiana Republicans since 2007, with $2,000 finding its way into Bennett's campaign chest.

Patricia Levesque also is named in the Indiana FOIA requests. A virtual schools lobbyist and director of Jeb Bush's Foundation for Excellence in Education and his Foundation for Florida's Future, Levesque cheered for Tony Bennett in April 2012 when she shot an email to several people asking them to contact the Indiana Select Commission on Education which was holding meetings on the state school superintendent. Levesque feared that the commission was going to "rake Tony over the coals," that a few commission members would show "hostility" because they are "legislative allies of charter schools who are concerned with the strong accountability Tony is putting in place to ensure all public schools, including charter schools are effectively educating their students." Levesque knows as well as anyone that charter schools have ways around so-called "accountability" and that Indiana officials wouldn't be looking closely at them anyway. It was merely Levesque's way to further hoodwink Bush and Bennett's ground troops, since Indiana Republicans didn't plan on reprimanding Bennett anyway. Calling Bennett a national hero, Levesque outlined talking points to use in emails to commission members and promised that, if operatives would "copy us" in the emails, she and crew would "let Tony's team know the volume of support that these legislative members will be receiving." Bush cohorts, too, could email Levesque their comments, and Levesque would "be helpful in getting the letters to" commission members. [63]

As current director of the Foundation for Excellence in Education and the Foundation for Florida's Future, Levesque maintains she doesn't take a paycheck for suggesting states buy their schools SendHub, a communications program which Jeb Bush, Foundation for Florida's Future's Garrett Johnson, and others own, but Levesque's own consulting company Meridian Strategies amassed $100,000 in 2008 and $123,000 in 2009 working for the Foundation for Excellence in Education. For contracts with Foundation for Florida's Future, Levesque's company scraped in $276,000 in 2010.[64]

When the Florida Assembly failed to pass more bills to benefit school privateers, a disappointed Levesque outlined a new strategy to fool the public and unions at an October 2010 corporate school conference. In "How Online Learning Companies Bought America's Schools," Lee Fang writes that:

> Levesque noted that reform efforts had failed because the opposition had time to organize. Next year, Levesque advised, reformers should "spread" the unions thin "by playing offense" with decoy legislation. Levesque said she planned to sponsor a series of statewide reforms, like allowing taxpayer dollars to go to religious schools by overturning the so-called Blaine Amendment, "even if it doesn't pass. . . to keep them busy on that front." She also advised paycheck protection, a unionbusting scheme, as well as a state-provided insurance program to encourage teachers to leave the union and a transparency law to force teachers unions to show additional information to the public. Needling the labor unions with all these bills, Levesque said, allows certain charter bills to fly "under the radar."[65]

Levesque is just one Florida corporate force who supported Bennett while he was in Indiana. Steve Hinnefeld has traced more Bennett money to hedge fund operators and others.[66] Karen Francisco noted that "Edward D. Easton, a Miami-based real estate official who was part of Jeb Bush's campaign finance team" tossed Bennett $1,000 for his reelection campaign.[67]

Campaign gifts obviously didn't surface in Indiana's public access counselor Joseph B. Hoage's cop-out over the Freedom of Information Act documents concerning Bush and Bennett's emails. Here is Hoage's conclusion, which is nowhere as severe as it should be:

> Based on the foregoing, it is my opinion that the Department has acted contrary to section 3(b) of the APRA by failing to provide all records in a reasonable period of time that were responsive to the reasonably particularized portions of Ms. Kaissal's February 22, 2012 request. However, it is my opinion that at this time the Department has complied with section 3(b) in its efforts to provide all records in a reasonable period of time that were responsive to the reasonably particularized request that was received on August 29, 2012.[68]

Hoage wants it both ways, claiming the IDOE was, in fact, stalling the request, but not really. The IDOE has no legitimate reason for the holdup, even though it blames a small staff in the Office of Legal Affairs. The IDOE held its feet on releasing these potentially damaging emails and other written files from Bennett because it was waiting until after the election. To make matters worse, IDOE's Heather Neal also is named in the FOIA request. Neal had Hoage's public access counselor's job before she started carrying Tony Bennett and Jeb Bush's dirty water.

JEB BUSH OPERATIVE Patricia Levesque was a member of Florida governor Rick Scott's transitional board team, alongside Imagine Schools' CEO Dennis Bakke—the billionaire member of the Fellowship, better known as the Family, a Christian Right secretive group in DC. Bakke is also known for his deals with Mitch Daniels. Bakke's dealings with Daniels go back to 2001, when Daniels was on the board of the Indianapolis Power and Light Company (IPALCO), which merged with Bakke's then-company AES Corporation, a monster utility corporation. Daniels and other IPALCO board members dumped their own stock before the merger took place. Afterwards, IPALCO stockholders and workers lost millions, including their 401k packages. While IPALCO board members and officials went home, "according to the lawsuit filings, with an estimated $43.6 million in profits and golden-parachute benefits," retirees and IPALCO workers lost $95 million, says a Republican lawyer who represented the workers and shareholders in an insider trading lawsuit against Daniels, Bakke, and others in 2003. Dan Coats, now an Indiana U.S. senator, and Barry Sharp, who works for Imagine Schools, were also involved. No criminal charges were ever filed, and the courts, quite conveniently, dismissed the civil lawsuits.[69]

Last count, Imagine Schools Inc. manages seventy schools in twelve states and DC, including one on Andrews Air Force Base in Maryland. Headquartered in Arlington, Virginia, Bakke sends his people into poverty-stricken US cities, handpicks a nonprofit branch to start a charter school, then uses School-house Finance, Imagine Schools' for-profit real estate branch, to buy the school buildings where the schools will be housed. Schoolhouse Finance then charges the school rent, which is sometimes nearly 40 percent of the school's overall budget.[70] In 2009, Imagine Schools sold twenty-seven school buildings for $206 million to Entertainment Properties Trust,[71] a real estate theater corporation which owns thirty-four charter school properties "accounting for $280.3 million of its $2.9 billion portfolio."[72] Imagine leases back the buildings and then sub-leases them to the charter school holders. If anyone on Imagines' school boards, or in the schools themselves, protests, Imagine quickly gets rid of them. Karen Francisco explains that for the Imagine MASTer Academy in Fort Wayne, "taxpayers will pay $790,000 in rent" in 2012, which comes to "almost $66,000 a month," which was "more than a quarter of the $2.9 million the entire property was sold for in 2007."[73]

In Fort Wayne in April 2006, Bakke picked Don Willis, a business man, private school owner, Mitch Daniels and Tony Bennett campaign funder, and later member of Bennett's education transition team, to found the schools. As Imagine-Fort Wayne Charter School board chairperson, Willis signed the contract with Imagine Schools in Virginia without a vote from others on the board and without a public meeting, which is illegal under Indiana's Open Door Law. This contract gave Bakke's company a 12 percent fee on all money brought into the school. The contract also gave away power of the local board to make decisions on hiring, curriculum, discipline, and all other issues of governance concerning the school. Willis then went on, without the school board's knowledge, to establish another Imagine Schools school in Fort Wayne. By the time the school board realized this, they had been board members of the new corporation for three months. This happened with a third Imagine school in Fort Wayne (as well as one in Texas), [74] the Imagine Bridge Academy, which didn't open because Ball State, who gets a 3 percent administrative fee to authorize

Imagine, was concerned about Imagine proposing to locate the school in a building with safety issues.[75]

After Fort Wayne *Journal Gazette's* reporters investigated Imagine's gimmicks, Ball State finally agreed to put Imagine in Fort Wayne on probation. As part of its probation, Ball State told Imagine to replace all board members whose terms were expiring. In March 2010, Willis' term on the board expired, and he was replaced. [76]

In February 2010, the same month as the Ball State mandate, Willis ran into trouble with Keystone, his own private, Christian-oriented school which his FourD Education Foundation managed. After Keystone fell into financial woes, Willis asked the students' parents to pay $2,000 more in tuition to keep the school open for the remaining school year because he had no cash to pay the teachers,[77] who finally walked out at the end of May and refused to return.[78] Willis and his school board (which included his daughter, Dacia Michael) agreed to step down and private investors took over the school. FourD Education Foundation's second Keystone school in Fort Wayne had closed down in 2009 because of financial problems.[79]

Indiana staff and teachers don't do much better under Imagine control. After being fired for not being a good "fit," Jennifer Murray, former dean of students at Imagine MASTer Academy in Fort Wayne, filed a racial discrimination lawsuit against Imagine after she and a principal both were let go in November 2008. According to Murray, African Americans were being disciplined more harshly at the Fort Wayne school (where teachers were paid an average of $32,000 for the 2008-2009 school year, compared with the $50,000 state average) than white teachers,[80] and black students were encouraged to not build good rapport with white teachers.[81]

Imagine received nearly $11 million under Obama's stimulus program,[82] but on April 17, 2012 St. Louis kicked out Imagine Schools, tired of the for-profit school management company's games. Officials finally closed six Imagine schools sponsored by Missouri Baptist University after reporter Elisa

Crouch and other *Post-Dispatch* reporters found that Imagine was using former cocaine importer Samuel Glasser for its real estate deals. Glasser—who spent time in jail in the 1970s—in February 2011 plead guilty to bank fraud in a case unrelated to Imagine. Glasser's dealings with Imagine, however, led to an FBI investigation since Elisa Crouch had found questionable bank statements where Glasser's company Samuel & Co. paid Imagine's midwestern manager Sam Howard $32,000. These payments to Howard "came shortly before or after Schoolhouse Finance, Imagine's real estate arm, had reimbursed Samuel & Co. for construction work done on several school buildings that opened in 2007." In the summer of 2011, "Imagine settled. . . a lawsuit filed by one of its own administrators in St. Louis who accused the company of firing her for reporting an alleged kickback paid to a co-worker."[83]

Bakke has used Eli Lilly officials, too, for his for-profit scheme. Lilly's Theressa Wright is on the board of Imagine Life Sciences Academy East in Indianapolis, as are two others from Lilly. Wright is a board member of the Indiana Public Charter Schools Association with former Indiana State Board of Education's Gwendolyn G. Adell.

GWENDOLYN G. ADELL was Mitch Daniels' ally and the principal at Gary's Thea Bowman Leadership Academy Charter School when she resigned[84] for what she said were family and personal reasons from the Indiana State Board of Education in July 2011 after the investigation I helped launch into her plagiarizing her Purdue PhD dissertation.

The fiasco unfolded in April 2011, when I stumbled upon an anonymous researcher's blog claiming that for her 2004 PhD[85] dissertation Adell had merely cut and pasted entire sections of a 1999 dissertation written by Lynn Amedy in the Department of Educational Leadership and Policy Studies at Virginia Polytechnic Institute and State University. I immediately contacted the blog's owner and purchased Adell's dissertation through ProQuest and compared the two. Sections were a complete match.[86]

On April 12, 2011, I detailed several examples of Adell's plagiarism in a letter to Mitch Daniels, Tony Bennett, Purdue's dean of students Danita M. Brown, Jeffery Stefancic, the associate dean in the Office of Students Rights and Responsibilities at Purdue, and Earl Goode, Daniels' chief of staff. In my letter, I noted how my anonymous source had contacted Purdue University officials who promised to look into the matter. But given that Purdue University officials had ties to Mitch Daniels, that Purdue may possibly sponsor charter schools in the near future, and that Tony Bennett sat on Purdue's Indiana Council for Economic Education's Director's Circle with the vice provost for engagement, I questioned if Purdue officials could or would do an unbiased, exhaustive investigation into the complaint. I also called on the governor and Purdue officials to arrange for an unbiased, outside research panel (along with, yet apart from, Purdue's) to examine the documents and for Daniels to kick Adell off the state board.[87]

Although I received a brief note from Earl Goode, I'm convinced that if Karen Francisco and *Journal Gazette* reporters hadn't have picked up my story[88] and printed, side by side, two passages from the two dissertations, one of which is below, the whole sordid affair would have been swept under the rug. Here, first, is the passage from the dissertation written at Virginia Tech:

> According to Ginn (1989), men dominated the teaching profession from colonial times until the twentieth century. Women gained access to the profession by teaching the younger students in the summer session because these jobs were easy to obtain. However, the salary for all teachers was extremely low and when the terms lengthened and the standards for certification rose, men began to look elsewhere for work. As the demand grew for literate, moral teachers at low wages, women began to monopolize the teaching profession. Women were accepted as teachers because they were thought to work well with children. Even though both genders left the profession at equal rates, women were seen as transient or waiting for marriage. Therefore, women remained segregated in the lower rungs of

the teaching professions while men, perceived to be more reliable managers, moved into the supervisory positions. For male administrators, marriage did not conflict with their career.

Compare Adell's dissertation now:

> According to Ginn (1989), men dominated the teaching profession from colonial times until the twentieth century. Women gained access to the profession by teaching the younger students in the summer session because these jobs were easy to obtain. However, the salary for all teachers was extremely low and when the terms lengthened and the standards for certification rose, men began to monopolize the teaching profession. Women were accepted as teachers because they were thought to work well with children. Even though both genders left the profession at equal rates, women were seen as transient or waiting for marriage. Therefore, women remained segregated in the lower rungs of the teaching professions while men, perceived to be more reliable managers, moved into the supervisory positions. For male administrators, marriage did not conflict with their career.[89]

Joining the conversation, Tom Matrka, a dissertation watchdog activist, pointed out that Adell also had lifted segments from Jude Isaacson's dissertation at Virginia Tech. Matrka, likewise, noticed that Adell even lifted text from the two dissertations for her acknowledgments and thank-you pages, in most cases merely changing the names of those mentioned.[90]

Proof that he could care less about plagiarism and genuine research, at his Valparaiso Economic Development Corporation report to taxpayers speech at the end of April, Daniels arrogantly praised Adell's Thea Bowman Charter School as a beacon of excellence, ignoring the charges against Adell entirely. Repeating a myth that corporate schoolers often voice about charter schools, Daniels declared that Thea Bowman, overseen by American Quality Schools, had one thousand students on its waiting list, and Indiana should have "three or four of those kinds of schools if there is that kind of demand for it."[91] Daniels also conveniently disregarded Indiana education department data showing that in 2009 only 33.6 percent of students at

Bowman's prized charter school passed both the English and math state tests, tests that Daniels and Bennett were exploiting to close down traditional public schools to give over to the likes of Adell and other opportunists.

To divert attention from her dissertation, Adell spread more myths to garner as much positive publicity as possible. On May 8, as the plagiarism story was breaking, Gwen Adell published an editorial in the *Times of Northwest Indiana*, claiming to "dispel" the falsehoods surrounding charter schools. Adell scripted that charter schools do accept special education students through a lottery system, because it is mandated by law. It is also a "misconception," Adell wrote, that "charter schools siphon money from traditional public schools," and charter schools as public schools also have a right to "funding to serve public school students."[92] Adell's statements were half-truths. If special needs students make the lottery, they are quietly shown the door out of the schools once their disabilities are discovered. Charter schools pick the best of the crop and outright discriminate against special education students, since these students cost more to educate and lower the schools' test scores. There is no debate about this among valid scholars of education, as Curt Dudley-Marling and Diana Baker detail in "The Effects of Market-Based School Reforms on Students with Disabilities," a review of the research.[93] Adell's own charter school, Thea Bowman, in 2010 had only 5.9 percent of its population classified as special education, which, along with the NBC-celebrated Charles Tindley school (5.9 percent), was among the lowest of all schools (whether charter or traditional public schools) in the state. Indiana Department of Education records show that in 2010 almost half of Indiana charter schools were enrolling low numbers of special needs students. Out of the fifty-eight charter schools listed in 2010, twenty-two of them had less than 10 percent special education enrollment. In contrast, only fourteen of the 292 traditional public school districts had enrollment numbers of special needs kids below 10 percent.

As for her second argument, charter schools are public schools that deposit money into the bank accounts of for-profit management companies or sham nonprofit organizations. To pack the wallets of CEOs and other wealthy investors, charter school officials slice budgets, often leaving students with no textbooks and monetary fines for minor behavior infractions. Mitch Daniels' pal Dennis Bakke at Imagine Schools is notorious for realty schemes where his schools pay so much in rent that teachers and students go into classrooms without books.[94] In Adell's backyard, Chicago's Noble Network of Charter Schools raked in $386,745 in three years by charging students fees for everything from chewing gum to not looking teachers in the eye. Noble's board also had a Northern Trust banker onboard, and the school was paying her bank $181,957 in interest from a loan to the network's Muchin College Prep from 2009 to 2010.[95] These schools are only public in that they recruit poor and minority public students and steal public money in the process, leaving communities dispersed and histories erased.

After Daniels returned from bragging about his "first-rate" corporate school roadmap at the free-market American Enterprise Institute in Washington, DC, the governor had to deal with Adell's critics. On May 18, in an interview with the *Journal Gazette*, Daniels took a swipe at me and others exposing Gwen Adell's plagiarism, saying: "It would be for Purdue to judge if there was anything amiss. We're not going to stand in judgment of whether she did or didn't meet their requirements. If they ever were to decide, we'd look at it then, but not based on some letter from people I suspect have a different agenda than academic purity."[96]

By July, Adell had vanished. Karen Francisco first noticed that Adell's name had mysteriously disappeared from the state board website, so she verified Adell's resignation with Bennett and Daniels' officials. Francisco criticized the IDOE for not announcing Adell's resignation publically. In an editorial, Francisco said Purdue officials had more or less closed their eyes, wishing for the controversy to go away, and "Mitch Daniels, who has responded quickly in other cases involving ethical concerns,"[97] had wanted the whole affair swept under the rug. "Adell served at the governor's pleasure, so it would have served him well to demand her resignation as soon as the alleged plagiarism involving her dissertation came to light," Francisco wrote.[98] It is, Francisco remarked, "embarrassing to have a top state education official and charter school leader accused of academic dishonesty when you're shoving through an education agenda that bolsters charter schools at the expense of traditional public schools."[99] Francisco connected the irony even more, saying the scandal "speaks to the credibility and integrity of the people driving so-called education reform in Indiana."[100]

Because records are confidential, no one knows how Purdue finally "judged" Adell, but her story illustrates that although corporate schoolers want higher standards and accountability for public school students and teachers, the only credential their cronies need is to be willing to carry on their profitable agenda. Even though Purdue was embarrassed, the embarrassment was short-lived. Purdue's board of trustees—many appointed by Mitch and many who funded his governor's campaign—went on to hire Daniels to become the school's twelve president. [101]

MITCH DANIELS IS just one of several Indiana legislators in Indianapolis and Washington who have been duped by or bought out with campaign money and gifts from Muslims who run Gülen schools in over a hundred countries, most for profit.

Controlling 135 charter schools in twenty-eight states in the US, Gülen brings in $400 million yearly in taxpayer money,[102] has six million members, and has even drawn concern from the US consulate in Istanbul[103] because the schools' founders are followers of Fethullah Gülen, a wealthy, controversial Muslim reformer living in exile in Pennsylvania. Fethullah Gülen was kicked out of Turkey in the late '90s for attempting to establish a neo-liberal and socially conservative Islamic state, and his followers have allegedly infiltrated the Turkish police force and other government offices. The goals of the Gülen movement are murky even to experts and US government officials who often disagree or change their opinions. Researcher Joshua Hendrick believes the Gülen movement seeks a "marketized Islam."[104] Our taxpayer money, filtered through Gülen's charter schools, is facilitating this free-market Muslim quest.

Despite the FBI and US Department of Labor and Education's 2011 visa fraud investigation[105] into the Gülen charter schools that has been hushed probably because of political ties, documents show that the group is using taxpayer money to fly teachers here from Turkey and other countries who agree to ship back a percentage of their taxpayer-funded paychecks to the Gülen movement in Turkey. In Ohio, auditors forced Gülen's Horizon Science Academy to repay taxpayers' money it was using for visas, stating there was "no authority that allowed these payments to be made, nor does the nature of the expense relate to the Academy's normal activities and operations."[106] Ohio auditor Mary Taylor also found that Gülenists used state money for legal fees to bring people from Turkey to America who were not even employed with the school. Many Gülenists in the Indiana movement are cited in the audit. The auditors wrote that:

> During the period ended June 30, 2006, Horizon Science Academy-Dayton issued the following payments to Concept Schools, Inc. (the Academy's Management Company), to reimburse the management company for expenditures made to the United States Citizenship and Immigration Services, the United States Department of Homeland Security, Robert A. Perkins & Associates, Karen D. Bradley, and Ant Travel for the purpose of assisting with the cost of Citizenship and Immigration applications and associated legal fees and travel in the amounts of:
>
> Kazim Eldes—Concept Schools, Inc. Invoice #1534
> Dependent Application Fee $ 195.00

Omer Yaliniz—Concept Schools, Inc. Invoice #1534
Legal Fees 600.00
Amanmyrat Gurdov—Concept Schools, Inc. Invoice #1614
Air Travel (Gurdov and his family) 1,597.75
Total Finding for Recovery $2,392.75[107]

The Kazim Eldes Ohio auditors mentioned was involved in the Indiana Math and Science Academy's founding and has served as Concept Schools' Indiana regional vice-president. Gülen's Indiana Math and Science Academy has two charter schools (North and West) in Indianapolis with another one opening in August 2013. The two older Indiana Gülen charters have applied for at least twenty-three visas for teachers and other individuals to come to Indianapolis and work.[108] A Gülen-affiliated for-profit charter management company, Concept Schools runs both Indiana Gülen schools and a total of twenty-seven Gülen schools nationwide. Concept Schools' vice president, Salim Ucan, is on the board of the soon-to-be opened Gülen Indy school, the Indiana Math and Science Academy-South. Ucan was the founding principal at the Chicago Math and Science Academy, which spent over "$113,000 of taxpayers' money in legal fees to fight the union"[109] after the school fired a pregnant teacher who was interested in organizing teachers. From 2007 to 2008, tax records show that Concept Schools got $235,114 for the Indiana schools.[110] The following year, when the Indiana Math and Science Academy spent over $7,000 on travel,[111] Concept raked in $187,322.[112] In 2010, the state awarded the Indiana Math and Science Academy-North with a $681,500 startup grant (renewed in 2011) to "pay Concept a fee that is equal to 10% of the per capita tuition" with the right to increase "the management fee 2 more percent."[113]

The Ant Travel cited in the Ohio audit was a now-defunct Chicago tour agency linked to the Gülen movement and Lyndsey and Bilal Eksili (often deceptively referred to as Eksila, not Eksili), Indiana's chief Gülen operative. In 2009, two years before the FBI would raid Gülen charter schools across the country, Bilal Eksili, ironically, won the FBI Director's Community Leadership Award, a national honor for those assisting the FBI with community partnerships.[114] Eksili and the Niagara Foundation, in turn, awarded Michael Welch, special agent in charge of the Indianapolis FBI division, a Community Leadership Award sometime in 2009, and Tony Bennett attended the event, as did US Indiana senator Richard Lugar.[115] Eksili sits on the Indiana Math and Science Academy-North and West boards and directs the Indiana branch of the eight-state Niagara Foundation and Indiana's Holy Dove Foundation, both Gülen-associated peace and interfaith groups almost indistinguishable. In June 2011, a few months after I first wrote about the Indiana Gülen story online, the Holy Dove Foundation changed its name to the Turkish American Society of Indiana, deleted its website and started a new one, and now passes itself off as a Turkish American Society of Chicago division. To confuse people tracking the Muslim movement, Gülen also now calls the Holy Dove Foundation Niagara Foundation Indiana. Oddly, besides giving luncheons and trips to Turkey for Indiana government people and Indiana Math and Science Academy board members, sitting on charter school boards, and using interns to organize meetings with Indiana government officials, religious leaders, and professors, the Holy Dove/Turkish American Society of Indiana/Niagara Foundation doesn't appear to do anything to promote diversity, love, peace, and friendship, as the mission statement suggests. Actually, Eksili seems to be running a one-man show.

To win support of government officials coast-to-coast, Gülenists like Bilal Eksili invite high-ranking state leaders to dinners to speak and then lavish the officials with awards and gifts. Nowhere is this tactic more at work than in Indiana. In 2008, Mitch Daniels and Indiana Pacers' Jim Morris both spoke with Eksili at a Niagara Foundation dinner and friendship event, where the governor was lavished with gifts.[116] In April 2011, Eksili, Bart Peterson, and Greg Ballard appeared at Indianapolis Public School #22 near Martin Luther King Jr. Park to remember the day forty-three years ago when Robert

Kennedy announced in Indianapolis the death of MLK. Peterson, in 2007, was given an award from the Holy Dove Foundation.[117]

Gülen and Eksili also have courted Virgil Madden and Indiana lieutenant governor Becky Skillman. Madden was Becky Skillman's education policy and faith initiatives advisor and an FBI Citizen Academy alumnus. In 2008, alongside state superintendent of public education Suellen Reed, Madden visited Turkey with the Holy Dove Foundation and Judy O'Bannon, Indiana's former First Lady whose husband legalized charter schools in the state. In Turkey, a WFYI crew filmed Mrs. O'Bannon for her TV program *Community Building Community*.[118] Virgil Madden posed for the Niagara Foundation cameras, too, with FBI's Welch, John Aytekin (Indiana Math and Science Academy-North's director), and Eksili at the Annual Inter-Cultural Friendship Reception with lawmakers in April 2011.[119] Madden now sits on the board of Gülen's Indiana Math and Science Academy-South, set to cut ribbons in Indianapolis in August 2013. In 2010, Becky Skillman herself presented Bilal Eksili the Governor's Distinguished Service Award.[120] Skillman staged a presentation to legislators in 2012, trying to convince them to go on trips to Turkey with Gülenists.

As they have done in Georgia, Hawaii, Texas, Oregon, Oklahoma, and Kentucky, Gülenists in Indiana have even tricked legislators into formally declaring partnerships with them. In March 2011, merely weeks before the FBI raid on Gülen charter schools, Indiana senators Brandt Hershman and Vi Simpson (both at the Gülen statehouse event in April 2011) convinced the Indiana Senate to voice-vote adopt a resolution "honoring the friendship between Indiana and Turkey" the Indiana House had already passed. After praising the Niagara Foundation, noting the constructive agricultural arrangements Indiana has with Turkey, and revealing that "400 civic leaders, elected officials, and academics traveled to Turkey to strengthen the relationship between Hoosiers and Turkish people," the Resolution 36 authors said that "the Indiana General Assembly honors the friendship between Indiana and Turkey" and that "the Secretary of the Senate is hereby directed to transmit a copy of this Resolution to Bilal Eksili," the leader of the Niagara Foundation.[121] The Niagara Foundation awarded Arne Duncan its Education Award in 2007. Duncan's award is just one example of the Gülen movement's influence in DC.

During a Washington, DC meeting at the Turkic American Alliance's second annual convention last November, when Fethullah Gülen's name came up thirteen different times, Indiana's federal legislators Andre Carson, Todd Young, Todd Rokita, and Dan Coats praised Turkish-American relations, Coats even thanking the Niagara Foundation for inviting him to the event. A 2009 speaker at one Holy Dove Foundation luncheon, Rokita said this at the Turkic American Alliance event: "On behalf of people, the great people of the state of Indiana, I thank you for your partnership, thank you for this leadership, the great charter schools that we have. They are run by the Turkish Community. We thank you."[122]

To help these Turkish community charter schools multiply without anyone asking questions, Gülenists bankroll the campaigns of Indiana's Washington legislators. In 2008, Numan Koca, a Holy Dove Foundation member and past board representative of the Indiana Math and Science Academy, gave Andre Carson's campaign $3,000. Mr. Eksili gave $2,000 to Mike Pence's campaign for Indiana governor. Lyndsey Eksili, Bilal Eksili's wife, has funded Todd Young ($250) and Pence ($1,000). In March 2010, Eksili and Concept Schools' Kazim Eldes each handed Carson's campaign for the US Senate $1,000, as did Mehmet Dundar, who is also associated with the Indiana Math and Science Academy. Hasan Yerdelen—a former Holy Dove comrade and now the American Turkish Association of Indiana's treasurer—donated $2,000 to Carson's 2010 quest and $1,000 to Mike Pence. Carson is a Democrat and a Muslim. Mike Pence is not, but his anti-women and conservative message registers with the Gülen crusade.

These political donations and relations may be one reason

why nothing became of the 2011 FBI investigation into visa fraud at Gülen's charter schools, but oil and other fishy US government deals could also play a sizeable role, as Sibel Edmonds has noted. Before she turned whistleblower, Sibel Edmonds was a language specialist for the FBI who had been translating wiretap conversations between Turkish lobby associates. An Iranian raised in Turkey before becoming a US citizen, Edmonds was fired from the FBI in 2002 for revealing to higherups security breaches and Turkish espionage at the bureau's language division. In 2009, Edmonds testified before the Ohio Election Commission in David Krikorian's defense case when Ohio Republican representative Jean Schmidt filed charges against him for alleging, during a 2008 campaign bid, that she accepted money illegally from Turkey interests. Besides discussing Gülen's US charter schools during testimony in the *Schmidt v. Krikorian* case, Edmonds said Gülen and the US State Department from 1997 to 2001 trained al-Qaeda in Central Asia with help from the Turkish military, Pakistani's Inter-Services Intelligence, and Azerbaijan officials.[123] In a subsequent interview with retired CIA counter-terrorism specialist Phil Giraldi (who believes her story), Edmonds details the Gülen and U.S training missions and Turkish drug-smuggling into Chicago and Paterson, New Jersey, two cities containing Gülen charter schools:

> GIRALDI: You also have information on al-Qaeda, specifically al-Qaeda in Central Asia and Bosnia. You were privy to conversations that suggested the CIA was supporting al-Qaeda in central Asia and the Balkans, training people to get money, get weapons, and this contact continued until 9/11. . .
>
> EDMONDS: I don't know if it was CIA. There were certain forces in the U.S. government who worked with the Turkish paramilitary groups, including Abdullah Çatli's group, Fethullah Gülen.
>
> GIRALDI: Well, that could be either Joint Special Operations Command or CIA.
>
> EDMONDS: Maybe in a lot of cases when they said State Department, they meant CIA?
>
> GIRALDI: When they said State Department, they probably

meant CIA.

EDMONDS: Okay. So these conversations, between 1997 and 2001, had to do with a Central Asia operation that involved bin Laden. Not once did anybody use the word "al-Qaeda." It was always "mujahideen," always "bin Laden" and, in fact, not "bin Laden" but "bin Ladens" plural. There were several bin Ladens who were going on private jets to Azerbaijan and Tajikistan. The Turkish ambassador in Azerbaijan worked with them.

There were bin Ladens, with the help of Pakistanis or Saudis, under our management. Marc Grossman was leading it, 100 percent, bringing people from East Turkestan into Kyrgyzstan, from Kyrgyzstan to Azerbaijan, from Azerbaijan some of them were being channeled to Chechnya, some of them were being channeled to Bosnia. From Turkey, they were putting all these bin Ladens on NATO planes. People and weapons went one way, drugs came back.

GIRALDI: Was the U.S. government aware of this circular deal?

EDMONDS: 100 percent. A lot of the drugs were going to Belgium on NATO planes. After that, they went to the UK, and a lot came to the U.S. via military planes to distribution centers in Chicago and Paterson, New Jersey. Turkish diplomats who would never be searched were coming with suitcases of heroin.[124]

The Turkish-American operation included, Edmonds says, paying off US officials to leak secrets and allow nuclear weapons technology to be sold to US enemies on the Pakistani, Iranian, and North Korean black markets.[125]

According to Edmonds, a corrupt scheme was also at work involving Turkey, Iraqi war architect Paul Wolfowitz, Marc Grossman, Bush's deputy undersecretary of state, and Indiana's own born-again Christian and conservative US House representative Dan Burton.[126] Under a "state secrets privilege" order, attorney general John Ashcroft gagged Edmonds from disclosing detailed information to the public, so Edmonds has not been able to say exactly what illegal activity Burton was enmeshed in with the Turkish lobby. Supposedly the crimes occurred from 1997 to 2002, the same time span the CIA was allegedly helping Gülen train al-Qaeda.[127] Gülen's name does not surface alongside Burton's during Edmonds' Ohio testimony, but Burton has accepted campaign donations from many

Gülenists tied to Indiana charter schools. Lyndsey Eksili, wife of Indiana Gülen leader Bilal, has given Burton $1000, and Hasan Yerdelen, the American Turkish Association of Indiana's treasurer, donated $1,000 to Burton in 2010, as well. A former Holy Dove official, Yerdelen's new group is part of the Assembly of Turkish-American Associations (ATAA), which Edmonds also names in her outing.

Burton receives money from the Turkish American Political Action Committee, which is linked to the American Turkish Council Edmonds exposes. In typical Gülen fashion, the Turkish American Political Action Committee has many names. Incorporated in Houston, Texas, it sometimes is called the Turkish Coalition PAC and the Turkish Coalition USA PAC. Until May 2008, its name was the Turkish PAC–Turkish American Heritage Political Action Committee. It is also tied to the TC-USA PAC. Federal Election Commission records show Burton, from 2007 to 2011, collected $11,000 from this association and its name variations.[128]

The Turkish Coalition of America's Lincoln McCurdy manages the Turkish Coalition USA PAC. A Hanover College, Indiana, graduate and former US diplomat in Istanbul, McCurdy was the American Turkish Council CEO from 1998 to 2004, during Burton's alleged shady activity. Through wiretaps, Edmonds was listening into conversations at the American Turkish Council (ATC), which is funded by US weapons contractors and drug and energy companies (including Imagine Schools' Dennis Bakke's former AES Energy, Eli Lilly, and Lockheed Martin). Edmonds' firing had involved ATC. When Edmonds told higher-ups an ATC spy was working as a FBI translator and attempting to conceal ATC's illegal activity, Edmonds was fired.

McCurdy and Turkish operatives are no strangers to Dan Burton. Burton has visited Turkey with McCurdy and the Turkish Coalition of America.[129] In a 2009 talk at the Gülen Institute Congressional Dinner, Burton praised how Dick Lugar—who that year received a community leadership award from the Niagara Foundation—was to be a future keynote speaker at the Holy Dove Foundation and how he himself is treated like a "king" when he takes trips to Turkey.[130] In the summer of 2010, Burton hired Turkish hand Baran Cansever to fact-find at congressional hearings. Cansever was an American Turkish Council intern in 2009, where he planned ATC-funded trips for congressional staffers and worked with the ATC "chairman during energy and defense sessions at the Annual Conference on U.S./Turkish Relations."[131]

Many have deemed credible Edmonds' finger-pointing, including the Department of Justice's inspector general[132] and senators Patrick Leahy and Chuck Grassley in interviews with CBS' *60 Minutes*.[133] Former Turkish intelligence chief Osman Nuri Gundes, in a recent memoir, writes that Gülen in his Central Asia charter schools in the mid-1990s gave cover to over 130 CIA agents posing as teachers, which may be the reason why the US government is okay with Turkish men on H-1B visas posing as educators in the US charter schools Gülen followers control.[134] Why was the CIA interested in Central Asia? Oil and gas, according to Edmonds.

When asked during the Ohio testimony if Fethullah Gülen with his 180 different organizations was a threat to United States interests, Edmonds, aware that Gülen's US charter schools were "spreading rapidly," said: "One hundred percent, absolutely."[135] The charter schools are "multiplying," and more of them are being proposed in Indiana with Gülen now having filed the paperwork for a nonprofit in Fort Wayne. Despite parents and officials in Ohio, Hawaii, Arizona, Utah, Texas, and elsewhere questioning Gülen charter schools' financial dealings, visa laws having been introduced in Oklahoma and Tennessee to curtail charter schools' recruitment of foreign workers, and a Texas investigation into Gülen, Indiana lawmakers remain silent. Despite former Ohio Gülen charter school employee Mary Addi detailing on *60 Minutes* how her husband, a former Gülenist who taught at the school, was forced to send much of his paycheck back to Turkey to support

Fethullah Gülen's quest for a radical free-market Islam,[136] nothing has changed. With the government-Muslim partnerships springing up all over the state, it looks like Indiana will remain "Turkey-tripped" into the near future, supporting a Muslim money-making scheme invading the US.

THE CHRISTIAN RIGHT backers behind the Challenge Foundation Academy Indy in the Avondale Meadows neighborhood owe a gratitude to Bart Peterson and Indiana Republicans. Peterson let the Challenge Foundation sneak into the city when he was mayor and now his acquaintances make money from the charter school.

A libertarian anti-climate change promoter started in Texas in 1988 which has given millions of dollars to over 182 charter schools across the US, the Challenge Foundation is the brainchild of former Georgia Gulf Corporation's millionaire John D. Bryan. In June 2010, John Bryan spoke on privatizing public schools at the Koch brothers' secret meeting in Aspen, Colorado, hobnobbing with Tea Party leaders, Glenn Beck, and other notable right-wingers. Bryan and son-in-law Ruppert Reinstadler have also hooked up with the Koch brothers in Washington, DC, hoping to acquire money for the foundation's charter school crusade.[137] A leadership board member at the Club for Growth (now led by former Indiana US representative Chris Chocola) and a key Scott Walker donor, Bryan—who is fond of viewing videos about the national anthem before beginning his school choice meetings—has given $151,000 to the Indiana House Republican Campaign Committee since 2006. Bryan gave $75,000 from 2005 to 2007 to the DeVos clan's All Children Matter, the Virginia Public Assess Project noticed.[138] Reporter Matt Dixon shows that Bryan recently handed $50,000 to DeVos' American Federation for Children.[139] The Challenge Foundation has also financed a school voucher program in Portland, Oregon, the Friedman Foundation, the Institute for Justice, the Black Alliance for Educational Options, Teach for America, and other corporate school groups, giving at least $100,000 to the Charles A. Tindley charter school in the Avondale Meadows neighborhood.[140] Combing through tax records, NC Policy Watch's Sarah Ovaska uncovered a mere sample of the Challenge Foundation's anti-public education contributions:

> * $10,000 that went to produce "The Cartel," a documentary criticized by many movie reviewers for its anti-public education slant. The Challenge Foundation described the project as exposing "corruption, waste and intimidation in the nation's public schools," according to a 2009 tax filing.
> * Another $10,000 grant for a group that planned to send all school districts in the country a film questioning the science behind global warming and what a greener economy will do to "working families whose livelihoods are dependent on energy production."
> * $690,000 went to a handful of public charter schools in North Carolina from 2007 to 2009, including $305,000 that went to Thomas Jefferson Classical Academy.[141]

The Challenge Foundation's Thomas Jefferson Classical Academy annually throws a diaper drive for an anti-abortion Christian group, has one student organization, the Young Republican's Club, and has Bryan's daughter Cheryl Reinstadler on its board. [142] Although this school has come under intense fire for the Challenge Foundation's Christian Right leanings, the Challenge Foundation brags that under former Atlanta pastor William Steinbrook's directorship, the group gave out over $18 million to charter schools nationwide.

Even though the Challenge Foundation controls the academy in Indy and eleven other schools in Arizona and North Carolina, Team Challenge Foundation Academy (Team CFA) wants to use corporate board members to multiply right-wing charter schools across several states. In a late 2011 board meeting in Phoenix, the group blueprinted plans to start fifty new charter schools in Indiana, Arizona, and North Carolina within the next twelve to fifteen years with $1.5 million from the Challenge Foundation. Team CFA and the Challenge Foundation have restructured agreements with new charter schools they manage. The Challenge Foundation now will give loans (and not grants) which can be forgiven, along with interest, after four, five, or six years, if the schools remain in good standing with the foundation. Good standing means rigging the board of directors and letting Team CFA call all the shots. Older schools where Bryan's group has invested over $500,000 will need to make Team CFA the corporate member of the school, allowing Team CFA to appoint and fire all local board members. This corporate control, according to Team CFA, is currently being reviewed, alongside Indiana law, for the Challenge Foundation Academy in Indianapolis.[143]

With Mayor Peterson's approval, the Challenge Foundation Academy corporate school model began in Indianapolis where it opened its first school. Using $5 million in new markets tax credits through the Charter Schools Development Corporation,[144] the Challenge Foundation's plan was to privatize everything at the Challenge Foundation Academy Indy. In its application to then-mayor Bart Peterson, Team CFA, posing as a locally supported group, wrote it would "use outside suppliers for many administrative services" and would "contract out janitorial services" to save money. Its "long-term intent" is "to bundle as many of the administrative services as possible into common outside suppliers."[145] Peterson, whose Mind Trust is requesting mayoral control and privatization for the entire Indy school system, must have loved the Challenge Foundation rulebook. In 2008, in what looks like a "scratch your back" moment, the Challenge Foundation gave Peterson's Mind Trust $486,400 to support its education fellowships, some which were named Challenge Foundation Fellows.[146]

Bart Peterson's old employer Strategic Capital Partners is partnering with the Challenge Foundation to charterize and gentrify Indianapolis' Avondale Meadows, where Challenge Foundation Academy Indy is located. Strategic Capital Partners is a private real estate investment management firm. Peterson, after he lost reelection for mayor in 2008, managed the firm's Strategic Partners Urban Fund. With offices in Chicago,

Indianapolis, and New York, Strategic Capital Partners has Al Gore's son Albert Gore III raising funds for Avondale Meadows and other projects. Albert III has had credentials with the corporate school crowd since Teach for America helped him launch *GOOD* magazine. Honored by Tony Bennett in 2010, Challenge Foundation Academy Indy's unelected board includes Strategic Capital Partners' Gene Zink, the trailblazer behind the Avondale Meadows gentrification project. A one-time Fifth Third Bank director, Zink in 2007 loaned $52,000 to the Charles A. Tindley Accelerated School,[147] another Avondale Meadows charter school run by Ed Power, the company the Indiana Department of Education chose to "turn around" Indianapolis' "failing" Arlington Community High School. Zink's colleague at Strategic Capital Partners, Charles Garcia, is on the Challenge Foundation Academy Indy board, too. A former board member of the Indianapolis Chamber of Commerce, the Indiana Chamber of Commerce, the Federal Reserve Bank of Chicago, and the Indiana Pacers, Garcia has make a handsome profit from the charter school. The Challenge Foundation Academy Indy recently paid Garcia's Garcia Construction $623,000 for work on a school project. Bart Peterson's friend and former Mind Trust fellow Earl M. Phalen did summer school for the Challenge Foundation Academy Indy. One hundred fifty thousand dollars went to Phalen's Entrepreneurial Ventures in Education in Quincy, Massachusetts. [148]

Last year, Team CFA members and the Challenge Foundation were present when Strategic Capital Partners and Atlanta-based Purpose Built Communities established the Strategic Community Venture Fund to develop "mixed income-housing" projects and charter schools in the Avondale Meadows community. To fulfill the corporate plan, in September 2011 Strategic Capital Partners and Purpose Built Communities hosted the Second Annual Network Member Conference at the Indianapolis Conrad Hotel. The conference included the Mind Trust's David Harris, Geoffrey Canada, the Harlem Children's Zone hero of *Waiting for Superman* whose school enterprise has

$128 million invested in hedge funds,[149] the KIPP Foundation's Richard Barth, Cynthia Kuhlman of Charles R. Drew Charter School in the East Lake Meadows district of gentrified Atlanta, and Indy mayor Greg Ballard, who was followed onstage by Tom Cousins who discussed how the East Lake "miracle" sparked Purpose Built Communities. On stage, Strategic Capital Partners' Gene Zink spoke with Warren Buffett (who even visited a kindergarten class at the Challenge Foundation Academy for a photo-op[150]) about "holistic revitalization." Indiana US congressman Andre Carson, Madelyn Adams, executive director of the East Lake Foundation, and Larkin Tackett, director of place-based initiatives in the US Department of Education's Office of Innovation and Improvement, which gives out grants to startup charter schools, also attended the event.

Apart from Warren Buffett donations, Purpose Built Communities was flooded with money from Julian Robertson, a retired hedge fund manager whose Robertson Foundation from 2007 to 2008, researcher Ken Libby found, gave the Democrats for Education Reform-affiliated Education Reform Now $250,000, Alliance for School Choice $250,000, the New Teacher Project $200,000, and Teach for America $7,120,000, among others.[151] The Tiger Foundation, Julian Robertson's other nonprofit, has donated millions to the school privatization movement and his family is deeply entrenched in the corporate overhaul of public schools. Leonie Haimson, founder of Class Size Matters, details one Robertson family controversy when then-CEO of the NYC Schools Joel Klein allowed the Robertson family charter schools to violate state law and expand inside public schools in New York City, despite "damaging effects on the students with disabilities."[152]

Strategic Capital Partners and Purpose Built Communities are counting on tax credits in Indy for their housing and charter school project. The Indiana Housing and Community Development Authority has "approved a reservation of more than $1.9 million annually in federal low-income housing tax credits from the State's 2010 allocation."[153] In 2011, the Department of Metropolitan Development donated land to the project. Indianapolis itself is geared to dish out a few million for the project. Additionally, Strategic Capital Partners and Purpose Built Communities' mission is to take advantage of new markets tax credits allowing investors who subsidize charter schools and other projects in inner-city communities to write-off their donations, dollar-for-dollar, on their taxes. The project's first stage calls for bulldozing down public housing projects and building 600 units of mixed-income apartments and 250 units of for-sale townhouses and single family homes, and no limit on charter schools.

Strategic Capital Partners and Purpose Built Communities' type of public-private investment in "mixed income housing" and charter schools hardly ever turns out well for anyone but the investors, as DePaul professor Kenneth Saltman outlines in *Capitalizing on Disaster: Taking and Breaking Public Schools*. Illustrating the Commercial Club of Chicago's Renaissance 2010 blueprint for Mayor Daley, Saltman details how in the guise of urban renewal to help the poor, the city and big business blended "real estate profiteering and land grabs at the expense of the most vulnerable," then called for ungodly guidelines making it impossible for the city's poorest to reenter the new mixed housing developments, "sometimes even restricting anyone with an extended family member with a [criminal] record."[154] This exemplifies gentrification nationwide, which is just a sly form of segregation. After decades of neglecting public housing and schools, big city mayors and privatizers move in with state grants, US Department of Housing and Urban Development money, and other funds, and build expensive housing projects to drive minorities into the suburbs or homeless shelters, so wealthier white residents can move in. Education scholar Pauline Lipman, an outspoken critic of Renaissance 2010 and gentrification and charter school schemes in general, adds that this real estate development breeds financial speculation, which, "in turn, causes increases in property values and rising property taxes, driving out low-income and working-class renters and home owners."[155] As Saltman notes, after Republicans took over the US House of Representatives in 1995, they ended the requirement that for each demolished public housing project a new public project be created.[156] At this point, the public schools are shut down and charter schools crop up to take taxpayer money for upper-middle-class kids and the poor students lucky enough to get new public housing with their families. Kids, from other neighborhoods, are bussed into the area to attend the charter schools.

To gentrify and open charter schools in Indianapolis' Avondale Meadows region and twenty-five other cities, Purpose Built Communities recently hired former Atlanta mayor Shirley Franklin, who was at the Indy kickoff event in September 2011. One doesn't have to look beyond the Shirley Franklin and Tom Cousins-led "holistic revitalization" housing project in Atlanta to see where Indy and these other cities are heading. By 2006, in the city where Martin Luther King Jr. was born, gentrification had forced many blacks out of the city entirely. In one Atlanta prior steel mill area, a new project called Atlantic Station developed 2,000 housing units with each loft starting at $160,000, despite a gentrification task force supposedly monitoring how lower-income residents were treated.[157] Even the event held in March 2007 to kick off the East Lake Meadows project, which the Woodrow Wilson International Center for Scholars' website highlighted, is chillingly a prophecy for Indianapolis. Philippa Strum, who directs Woodrow Wilson's Division of US Studies, writes:

> Former Mayor William Hudnut of Indianapolis, Indiana and Chevy Chase, Maryland spoke about the need for mixed-income housing as a major element in urban renewal, emphasizing that it can be both profitable for investors and the creator of enormous social capital. Fifty percent of East Lake's housing is market rate. Apartments are organized, Cousins said, so that the few families on welfare live in-between two working families and are literally surrounded by examples of what they can accomplish. That, along with job training and education, helps move additional members of the community into the paid workforce.[158]

But when wealthier white people move into these areas and new businesses open, blacks, other minorities, and the poor find it hard landing jobs. Tom Cousins' statement "surrounded by examples of what they can accomplish" blames the victims. *Black Commentator's* Glen Ford has pointed the finger at black mayors like Franklin and Washington, DC's Anthony Williams who have handed over the keys of their cities to the white establishment, dislocating their own in the process, because these leaders only "are loyal to their own tiny but crafty class of Black hustlers, for whom the masses of African Americans are simply pawns, marks and suckers, eminently unworthy of self-determination or even simple protection."[159]

After the 2008 Wall Street meltdown, Shirley Franklin's "real-life Cinderella story" (as *Education Week's* Alexandra Rice called it) turned ugly. As Naomi Spencer notes, the metro Atlanta region in 2009 lost 143,000 jobs and 97,000 homes. Homeless shelters were overflowing with people, some with PhDs. Even the Salvation Army had run out of money to build a new shelter. Spencer describes that over "the past 15 years, the city has torn down some 15,000 units in 32 housing projects," swapping them with "mixed-income communities," where "only one third of displaced residents were able to resettle." Mayor Franklin, in fact, in 2003 started "banning such acts as donating food to the homeless on downtown streets, soliciting donations and sleeping in public areas." Spencer writes that "Atlanta police, posing as tourists, have staged a series of undercover street sweeps, arresting dozens of homeless people for asking for money."[160]

Kicking people to the curb and then handcuffing them for being homeless isn't the official narrative the Bill Gates-funded *Education Week* passes on about Franklin and Purpose Built Communities' projects. In a blaringly distorted article, Alexandra Rice says the East Lake crime rate is down and "mixed-income housing is woven between shops, local eateries, schools, a family center, a YMCA, and two golf courses,"[161] where students who all dress the same way in charter school uniforms learn to play golf. But tee tricks and test scores measure superficiality, and the lowering crime-rate in East Lake has just been moved to a different location.

Indianapolis is the present location for the Purpose Built Communities plan. While there in 2011 to support the Avondale project, Challenge Foundation's wealthy donor John Bryan quoted the US Constitution but didn't publicize his Indiana charter school problems.[162] Challenge Foundation Academy Indy had only 52.4 percent of its students passing the math and English state tests in 2010, and state investigators found that from October 2006 to May 2007 payments made to Fifth Third Bank (Gene Zink's old stomping grounds) "were not supported by original bills or invoices" and some payments "were made to employees that were not included in the payroll system or on a salary schedule or contract." Payroll taxes "were not properly withheld or remitted" either.[163] Yet, in 2010, the Indiana Department of Education gave $1.6 million to Challenge Foundation Academy Indy to start a 200-day school year and implement teacher merit-pay.[164] More good news came on April 20, 2012, when charter school sponsor Ball State gave GEO Foundation's mayor-closed Fountain Square charter school over to the libertarian Challenge Foundation, kept Rollin Dick, the former Conseco scandal guru from GEO, onboard, and added Gene Zink.[165] This is not surprising. GEO's Kevin Teasley recently sat on the Team CFA national board.

Bryan and Team CFA don't believe in "government schools," but they don't turn down state and federal money. Their plan seems less about personal profit than about helping destroy the public school system so future corporations and the Gene Zinks of the world can gain handsomely, where local control is abolished and fake patriotism conceals a more undemocratic ploy.

THE PROJECT SCHOOL was unique, and its board of directors was even more unique, for it, unlike other Indianapolis charter schools, did not contain corporate members and cronies of the Indiana government-corporate school complex. Plain and simple, as one of the few Indiana community-led charter schools meant to fulfill what the original creators of the charter school idea envisioned, The Project School didn't play by the same capitalistic blueprint the powers-that-be in Indianapolis have insisted be the standard. That is why, on July 17, 2012, after the Mind Trust's David Harris had made the recommendation in the *Indianapolis Business Journal*, mayor Greg Ballard axed The Project School (TPS).[166] Blaming low test scores and financial problems, the mayor gave TPS officials only fifteen days to respond to his closing the school and held no public meeting besides a press conference, after which local reporters quickly aped the "official" narrative.

The closing came out of the blue. TPS leader Tarrey Banks, in an email to the school's community, said that the week before, Beth Bray, Ballard's charter school director, emailed and said not to "worry about" the school's upcoming year, since in early fall the mayor's office would meet with TPS' board to discuss the school's fourth year review. After a parent notified Banks that someone had heard the closing announced at a meeting, he called the mayor's office but was ignored. Bray finally emailed TPS about revoking its charter at 4:45 that day, while Jason Kloth, deputy mayor of education, was holding the press conference.

The mayor accused the school of inappropriately using funds from a federal startup grant to pay teachers and other financial improprieties. Tarrey Banks responded: "We have been fully transparent about all grant expenditures. The 'issue' they are stating in terms of grant mismanagement is an issue from the 2nd year of the school and is inaccurately articulated in the media. The Mayor's office has had this report for well over a year and has NEVER expressed any concern or even questioned us about it." Banks went on to refute other statements from the mayor's office, saying the school has never missed payroll, and the audit proved the school "had strong enough financials to fully finance and purchase our building in one of the toughest economic and development times in our state's history." TPS, according to Banks, was also "in good standing with our bank and bankers."

Winner of *NUVO's* 2012 Cultural Vision Award, TPS was a hands-on learning center taking in students other charter schools, IPS, and private schools ran from. TPS school board figures said that "a quarter of all sixth graders have been retained at least once, more than two-thirds of fifth graders qualify for free or reduced lunch, twenty-six percent of fourth graders have been in three or more schools, a tenth of all third graders have attended five or more schools, and a quarter of all second graders qualify for special education services."[167]

Because it came only a few weeks before classes started and gave TPS no time to find another authorizer to grant the school a new charter, the school closing outraged parents, students, and teachers. Elizabeth Annarino had many complaints. Annarino and her husband found TPS to be the perfect school to look "at my children as whole persons, that would help them develop their emotional intellect, which leads to intellect and introspection at not a private school price." Noting that her daughter, like most creative thinkers, didn't do well on standardized tests, Annarino said "there is a witch hunt on to weed out schools that make successes that aren't easily plotted on the datagraph. The bottom line for me is I don't want my children plotted on a national datagraph." Annarino was referring to another mayor complaint about TPS—its low test scores, which have seldom factored into the evaluations of other Indianapolis charter schools.

As part of the Opt Out and Save Our Schools movements, several TPS parents are on the national forefront to stop the corporatization of our public schools, seeing standardized testing as a waste of tax money and children's minds. Matthew Brooks is one of these parents. Brooks, who is anti-standardized testing, believes that TPS students with their Curricular Summit Program were getting a unique schooling because they were taught that "Heart/Mind/Voice is the key to total and whole growth" as human beings. Another TPS parent said that "this is why we chose The Project School. The Opt Out movement is not going away. We are increasing in numbers thanks to Mayor Ballard's actions and the support he is getting from IDOE." [168] Shaun Johnson, a Towson University elementary education professor in Baltimore, echoed this sentiment. "Reducing young persons and dedicated professionals who work with them to quantitative data points is humiliating, destructive, and thoroughly misguided," he says in an email to the powers-that-be. "This is what makes the potential closure of TPS so tragic, that they have taken powerful positions in support of their students rather than capitulating to the prevailing education reform model that puts profits over people."[169]

That Mayor Ballard "puts profits over people" and is "accountable" not to school children but adults is confirmed by his campaign chest, jam-packed in 2011 with what I estimate to have been around $57,000 in corporate school money. These donors included Ballard's former economic and workforce development deputy mayor Nick Weber, who helped Ballard direct his "mayor-sponsored charter school operations;" Tony Bennett; mega-Bennett donor and popcorn "entrepreneur" Mike Weaver; Brian Bosma; millionaire Fred Klipsch, operative for the DeVos and Walmart American Federation for Children's Indiana branch; the Mind Trust, Teach for America, and Lilly hand Anne Shane; Bill Shrewsberry, from the Mind Trust and a member of the Indiana Charter School Board; Todd Huston, another Indiana Charter School Board member and former Bennett advisor; Eli Lilly CEO John Lechleiter and Sarah, his wife; former Lilly Endowment leader John Mutz, who is now a member of Ballard's education innovation committee; and even Deborah Daniels, Mitch's sister.[170]

KIPP INDY IS a team player in the Indiana government-corporate school complex, as was apparent when on March 14, 2012 Greg Ballard selected Jason Kloth as his deputy mayor of education.[171] Before his appointment, Kloth had been roving Teach for America's DC offices, concocting ways for the temporary teachers group to invade the personal space of US schools. Kloth had also led Teach for America Indianapolis and the Indy KIPP board, hiring other TFAers to the equation. Corporate school champions like to sell the story that sometime in 2008 Kloth appointed two of his TFA comrades, Emily Pelino and Aleesia Johnson, to drag the KIPP school out of its financial and testing mess. DFER's Whitney Tilson posted online an email from Patrick O'Donnell, another TFAer, glorifying Kloth's brilliance, just after Mayor Ballard chose his new henchman. In part, the email reads:

> Jason was the KIPP: Indy board chair a few years back who reconstituted the entire board and staff, brought in Emily Pelino and Aleesia Johnson as the school leaders, and brought in 2/3 of the teachers (over 80% of staff is now TFA CMs/alums actually). The school has since had some of the most significant student achievement growth in the state and is poised to expand with a great executive director. All of this wouldn't have happened without Jason. Great stuff![172]

Despite the fanfare, not much has changed since 2008, when KIPP Indy wasted "$8,000 in Title I funding that had been improperly used on items ranging from teacher salaries to spa services at a professional development retreat."[173] From 2005 to 2009, KIPP Indy's yearly progress was lacking. The school took several years to show anything that could remotely be considered so-called progress, something Ballard has conveniently ignored.[174] KIPP Indy's dropout rate is shocking. Hammering the school in August 2011, Jim Horn quoted page 12 of the October 2010 KIPP Indy report from Ballard's own office:

> "KIPP Indianapolis has been consistently under-enrolled during the past four years. The school's attendance rate has fallen below the target established by the IDOE for the past two academic years. The school's retention rate was above or near 70% for the first three years, but dropped each year since, reaching only 33.3% this past year. Accordingly, the school receives a Does Not Meet Standard for

this indicator."[175]

At the end of his analysis, Horn, the education professor who with Caroline Grannan has shown how KIPP at its 141 schools across America highly inflates how many of its students actually go to college, asks what the Indy mayor plans "to do about it."[176] The mayor did nothing. While reviewing KIPP Indy in late 2011, Ballard had no difficulty renewing the school's charter, despite the school's history of lousy tests schools, a high dropout rate, financial issues, and an alleged sexual assault by four males on an eleven-year-old special needs student during a 2007 field trip to Boston, for which the school was sued in 2010.[177] In the KIPP Indy renewal report, the mayor's office didn't appear concerned that in 2008 only 36.6 percent of KIPP Indy students passed both state tests in math and English and only 27.6 percent the year after.

Financially, the KIPP school in Gary, Indiana, in 2008 was also in shambles, and it still appears to be. In a State Board of Accounts audit covering July 2009 to June 2011, auditors noted that KIPP paid penalties, late fees, and finance charges, and failed to "pay claims and remit taxes in a timely fashion," which indicated "serious financial problems which should be investigated by the governmental unit." Even an official bond for the school—run by American Quality Schools—was not filed in the county recorder's office. Auditors noted this same violation in an earlier report to the school. Auditors similarly discovered that several different people were running school credit cards over a five month period, and in 23 instances no receipts could be found. Auditors emphasized this problem, too, in an earlier report. The auditors said the "Director of Finance and Administration handles the daily collections, issues receipts, prepares bank deposits, takes deposit to the bank, and handles student billings and postings on accounts." Regarding the school's paying system, the auditors wrote that: "Offers to employees are signed only by the School Leader and the Employee without the signature of a board member representative," so that it was unclear if the board approved the pay and contract at all.[178]

Financial fuzziness aside, KIPP, nationwide, has come under fire for its tough-love discipline, where both teachers and students are forced into "no excuses" psychologically abusive environments which KIPP founder David Levin adapted from the overhyped learned helplessness and positive guru Martin Seligman. Students who don't follow rules or do their assignments are made to wear "a large sign pinned to their clothes labeled 'miscreant.'" Poor students "are indoctrinated to feel okay when they are berated or screamed at, which is a common occurrence."[179] Special education kids are often yelled at, too, for not following S.L.A.N.T (Sit straight. Listen. Ask a question. Nod your head. Track the speaker, i.e. make eye contact). One New York City special education student told Class Size Matters that:

> Teachers would scream at us all the time. Sometimes for things we did, and sometimes for things we didn't. A kid would raise his voice. Then the teacher would raise his voice. Kid would raise his voice higher and the teacher raised his voice higher. Until it was a screaming match between the kid and the teacher. And then the principal comes in, and it's three people all screaming at each other. It would give me such a headache![180]

IT DOESN'T LOOK like any of these politically connected, low- performing, financially shady, and sometimes abusive charter schools will be shut down, and many more will open. Not only can schools shop around at universities and religious colleges to get sponsorship if they are closed, a stacked Indiana Charter School Board intends to rubberstamp new charter schools to give the corporate leaders more opportunity to grab taxpayer money. Consisting of representatives appointed by Daniels, Brian Bosma, Bennett, and other legislators, the Indiana Charter School Board was recently led by former Mind Trust and Eli Lilly official Claire Fiddian-Green, alongside Stand for Children's Karega Rausch. If that isn't enough, Indiana Charter School Board member Todd Huston should warn of the cronyism to come. After Huston left his job as Tony Bennett's chief of staff to land a gig with Cisco Systems, Bennett turned around and used $1.7 million of state money to buy video-conferencing equipment from Cisco which was never used, some of it never even delivered.[181] Then there's Indiana Charter School Board member Jamie Garwood, a Marian University student. When the Indiana State Ethics Commission ruled that Garwood could not participate in the authorizing board discussions concerning the Urban League's charter school application for Fort Wayne, since she was the Urban League's director of development, the Indiana Charter School Board approved Urban League's request to allow American Quality Schools to run the charter school anyway, after Garwood promoted it.[182] With another stacked board established, Indiana has all the wheels in place to start the Walmartization of public schools, and the Walton family has been here all along and isn't going anywhere. ■

4.
CONCLUSION: SAM'S CLUB'S
HERO DEFEATED

The primal need of the working class is education. By education I mean revolutionary education; the kind that enables men to see that the twenty odd millions of wage-workers in the United States are wage-slaves.
Eugene V. Debs

The government has ceased to function . . . the corporations are the government.
Theodore Dreiser

T EARING UP BEFORE THE CAMERAS, AN EMOTIONAL Bill Oberndorf was remembering the first time he telephoned Walmart heir John T. Walton in 1990 about calculating a school heist for billionaires. As Betsy DeVos' companion on the board of Jeb Bush's Foundation for Excellence in Education who has shoveled millions of dollars to the Center for Education Reform, Walmart and DeVos' All Children Matter and American Federation for Children, Oberndorf quoted former Hoosier and Black Alliance for Educational Option's Kevin Chavous then introduced Tony Bennett to receive the 2012 John T. Walton Champions for School Choice Award at American Federation for Children's National Policy Summit.

Beginning his May 7, 2012 sermon, a proud Bennett stood behind an American Federation for Children banner. Receiving the award Walmart and Bradley Foundation's Black Alliance for Educational Options' founding father Howard Fuller received the year before, Bennett had reached the big time, a lapdog for the filthy rich. Bennett first honored the Indiana Chamber's Derek Redelman and Leslie Hiner, Brian Bosma's former chief of staff now with the Friedman Foundation, both in the audience. On several occasions, Bennett addressed the cash princess Betsy DeVos herself. Then he said he loved "the little guy who occupies the big office down the hall," Mitch Daniels, the best governor in America. Mitch, Bennett said, "opened up a big checkbook" and granted him and Indiana Republicans free rein. [1]

Besides DeVos and Daniels, Walmart had "opened up a big checkbook" in Indiana, too. In 2011, the Walton Family Foundation flooded $1.3 million to Indianapolis mayor Greg Ballard's CEOs for New Schools Initiative to back new corporate charter schools across the city. The mayor paid some of the Walmart money to Indiana University Health, so the healthcare provider could "explore" its own charter school franchise; some cash went to Ballard's alma mater, Cathedral High School, to supplement the Mind Trust money it was already spending.[2] In 2012, the Waltons dropped another $3 million into the Indianapolis corporate school movement, chump change for a family hoarding as much wealth as 48 million Americans combined.[3]

Ballard was just one of Walmart's beneficiaries. In 2011, Walton Family Foundation money loaded the bank accounts of several corporate school groups active in the Hoosier state: the Alliance for School Choice, $1,202,000; Andy Rotherham's Bellwether Education Partners, $90,000; the Black Alliance for Educational Options, $796,000; Stand for Children Leadership Center, $1,136,016; Charles A. Tindley Accelerated School, $250,000; Christel House DORS, $30,000; Damar Charter Academy, $250,000; IFF (Illinois Facilities Fund), $2,190,000; Institute for Justice, $443,885; KIPP Foundation, $6,404,020; New Teacher Project, $2,941,239; Indiana Public Charter Schools Association, $380,000; School Choice Indiana, $200,000; Indiana Department of Education, $25,000; Friedman Foundation, $565,000; and the Mind Trust, $500,000. In

2012, out of the $157 million the Walton Family Foundation gave out to corporate schoolers nationwide, the Alliance for School Choice got $2.3 million, the Friedman Foundation received $735,000, and the Indiana Public Charter Schools Association pocketed $594,000.

According to a 2004 *USA Today* report, the Walton family has given at least $701 million to "education charities" since 1998, the majority of it promoting school privatization.[4] Now the family's national funding to promote vouchers and finance charter schools has shattered the billion dollar mark.

During Bennett's Champions for School Choice Award speech, Walmart was busy hurling other countries and America back to the 1890s. To shoot profits out the roof, the world's largest retailer contracts with factories worldwide, with almost 300 factories in Bangladesh alone, at least one employing children, and one where over 1,000 people recently died after an unsafe building collapsed.[5] These workers are paid just cents upon the hour, unable to afford food and toothpaste.[6] As Walmart pulled in $405 billion in sales in 2010,[7] Walmart employees in America—though treated a bit better—were being paid wages that barely kept them above water. A few months before Bennett's school choice appearance, watchdog Good Jobs First, using data from state health departments, found that Walmart ranked at the top of US corporations where workers are getting health coverage from state-administered low-income programs, Medicaid, and the Children's Health Insurance Program, the type of programs the Bradley Foundation, the Walton family's partner in school privatization, tries hard to eliminate.[8] The Walmart worker plan has included this. Walmart cashed in on "peasant death" insurance in the 1990s when it took out insurance on 350,000 workers. When workers died, the company stuffed its pockets, getting $80,000 in one case, while many families whose loved ones died were handed loose change or no money at all and ended up footing the bills for the funerals.[9] The month before Bennett's speech, news had surfaced that anti-union Walmart had been bribing Mexican officials to open stores across the entire country.[10] In America, thanks to the shattering of FDR's New Deal, Walmart gets millions in tax breaks and state and local government subsidies each year. In Indiana, according to Good Jobs First, Walmart recently closed deals with several cities worth a total of $15.8 million to the corporation, money that could have been invested in real public schools.[11]

The money the Walton family gives out for teacher gift cards pales in comparison to the amount it contributes to the temporary teacher workforce. In 2011 alone, the Waltons handed over $49 million to Teach for America. You can't blame the teachers who buy school supplies for poor kids at Walmart for spending their way to their own dismiss, for the mom-and-pop shops in their communities have been boarded up because of Walmart. The Waltons want the community schools boarded, too, so that only corporate charter schools are left to duke it out with the school voucher "David Duke academies." This is the future of American education, where teachers have the pay and benefits of Walmart greeters and work at for-profit charter schools.

The school champion award named for John Walton was just another show of affection in Walmart's love affair with Tony Bennett. In addition to Walmart money through front groups, Walmart daughter Alice Walton personally presented the Tony Bennett reelection campaign with $200,000.

FOR HIS SECOND superintendent run, Bennett accumulated over $1.8 million. Almost every person or group in the Indiana government-corporate-theocratic school movement mentioned in this book donated to Bennett's campaign since his 2008 election, as did New York City mayor Michael Bloomberg, who (along with his gift of $20,000 to the Indiana branch of the Democrats for Education Reform and $15,000 to hedge fund Democrat Mary Ann Sullivan) slid Bennett $40,000. William Oberndorf, for his part, handed Tony Bennett $10,000 toward the reelection campaign. Obama supporter Eli

Broad, whose "broadies" (like past members of Bill Gates' foundation) make up a chunk of Arne Duncan's Department of Education, donated $50,000 to Bennett. Others who gave big were Angie's List's William Oesterle, popcorn business man Mike Weaver, hotel and billboard billionaire Dean White, and Anne Griffin, a hedge fund manager who is unveiling a digital media company to "reform" education and fiscal policy in Illinois and the Midwest. From 2008 through 2012, Hoosiers for Economic Growth—the DeVos family and Alice Walton-funded parent organization of School Choice Indiana—gave Bennett $160,150.

But Tony Bennett's corporate and free-market Christian money was not enough. When Glenda Ritz defeated Bennett for the superintendent's office in November 2012, receiving more votes than both Romney and governor Mike Pence, Mitch Daniels threw in his two-cents from the almost half-a-million he was about to get at his new job as Purdue's president, quickly blaming illegal activity by teachers and the Indiana State Teachers Association for Bennett's defeat.[12] It was merely more of Daniels' gobbledygook. Bennett lost because social media savvy activists educated thousands across Indiana as to how he was merely a duped puppet of the 1 percent.

But Bennett's real defeat came in July 2013[13] when Associated Press' Tom LoBianco got tipped to what was really going on during the Bennett and Daniels regime in Indiana school reform. Emails LoBianco dumped prove Tony Bennett, while in Indiana, rigged the grade of an Indianapolis charter school run by multi-millionaire exchange vocation princess, campaign donor, and mansion owner Christel DeHaan. Christel DeHaan has given $2.8 million in campaign donations to both Indiana Republicans and Democrats since 1998, and large sums have traveled to Mitch Daniels. DeHaan handed Tony Bennett $130,000 in campaign funding. The scandal that erupted led to Bennett, Dale Chu, the aide Bennett took to Florida, and two others involved in the Indiana grade scandal resigning from their jobs. The Indiana media had to finally answer some questions about its role in all the crony capitalism it had concealed or ignored for several years.

And reporters still left out several things when reporting on the DeHaan debacle. School envoys at DeHaan's Christel House Academy where the grade was changed squandered over $70,000 the last few years travelling, according to tax records. Even as the school paid out $15,000 on advertising for the 2011 calendar year, it poured out a staggering $40,000 on travel alone.[14] No details are given as to where this travel took place, but this is not money spent on school bus transportation, which is separately itemized in 990 documents. The school received only a little over $12,000 in private donations that year,[15] so this travelling money came out of taxpayers' pockets or from school fees or other revenue. DeHaan owns charter schools across the world, but one wonders how much of the $70,000 was even spent on travel, since DeHaan has surrounded herself with dishonorable people like Mitch Daniels and Randall Tobias.

When DeHaan broke ground for high school students a few years back, naming the new section of the charter school after a former Eli Lilly executive, then-governor Mitch Daniels (wanting to keep DeHaan's Indiana GOP campaign donations rolling) and Randall Tobias (another big Daniels donor) were there for the photo-op.[16] Tobias, then Eli Lilly's chairman emeritus, is known for his job in George W. Bush's administration promoting an anti-AIDS and anti-prostitution public policy inspired by the Religious Right while he himself was sleeping with prostitutes.[17] Tobias, for the charter school, went a step further, chairing with DeHaan a $4 million "capital campaign" to raise corporate money. The school did draw in private investors for a couple of years after Tobias' "capital campaign," but the money they gave is trivial compared to the millions taxpayers are giving. This money isn't going to paying janitors, since the school outsources those jobs.

The corporatists and banks who have donated to the Christel House Academy are the regular suspects:[18] temporary teacher-

promoting Eli Lilly, Klipsch Audio Technologies (owned by
millionaire and Betsy DeVos front man Fred Klipsch, who recently bragged that his Hoosiers for Economic Growth and
other astroturfers spent $4.4 million to ram through "school
choice" bills in Indiana[19]), JP Morgan, and Fifth Third Bank.
As I pointed out earlier, JP Morgan—which has collected interest on charter school loans in Indiana for years[20]—recently
set aside $325 million to loan to charter schools nationwide to
profit from public money, destabilize schools, and take advan-
tage of new markets tax credits.[21] In 2008, Fifth Third Bank
charged a stunning 8.74 interest rate on a loan to a charter
school in Florida.[22]

DeHaan also plays a role in the Mitch Daniels emails Lo-
Bianco unleashed on the public. In AP-released emails from
2009,[23] Daniels targeted professor Chuck Little, suggesting the
state audit Little's Indiana Urban Schools Association, an Indiana University-Purdue University Indianapolis (IUPUI) organization representing poor and minority kids across the state.
The Indiana Urban Schools Association was, in fact, audited
by the state in 2005 and 2007 because of Little's political op-
position to Daniel's school privatizing agenda.[24] Little publically opposed the corporate-theocratic school bills that Jeb
Bush, Amway, Walmart, Democratic and Republican hedge
fund managers, and the Bradley Foundation (the Milwaukee
group behind anti-affirmative action laws, school vouchers,
workfare, and *The Bell Curve,* which just awarded Mitch
Daniels with $250,000)[25] shoved through Indiana, and the audit
was an attempt to shut him up. Moreover, DeHaan is a board
member of the Woodrow Wilson National Fellowship Foundation. This group hands out the teaching fellowships that Mitch
Daniels, as his emails attest to, didn't want professor Chuck
Little's IUPUI students to get, so the governor attempted to
boot the Indiana Urban Schools Association out of the program.

Another thing revealed in Daniels' emails from 2010 was
how he attempted to ban teachers from getting credit for classes
that taught Howard Zinn, the liberal scholar who wrote the

best-selling book *A People's History of the United States*, a text which throws light on how billionaires throughout America's founding have oppressed and even sometimes massacred women, minorities, and workers in order to remain wealthy.[26] Daniels has been out to ban history books for decades, in fact. In 1988, when Daniels was leading the Hudson Institute, the Bradley Foundation funded Hudson to publish a study entitled *Building a History Curriculum: Guidelines for Teaching History in Schools* "in response to widespread concern over the inadequacy of history education in American elementary and secondary schools."[27] This was published by Hudson's Educational Excellence Network, a school privatization supporter that was one of the earliest groups to call for school vouchers and charter schools in Indiana and across the country which the Bradley Foundation later gave $780,000 to from 1990 to 1992.[28] The Bradley project morphed into the National Council for History Education, which didn't turn as far-right as the Bradley Foundation probably had hoped, but now includes, nonetheless, anti-Howard Zinn professor Sam Wineburg.

In his response to the emails concerning his attempts to ban Howard Zinn's work from classrooms, Mitch Daniels, now president of Purdue University, used Sam Wineburg when he first lifted words from someone else's writing and passed them off as his own. On the heels of a $58,000 bonus for Daniels,[29] Josette Torres and Aaron Hoover, an Ivy Tech Lafayette English instructor, first noticed Indiana's former governor used five words ("heavily filtered and weighted interpretation") written by David Plotnikoff without mentioning Plotnikoff or putting Plotnikoff's phrase into quotations. Daniels also helped himself to the same quotation Plotnikoff published in his "Does Zinn's Alternative History Teach Bad Lessons?" Although Daniels deleted the stolen section sixteen hours or so after Torres and Hoover's discovery made its rounds around facebook, the Purdue president's original statement can still be found online with Aaron Hoover's commentary. It reads:

> Stanford history education expert Sam Wineburg cautioned that exposing children to a heavily filtered and weighted interpretation such as Zinn's work is irresponsible when "we are talking about how we educate the young, those who do not yet get the interpretive game."
> [30]

Here is David Plotnikoff's passage at a Stanford University website:

> Wineburg writes that a heavily filtered and weighted interpretation becomes dangerous when "we are talking about how we educate the young, those who do not yet get the interprctive game."[31]

Either Daniels' cronies stumbled upon the facebook outrage or someone pointed out the word-lifting and Daniels' sloppy research to them. Sadly, as I detailed earlier, this is not Daniels and Purdue's first plagiarism-rodeo together.

In one email, Daniels stresses[32] his desire to sneak into Indiana classrooms as quickly as possible William J. Bennett's *America: The Last Best Hope*, a pseudo-history book which whitewashes all the truth behind America's so-called exceptionalism and has the Bradley Foundation propaganda written all over it. Bill Bennett, Ronald Reagan's secretary of education, former Bradley Foundation board member, and past Hudson Institute operative, was the founder of online learning K12 Inc. and now sits on the board of the workforce-ready school training program Project Lead the Way, which is funded by Eli Lilly and the right-wing Kern Foundation, both involved in Marian University's Turnaround Leadership Academy. Besides being an opportunist and school privatizer, Bennett is best known for his racist comments about how if every black kid was aborted in America, there would be no crime.[33] For Bennett and Daniels' agenda to place right-wing textbooks in Indiana schools, the governor called upon his buddies at the Sagamore Institute, Dan Coats' faith-based free-market think tank which Daniels' sister Deborah directed from 2006 to 2008 while the group was getting state money to work with meth addicts. Sagamore is a branch of the State Policy Network, a

Bradley, Devos, Koch-funded interlocking chain of right-wing organizations. It helped set up Marian University's Turnaround Leadership Academy. An operative with Sagamore, the Woodrow Wilson National Fellowship Foundation, Edison Learning, and Project Lead the Way, Rex Bolinger helped Bill Bennett recruit several "educators" funded by TAP teacher merit-pay promoter and convicted felon Michael Milken's family foundation, who set up Sagamore's Team HOPE (History Opens Eyes) to promote Bennett's book in Indiana schools. The Sagamore Institute is now led by Christian Right's Jay Hein, a former Hudson Institute member who worked with governor Tommy Thompson on the Bradley Foundation's poor-bashing welfare overhaul agenda in Wisconsin, the Bradley Foundation-inspired Bush Office of Faith-Based and Community Initiatives, and Daniels' Indiana Commission on Community Service and Volunteerism. In a newsletter, Sagamore writes that in 2009 the Indiana "State Board announced that *The Last Best Hope* was the only history textbook that enhanced student interest in history. Approximately twenty Indiana schools and districts have adopted the text and curriculum."[34] Along with Lilly, Bradley funded the Sagamore Institute when it was founded. Bill Bennett visited the Sagamore Institute to pump his book, and emails show that Tony Bennett attempted to use Republican donor Jerry Slusser, who was fined "$600,000 by federal regulators for defrauding German investors in the late '90s," to fly Bill Bennett to a Jeffersonville fundraiser in 2012.[35]

Although Daniels accused teachers of doing illegal things to get Glenda Ritz elected as state school superintendent,[36] it turns out it was Tony Bennett who was using his state email address and state time to email battle plans to his various Indiana Department of Education operatives on how best to derail Ritz' campaign by examining her videos and calling out her "stupidity." By way of a Freedom of Information Act request, Fort Wayne *Journal Gazette's* Niki Kelly also found that Bennett hated Karen Francisco, who dug up dirt and threw it.

While writing to Michael Malone from the Jeb Bush-bailed out Edison Learning after the election, Bennett says he will not miss Fort Wayne for various reasons. Malone says "of which the first six are named Karen." Bennett answers: "Maybe 11 of the first 12 are named Karen, but FWCS is also on that list," meaning Karen Francisco and the Fort Wayne Community Schools.[37]

Bennett, still naively believing he was a leader and not a lapdog, was up in smoke. Indiana and Florida students, teachers, parents, and activists for the public schools had won.

ACTIVISTS LOST, HOWEVER, when Douglas Storm, my editor at the *Common Errant*, was fired from his aide job at Unionville Elementary in Monroe County after just three weeks. The reason school district officials gave was that Storm, who has been an avid defender of public education against the corporatists and Christian Right, was writing blog posts that "ridiculed the administration" and were "not conducive to a collaborative environment." School district officials never did name specific blog posts and denied Storm's appeal.[38] Storm went well beyond the mere yelling. In intellectually-charged blog posts, he asked how we could make our public schools more progressive. He spread the guilt wide and envisioned a public school founded on social justice principles, something like The Project School. Instead of feeling fortunate they employed someone as determined and brilliant as Storm to fight for school kids who have no voice, school officials deleted him from the payroll, violated his freedom of speech, and lost one of the most attuned people attempting to save the public schools. We must support teachers, students, and activists who rail against the corruption and hypocrisy, like Douglas Storm, because the government-corporate-theocratic assault is far from over.

Truthfully, the situation remains bleak. Instead of hiring teachers, local school districts now take out billboard ads to compete with the privatizers, cut art classes, and lay off staff.

From layoffs or attrition, 685 Indiana teachers lost jobs in 2011 alone,[39] while Teach for America and the corporate temporary teacher force gained many. Following the billionaire Eli Broad playbook, Indiana legislators recently approved former Tony Bennett chief of staff Todd Huston's bill so that superintendents of school districts no longer are required to have educational backgrounds or certification, paving the way for more business CEOs to take over, slash the teacher force, hire scab workers, and disrupt the lives of students.

With privatization kicked in high gear, voucher and charter schools are expanding without accountability and with bad results. Indiana now has 9,000 kids using school vouchers,[40] with many in thirty-seven schools teaching creationism.[41] A family of four earning up to $62,000 a year can qualify to get taxpayer money for private school now. For the 2013-2014 school year, 456 private and mostly religious schools plan on taking advantage of school vouchers.[42] Even though more than 20 percent of voucher students so far have selected private schools that the state has rated C, D, and even F,[43] Mike Pence, the new Koch brothers-backed governor, recently signed into law the voucher expansion bill allowing kids attending so-called F public schools to now show up at private schools without first going a year to a public school, as the original school voucher bill required. The new law also cracks wide the door for more special education kids to attend voucher schools, as they do in Florida. Thirty thousand Hoosier students now are taught in seventy-two charter schools,[44] even though "more than three-fourths of Indiana charter schools perform worse or at least no better than local public schools,"[45] and those charter schools supposedly performing well have ways around the system. The charter schools not performing are being bailed out by taxpayer money. In 2013, Hoosier legislators set aside $91 million to forgive startup loans to charter schools, even ones with horrible track records and whose sponsorships were not renewed and their schools bolted shut. After being closed by its sponsor Ball State, Imagine Schools' charter school in Fort Wayne merged with the Horizon Christian Academy and will collect state money through vouchers, its $3.6 million charter school tax-payer loans forgiven by the state. The merger details will not be released to the public.[46] Once again, for the crony capitalists, standards, accountability, and transparency do not apply.

With no public input, the Indiana State Board of Accounts also decided Indiana voters should be kept in the dark about charter school finances. On December 11, 2012, while describing how the problem-stricken 21st Century Charter School in Gary passed an "independent" audit with flying colors, the *Times of Northwest Indiana's* Carmen McCollum wrote that "state officials said because of the growing number of charter schools across the state and the number of traditional public schools, independent auditors will conduct audits of the 72 charter schools in Indiana."[47] In other words, corporate auditors will be hired to pull one over on the public. When 990 tax records and other public documents often don't detail how these schools are financially managed and leave many questions and gaps, this move adds to the lack of transparency concerning charter schools.

A school is a small town—not a company town. In a society where government-embedded corporations run schools and Jesus is painted as a Milton Friedman crusader, the bottom line becomes more important than children, as it has in Indiana. By reducing kids to "commodities" and parents to "buyers," corporate schoolers stress that teaching young people to splurge on material objects is a main educational goal. School privatization diminishes teachers, parents, students, and education to something one can sell and make money from, and it eliminates any quest for knowledge for knowledge's sake. If the corporate school assault is not stopped and we still have a public school system left, the best we can hope for is that children of the labor class will be trapped in for-profit public institutions (where teacher turnover is high) legislated by a New World Business Order where class division is applauded as a national standard. Public school students will be left with only faulty measurements like test scores to dumb them down and classes targeting the workplace or ones sending them off to drown in student loan debt, unable to find employment after college. If they can find a job at all, overworked teachers in for the long haul will be paid less and incessantly worried about becoming the latest victims of faulty test scores.

Poor teacher pay just exacerbates what is really at issue in the education of our children: poverty. The filthy rich behind school privatization know this, and they don't care. Instead of giving money to the few real charities left and offering a living wage to workers, they are widening the income gap even more by stealing from the middle class, shipping more jobs overseas, and gambling away our money on Wall Street. "School choice" is their choice and will only make the gap worse.

Sadly, only a fundamental overhaul of American society is going to turn the school bus around, as it did in the years leading up to the New Deal, after the robber barons stole everything. Albert Einstein had it right in 1949 when he wrote the following in the *Monthly Review's* first issue:

> This crippling of individuals I consider the worst evil of capitalism. Our whole educational system suffers from this evil. An exaggerated competitive attitude is inculcated into the student, who is trained to worship acquisitive success as a preparation for his future career.
>
> I am convinced there is only *one* way to eliminate these grave evils, namely through the establishment of a socialist economy, accompanied by an educational system which would be oriented toward social goals. In such an economy, the means of production are owned by society itself and are utilized in a planned fashion. A planned economy, which adjusts production to the needs of the community, would distribute the work to be done among all those able to work and would guarantee a livelihood to every man, woman, and child. The education of the individual, in addition to promoting his own innate abilities, would attempt to develop in him a sense of responsibility for his fellow men in place of the glorification of power and success in our present society.[48]

The "power and success" of a few greedy people are destroying the lives of the rest of us and our children and grandchildren. Corporatists and wealthy theocrats have no "sense of responsibility" to anyone but themselves and their government friends. And although America probably will never develop into a wholly Christian Right free-market nation as some on the Religious Right want, we are quickly sliding into a fascist country, where the corporations and the government are one, the type Hoosiers Eugene V. Debs and Theodore Dreiser railed against a hundred years ago. As Katherine Stewart writes: "We may well find, in a future world—where the rich have their own system of education, the religious have theirs, the poor don't get educated at all, and everyone is schooled in contempt for those who are different—that we have kept all of our rights, yet lost everything but the pretense of democracy."[49] This is where we stand or fall, where we truly stand for children, not hedge fund managers. If we don't stop the corporate-government-theocratic forces heisting the little bit of democracy we still have left in education, in Indiana, and in America, we are in deep, deep trouble. ■

Notes

To CITE EVERY SINGLE SOURCE I'VE ACCESSED FOR THIS BOOK WOULD BE impossible. Campaign funding information comes from the Indiana Campaign Finance website (http://campaignfinance.in.gov/PublicSite/Homepage.aspx) and from the Indianapolis Campaign Finance website (http://www.indy.gov/eGov/County/Clerk/Election/Candidate_Info/). Internet links to these sources are extremely long, so I have not included them here. Many numbers and statistics of various organizations were gathered from their websites. Much information in this book comes from press releases. I have only cited them when the information within the note (such as the date) shines further light on the given topic or if this information is not readily available online or is not public knowledge. Sources that do not have cyberlinks are no longer online or are printed documents. Please see hoosierschoolheist.com for live links to all sources below.

INTRODUCTION: MYTHS, MINIONS, MISINFORMATION, AND TORTURE

1. Orlando Letelier, "The Chicago Boys in Chile: Economic Freedom's Awful Toll," *The Nation*, August 28, 1976.

2. Naomi Klein, *The Shock Doctrine: The Rise and Fall of Disaster Capitalism* (New York: Picador, 2007), 98-100.

3. Jason Farbman, "Chile's Long Hot Winter," *Socialist Worker*, August 31, 2011, http://socialistworker.org/2011/08/31/chiles-long-hot-winter.

4. Friedman's 1955 essay is reposted at http://www.edchoice.org/TheFriedmans/The-Friedmans-on-School Choice/The-Role-of-Government-in-Education-%281995%29.aspx.

5. Rachel Tabachnick, "The DeVos Family: Meet the Super-Wealthy Right-Wingers Working with the Religious Right to Kill Public Education," *AlterNet*, May 6, 2011, http://www.alternet.org/story/150868/the_devos_family:_meet_the_superwealthy_rightwing ers_working_with_the_religious_right_to_kill_public_education.

6. Gus Garcia-Roberts, "McKay Scholarship Program Sparks a Cottage Industry of Fraud and Chaos," *Miami New Times*, June 23, 2011, http://www.miaminewtimes.com/2011-06-23/news/mckay-scholarship-program-sparks-a-cottage-industry-of-fraud-and-chaos/.

7. Joseph L. Bast and David Harmer, "The Libertarian Case for Vouchers and Some Observations on the Anti-Voucher Separationists," *Cato Policy Analysis*, no. 269 (March 12, 1997), http://www.cato.org/pubs/pas/pa-269.html.

8. Mary Wisniewski, "Struggling Catholic Schools Strategize to Draw New Students," *Reuters.com*, May 2, 2013, http://www.reuters.com/article/2013/05/02/us-usa-education-catholic-idUSBRE9410PN20130502.

9. Milton Friedman, "The Promise of Vouchers," *Wall Street Journal*, December 5, 2005, http://online.wsj.com/article/SB113374845791113764.html.

10. Klein, *The Shock Doctrine*, 5-6.

11. Juan Gonzalez, "Big Banks Making a Bundle on New Construction as Schools Bear the Cost," Democracy Now!, May 7, 2010. You can examine the video online at http://www.democracynow.org/2010/5/7/juan_gonzalez_big_banks_making_.

12. Matt Taibbi, "Dan Loeb Simultaneously Solicits, Betrays Pension Funds," *Rolling Stone*, April 11, 2013, http://www.rollingstone.com/politics/blogs/taibblog/dan-loeb-simultaneously-solicits-betrays-pension-funds-20130411#ixzz2QBgEWGZh.

13. Even though charter schools are non-unionized, Obama, for his Recovery Act to supposedly put people back to work after Wall Street destroyed the economy, gave taxpayer money to

Notes

approximately 700 charter schools in the US, many like Imagine Schools—owned by Mitch Daniels' friend Dennis Bakke—with a profit mindset to fire teachers instead of hiring new ones. If you have about a year of free time for research, you can examine all the money Obama's Recovery Act gave out to charter schools at http://www.recovery.gov.

14. Kathy Emery and Susan Ohanian wonderfully outline the progress of the corporate education movement from *A Nation at Risk* report to the No Child Left Behind era. See *Why Is Corporate America Bashing Our Public Schools?* (Portsmouth, NH: Heinemann, 2004). For the fake education crisis, see David C. Berliner and Bruce J. Biddle's highly researched *The Manufactured Crisis: Myths, Fraud, and the Attack on America's Public Schools* (Reading, MA: Addison-Wesley, 1995).

15. Many studies expose the corporate school myth that students are not prepared for the twenty-first century workforce and that America is running out of engineers. For a good take on this, read Vivek Wadhwa, "The Science Education Myth," *Bloomberg Businessweek*, October 26, 2007; Beryl Lieff Benderly, "The Real Science Gap," *Miller-McCune*, June 14, 2010, http://www.miller-mccune.com/science/the-real-science-gap-16191/#. See also Economic Policy Institute, "H-1B Visa Program Is Not Attracting the Best and Brightest Workers, New EPI Paper Finds," news release, February 28, 2013, http://www.epi.org/press/1b-visa-program-attracting-brightest-workers/. Visit, too, Roger Bybee's "Study Demolishes the Myth That U.S. Workers Lack Skills," *In These Times*, February 27, 2013, inthesetimes.com/working/entry/14 660/the_medias_skills_gap_thesis_is_a_myth/.

16. Valerie Strauss, "The Hardest Jobs to Fill (Think Plumbers)," *The Answer Sheet* (blog), *Washington Post*, July 7, 2012, http://www.washingtonpost.com/blogs/answer-sheet/post/the-hardest-jobs-to-fill-thinkplumbers/2012/07/07/gJQA4wW3UW_blog.html.

17. Center for Evaluation and Education Policy, Indiana University School of Education, "CEEP Report: Indiana Eighth-Graders Outperform Much of World in Math, Science," news release, March 25, 2013, http://newsinfo.iu.edu/news/page/normal/23979.html.

18. Indiana Business Research Center, Indiana University Kelly School of Business, *Major Unemployment: How Academic Programs of Study Affect Hoosier Unemployment Patterns*, August 2012, http://www.iwis.iupui.edu/documents/MajorUnemployment_2012.pdf.

19. Peter Cappelli, *Why Good People Can't Get Jobs: The Skills Gap and What Companies Can Do about It* (Philadelphia: Wharton Digital Press, 2012).

20. Tracy Warner, "Policing the Rush to Charter Schools," *Journal Gazette* (Fort Wayne, IN), January 16, 2011, http://www.jg.net/article/20110116/EDIT0502/301169950/1144/EDIT05.

21. These studies were done in 2009 and 2013 by Stanford University's Center for Research on Education Outcomes (CREDO). You can find the summary of the 2009 study at http://credo.stanford.edu/reports/National_Release.pdf. For a good take on the 2013 study, see Jim Horn's "Charter Schools Are No Better than Public Schools, and Don't Expect Them to Change," *Common Dreams*, January 31, 2013, https://www.commondreams.org/view/2013/01/31-9.

22. Vic Smith, "Summary of Ten Improvement Indicators in Indiana Education," *Battle for Indiana Public Education* (blog), June 28, 2013, http://indianapubliceducation.blogspot.com/2013_06_01_archive.html.

23. Niki Kelly and Julie Crothers, "500 More Students Lost to Vouchers: More Than 1,100 Have Left FWCS for Private Schools," *Journal Gazette* (Fort Wayne, IN), November 21, 2012, http://www.journalgazette.net/article/20121121/LOCAL04/311219976/1026.

24. Elle Moxley, "Why Construction Referenda Could Lead to Inequalities in School Facilities," *State Impact Indiana*/NPR, May 3, 2013, http://stateimpact.npr.org/indiana/2013/05/03/why-construction-referenda-could-lead-to-inequalities-in-school-facilities/.

Notes

25. Dan Stockman, Associated Press, "Poverty Crippling Social Development of Hammond Kindergarteners,"June 24, 2011, *Chicago Sun-Times*, http://www.suntimes.com/news/education /6150007-418/poverty-crippling-social-development-of-hammond-kindergarteners.html.

26. Children's Defense Fund, "Children in Indiana: January 2012," January 26, 2012, http:// childrensdefense.org/child-research-data-publications/data/state-data-repository/cits/2012/2012-indiana-children-in-the-states.pdf.

27. Kevin Connors, "A Closer Look at States' Charter School Performance," *Education Week*, June 26, 2013, http://blogs.edweek.org/edweek/charterschoice/2013/06/charter_school_ performance_varies_widely_across_states_according_to_credo_report.html.

28. Matthew Di Carlo, "The Structural Curve in Indiana's New School Grading System," *Shanker Blog*, November 1, 2012, http://shankerblog.org/?p=7090.

29. Phil Harris, Bruce M. Smith, and Joan Harris, *The Myths of Standardized Tests: Why They Don't Tell You What You Think They Do* (Lanham, MD: Rowman & Littlefield Publishers, 2011).

30. Vic Smith, "Observations on Education Items in the 2011 Budget," memo, May 12, 2011.

31. Dan Dimaggio, "The Libyan Dictatorship Partially Owns the Company Scoring Your Kids' Standardized Tests," *Buzzflash*, March 9, 2011, http://www.truthout.org/buzzflash/commentary/item/10561-the-libyan-dictatorship-partially-owns-the company-scoring-your-kids-standardized-tests.

32. William L. Bainbridge, "Bush Ties Prove to Be Lucrative," *Columbus Dispatch* (OH), August 19, 2006, http://schoolmatch.com/articles/cd2006Aug19.cfm.

1 KIDNAPPING KIDS' TEACHERS: THE PRETEND-LIBERAL SAVIORS

1. Pauley's speech at the 2010 Mind Trust event is posted at http://indianapolis.granicus.com/MediaPlayer.php?publish_id=531.

2. Mind Trust, "The Mind Trust Seeking Fellows," news release, *Inside Indiana Business*, January 2, 2011, http://www.insideindianabusiness.com/newsitem.asp?id=45958.

3. Ben Gose, "Midwest Group Serves as Magnet for Innovation," *Chronicle of Philanthropy*, September 6, 2010, reposted at http://edposa.wordpress.com/2010/11/16/david-harris-and-the-mind-trust-article-in-the-chronical-of-philanthropy/. Fairbanks has given the Mind Trust at least $4.6 million.

4. David Harris' Mind Trust paycheck is noted in the group's 2010 Form 990 on page 7, http://www.guidestar.org/FinDocuments/2010/204/560/2010-204560286-07717705-9.pdf. Harris, in 2011, made $229,000, not counting other compensation. See page 7 of the Mind Trust's 2011 Form 990 at http://www.guidestar.org/FinDocuments/2011/204/560/2011-204560286-087808fa-9.pdf.

5. David Skinner coined the "Peyton Manning of Charter Schools" phrase in "Indianapolis Mayor Bart Peterson: The Peyton Manning of Charter Schools," *Education Next* 7 (Summer 2007), no. 3, 33-39.

6. CELL, University of Indianapolis, "School Thrives under Dr. Scott Syverson's Leadership: Stonegate Early College High School—Solid as a Rock," reposted at *Scott Syverson Leadership News* (blog), May 1, 2010, http://elprpal.blogspot.com/2010/05/school-thrives-under-dr-scott-syversons.html. For Peterson's family pay, examine Stonegate Early College High School, Form 990, covering July 1, 2009 to June 30, 2010, page 8, http://www.guidestar.org/FinDocum

Notes

ents/2010/205/145/2010-205145009-06d7fc6f-9.pdf.

7. *Program-Related Investments: Social Investments* (Baltimore, MD: Annie E. Casey Foundation, 2006), 11-12, http://www.aecf.org/~/media/Pubs/Other/P/ProgramRelatedInvesting andtheIndianapolisChar/accion.pdf. See also Local Initiatives Support Corporation, "LISC Stakes New Ground in Charter Schools," news release, June 20, 2005, http://www.lisc.org/content/article/detail/646.

8. For Eli Lilly's various problems, witness Kris Hundley, "Dementia Relief, with a Huge Side Effect: The Off-Label Use of Some Drugs Is Helping Elderly Patients, but May Be Killing Thousands," *Tampa Bay Times*, November 18, 2007, http://www.sptimes.com/2007/11/18/Wor ldandnation/Dementia_relief__with.shtml; Heidi Turner, "Zyprexa Side Effects Are Deadly," *Lawyers and settlements.com*, November 21, 2007, http://www.lawyersandsettlements. com/features/zyprexa/zyprexagroup.html#.UX1U04zD9jo; Duff Wilson, "Side Effects May Include Lawsuits," *New York Times*, October 2, 2010, http://www.nytimes.com/2010/10/03 business/03psych.html?pagewanted=all&_r=0; and Matthew Perrone, "Elderly with Dementia Are Wrongly Given Antipsychotic Drugs, Inspectors Say," *Huffington Post*, November 30, 2011, huffingtonpost.com/2011/12/01/elderly-dementia-antipsychotic-drugs_n_ 1123195.html.

9. Jeffrey Smith, "Is Eli Lilly Milking Cancer by Promoting *and* Treating It?," *Huffington Post*, October 7, 2009, http://www.huffingtonpost.com/jeffrey-smith/is-eli-lilly-milking-canc_b_312754.html.

10. Joanne Kenen and Rochelle Sharpe, "During Mitch Daniels' Decade at Eli Lilly, the Drug Giant Paid Billions in Fines and Settled Thousands of Lawsuits," Center for Public Integrity, last modified June 24, 2011, http://www.publicintegrity.org/2011/05/09/4499/during-mit ch-daniels-decade-eli-lilly-drug-giant-paid-billions-fines-and-settled.

11. Bruce Levine, "Eli Lilly, Zyprexa, and the Bush Family," *Z Magazine* 17, no. 5 (May 2004), http://psychrights.org/articles/LevineLillyandBush.htm.

12. The warning letter to Lilly is displayed at the FDA's website: http://www.fda.gov/ICECI/EnforcementActions/WarningLetters/ucm200845.htm.

13. For articles and takes on Peterson's tax breaks to Lilly while mayor, see Ted Evanoff, John Russell, and Bill Ruthhart's "Lilly's Pain Could Be Shared by Indianapolis: Cuts Could Eliminate 3,600 More Jobs in Wider Economy, While Restructuring Could Speed Drugs from Pipeline to Market," *Indianapolis Star*, September 15, 2009, and Gary R. Welsh's "City Doled Out $1.6 Billion in Incentives to Eli Lilly," *Advance Indiana* (blog), September 15, 2009, http://advanceindiana.blogspot.com/2009/09/city-doled-out-16-billion-in-incentives.html. It is not known if any of this incentive money made its way back to taxpayers or not. For Lilly's tax havens, see *Bloomberg News*, "Overseas Tax Savings for U.S. Drugmakers under Threat," March 11, 2013, reposted at http://www.ibj.com/overseas-tax-savings-for-us-drugmakers-under-threat/PARAMS/article/40105.

14. History of University of Indianapolis' CELL, http://cell.uindy.edu/aboutcell/history.php.

15. For Michael Milken's crimes, read Kurt Eichenwald, "Milken Set to Pay a $600 Million Fine in Wall St. Fraud," *New York Times*, April 21, 1990. Witness, also, Kenneth J. Saltman, "Michael Milken and the Corporate Raid on Education," *Electronic Book Review*, October 3, 2003, http://www.electronicbookreview.com/thread/technocapitalism/rehab?mode=print.

16. Funding for TAP is detailed at http://cell.uindy.edu/TAP/TAPinindiana.php.

17. Page 1, http://www.lillyendowment.org/annualreports/2007/Grants_Education.pdf, for-Lilly's 2007 Mind Trust funding.

18. Eli Lilly and Company, "Eli Lilly and Company Invests $2.5 Million to Launch the Mind Trust's Grow What Works Campaign," news release, May 5, 2011, reposted at *Bloomberg News*, bloomberg.com/apps/news?pid=newsarchive&sid=avklaynkT.Es.

Notes

19. Gail Payne, "The Mind Trust Announces $3.5 Million Gift from Lilly Endowment to Expand Teach for America and the New Teacher Project," news release, November 7, 2011, http://www.themindtrust.org/files/documents/1111111114-final-lei-tfa-tntp-2011-press-release-11-7-11.pdf.

20. See page 15 in the Mind Trust's *A Landscape Transformed: A Report on the Impact of the Grow What Works Campaign*, October 2012, http://www.themindtrust.org/files/file/final impactdoc-2012-10-3.pdf.

21. New Teacher Project, Form 990, covering October 1, 2011 to September 30, 2012. For TNTP's revenue, see page 1; for Rozman's salary, see page 7 at http://www.guidestar.org/FinDocuments/2012/133/850/2012-133850158-090760a2-9.pdf.

22. Diane Ravitch, "Confessions of a Teaching Fellow," *Diane Ravitch.net* (blog), July 31, 2012, http://dianeravitch.net/2012/07/31/confessions-of-a-teaching-fellow/.

23. Valerie Strauss, "Guess What Michelle Rhee Charged a School to Speak," *The Answer Sheet* (blog), *Washington Post*, October 26, 2011, http://www.washingtonpost.com/blogs/answer-sheet/post/guess-what-michelle-rhee-charged-a-school-to-speak/2011/10/24/gIQAen6GJM_blog.html.

24. Jim Horn, "An Indiana Teacher's Close Encounter with 'Red Menace' Daniels," *Schools Matter*, February 13, 2011, http://www.schoolsmatter.info/2011/02/indiana-teachers-close-encounter-with.html.

25. Scott Elliott, "Interview with Michelle Rhee, Ex-D.C. Schools Chief Champions Reform," *Indianapolis Star*, March 30, 2011, http://www.indystar.com/article/20110330/LOCAL18/103300329/Ex-D-C-schools-chief-champions-reform.

26. For the Thomas Nida story, study the following: David S. Fallis and April Witt, "Public Role, Private Gain," *Washington Post*, December 14, 2008, http://www.washingtonpost.com/wp-dyn/content/article/2008/12/13/AR2008121302079.html; James V. Grimaldi and Theola Labbé-DeBose, "In One School Deal, Chairman Played Three Roles," *Washington Post*, December 14, 2008, http://www.washingtonpost.com/wp-dyn/content/article/2008/12/13/AR2008121301779.html?sid=ST2008121302293; David S. Fallis and April Witt, "Credit Committee's Actions Benefited Associates," *Washington Post*, December 14, 2008, washingtonpost.com/wp-dyn/content/article/2008/12/13/AR2008121301783.html and David S. Fallis and James V. Grimaldi, "Review Finds No Breach by Charter Board Leader," *Washington Post*, January 15, 2009, http://www.washingtonpost.com/wp-dyn/content/article/2009/01/14/AR2009011403534.html.

27. For Rhee's cheating scandal, see Jack Gruber and Marisol Bello, "When Standardized Test Scores Soared in D.C., Were the Gains Real?," *USA Today*, March 28, 2011, http://usatoday30.usatoday.com/news/education/2011-03-28-1Aschooltesting28_CV_N.htm; Greg Toppo, "Memo Warns of Rampant Cheating in D.C. Public Schools," *USA Today*, April 11, 2013, http://www.usatoday.com/story/news/nation/2013/04/11/memo-washington-dc-schools-cheating/2074473/; and John Merrow, "Michelle Rhee's Reign of Error," *Taking Note*, April 11, 2013, http://takingnote.learningmatters.tv/?p=6232.

28. Julian Vasquez Heilig and Su Jin Jez, *Teach for America: A Review of the Evidence* (Boulder and Tempe: Education and the Public Interest Center & Education Policy Research Unit, June 2010), http://epicpolicy.org/publication/teach-for-america.

29. Amanda M. Fairbanks, "Walton Family Foundation Gifts Teach for America $49.5 Million," *Huffington Post*, July, 27, 2011, http://www.huffingtonpost.com/2011/07/27/walton-foundation-teach-for-america-walmart_n_910615.html. If not otherwise noted, information on Walmart's funding to corporate school reform has been gathered from the Walton Family Foundation website at http://www.waltonfamilyfoundation.org.

Notes

30. Teach for America's CEO's pay is mentioned on page 18 of the group's Form 990 for 2010: http://www.greatschoolsforamerica.org/images/fin_docs/000056_2011.pdf.

31. Mind Trust, *A Landscape Transformed*, 6.

32. Gabriel Leiner, "Questions Raised about Lack of Fine in Wayland Campaign Law Violation," *MetroWest Daily News* (Framingham, MA), July 2, 2008, http://www.metro dailynews.com/news/x19929117/Questions-raised-about-lack-of-fine-in-Wayland-campaign-law-violation.

33. See page 7 of the Challenge Foundation Academy Indy's 2010 to 2011 Form 990 at http://www.guidestar.org/FinDocuments/2011/134/289/2011-134289579-08409882-9.pdf.

34. Dan Carden, "Out-of-State Money Paying for Ads Criticizing House Democrats for Leaving State," *Times of Northwest Indiana* (Munster, IN), March 13, 2011, http://www.nwit imes.com/news/local/lake/hammond/article_1d3b8ee5-6d17-5b35-b9b79e6a119d13c3.html.

35. Davis Guggenheim, "My Picks: Educators," *Forbes Magazine*, November 22, 2010, http://www.forbes.com/forbes/2010/1122/powerful-people-10-davis-guggenheim-kopp-klein-my-picks-educators.html.

36. Kevin Rader, "Indiana Lawmakers Consider Merit Pay for Teachers," WTHR, last modified April 27, 2011, http://www.wthr.com/story/14419977/indiana-lawmakers-to-consider-big-education-proposals.

37. For Rob Smith, Jason Kloth, and Sagamore's involvement, see pages 20-21, Marian University, *Turnaround Leaders Academy for Transformative Teaching and Learning Leadership, Grant Proposal Respectfully Submitted to the Indiana Department of Education*, March 26, 2010, Indianapolis, Indiana. For Sagamore's role with Marian, Notre Dame, and the IDOE's CEO-based guidelines for principals, see J.K. Wall's "Education Trend Targets Training for Principals," *Indianapolis Business Journal*, May 1, 2010, http://www.ibj.com/article/print?articleId=19672.

38. Editorial, "Bennett's Education Ties," *Journal Gazette* (Fort Wayne, IN), February 7, 2011, http://www.journalgazette.net/article/20110207/EDIT07/302079998/1021/EDIT.

39. Daniel Weisberg, Susan Sexton, Jennifer Mulhern, and David Keeling, *The Widget Effect: Our National Failure to Acknowledge and Act on Differences in Teacher Effectiveness*, 2nd ed. (n.p.: New Teacher Project, June 2009). This quotation comes from the first ed. of *The Widget Effect*, which is no longer available. In the 2nd ed., the quotation has been slightly revised, but the content remains the same. It appears on page 6. You can download the 2nd ed. at http://widgeteffect.org/.

40. Diane Ravitch, "Carol Burris and I Dissect a Bizarre *New York Times* Editorial," *Diane Ravitch.net* (blog), September 17, 2012, http://dianeravitch.net/2012/09/17/carol-burris-and-i-dissect-a-bizarre-new-york-times-editorial/.

41. Bruce Baker, "On Misrepresenting (Gates) MET to Advance State Policy Agendas," *School Finance 101* (blog), April 10, 2013, http://schoolfinance101.wordpress.com/2013/04/10/on-misrepresenting-gates-met-to-advance-state-policy-agendas/.

42. Jane Roberts, "Outsiders Get a View of Memphis City Schools' Vision," *Commercial Appeal*, September 11, 2010, http://www.commercialappeal.com/news/2010/sep/11/outsiders-get-a-view-of-city-schools-vision/.

43. Diane Ravitch, "Confessions of a Teaching Fellow."

44. For Coggin and Thompson's pay, inspect page 7 of Form 990 for the year beginning October 1, 2010 and ending September 30, 2011, http://www.guidestar.org/FinDocuments/2011/263/849/2011-263849472-087520e9-9.pdf.

Notes

45. Gose, "Midwest Group Serves as Magnet for Innovation." See also Sam Dillon, "Behind Grass-Roots School Advocacy, Bill Gates," *New York Times*, May 21, 2011, http://www.nytimes.com/2011/05/22/education/22gates.html?pagewanted=all&_r=1&.

46. Susan Ohanian, "Notes to Michael Winerip's 'Lesson Plan in Boston Schools: Don't Go It Alone,'" *SusanOhanian.org*., n.d., http://susanohanian.org/show_nclb_outrages.php?id=4014.

47. Celine Coggins and Casey Patterson, *The Domino Effect: How Seniority-Based Reassignment Impacts Teachers and Students* (Indianapolis: Teach Plus, Winter 2011), http://www.teachplus.org/uploads/Documents/1297365387_TheDominoEffect.pdf.

48. James Larson, "Opinion: Lessons Learned," NBC, September 22, 2010, http://www.educationnation.com/index.cfm?objectid=C984E860-C69D-11DF8243000C296BA163&aka=0.

49. Tindley, in 2007, had a $52,000 loan from Darrell Gene Zink (see page 27 in Tindley's Form 990 starting July 1, 2007 and ending June 30, 2008), http://www2.guidestar.org/FinDocuments/2008/352/151/2008-352151971-04c05f19-9.pdf.

50. City of Indianapolis, Office of the Mayor, *Charles A. Tindley Accelerated School, Supplemental Report #3, Detailed Performance Assessment and Profile*, n.d., 10, http://www.indy.gov/eGov/Mayor/programs/education/Charter/Documents/PDF/S3FINAL.pdf.

51. This information comes from the Indiana State Board of Accounts, *Financial Statement and Federal Single Audit Report of Charles A. Tindley Accelerated School*, July 1, 2009 to June 30, 2011, 22-28, http://www.in.gov/sboa/WebReports/B40128.pdf and the Indiana State Board of Accounts' audit of Tindley for July 1, 2007 to June 30, 2009, 28, http://www.in.gov/sboa/WebReports/B35967.pdf.

52. This school board "failure" was noted in a *Republic* (Columbus, IN) article, which is no longer outline. Although I have no memory of who exactly was painting the school board as failing, it does represent how Indiana newspapers played their part in promoting the privatization of schools from the beginning.

53. Public Impact, *Opportunity Schools: A Bold Plan to Transform Indianapolis Public Schools* (Indianapolis: Mind Trust, December 2011), http://www.themindtrust.org/files/file/opportunity-schools-executive-summary-mediaresourcesmediakit5.pdf. See, also, Rebecca Townsend, "In the Mind Trust We Trust?," *NUVO*, June 8, 2012, http://www.nuvo.net/indianapolis/in-the-mind-trust-we-trust/Content?oid=2456165&showFullText=true#.USpct1e2UuI.

54. Alexander Russo, "Who's Who: Edison Lobbyist Heather Podesta," *This Week in Education* (blog), *Education Week*, February 15, 2007, http://blogs.edweek.org/edweek/thisweekineducation/2007/02/whos_who_heather_podesta.html.

55. Michael J. Petrilli, "One Size Fits Most," *Flypaper*, August 25, 2011, http://www.edexcellence.net/commentary/education-gadfly-daily/flypaper/2011/one-size-fits-most.html.

56. Michael F. Shaughnessy, "An Interview with Michael Petrilli: Are Local School Boards Still Necessary?," *Education News*, May 1, 2011, http://www.educationnews.org/commentaries/155109.html.

57. John Harris Loflin emailed me his research and I wrote about it at *Schools Matter*. See Doug Martin, "Corporate School Boarding Indy Style," *Schools Matter*, November 5, 2012, http://www.schoolsmatter.info/2012/11/corporate-school-boarding-indy-style_5.html. For Hubbards' behind-the-scenes maneuvering, see Tom LoBianco, Associated Press, "Emails Reveal GOP Powerbrokers' Role in Crafting Indiana Education Policy," *Journal Gazette* (Fort Wayne, IN), August 31, 2013, http://www.journalgazette.net/article/20130831/NEWS07/130839895.

58. George N. Schmidt, "The Union-Busting Billionaires behind Phony 'Grass Roots' Groups like Stand for Children and Advance Illinois Have Emerged from the Shadows... Com-

Notes

plete Transcript of the Remarks of Ross Wiener, James Crown and Jonah Edelman at the Aspen Institute," *Substance News*, July 12, 2011, http://www.substancenews.net/articles.php?page=24 27.

59. Rick Pearson and John Chase, "Education Activist Boasts of Power Plays, Then Apologizes: Stand for Children Leader Brags of Outsmarting Unions on School Reform," *Chicago Tribune*, July 13, 2011, http://articles.chicagotribune.com/2011-07-13/news/ct-met-madigan-education-reform-0713-20110713_1_edelman-teachers-unions-aspeninstitute.

60. Corey Paul, "Stand for Children Leader Taking Heat," *Willamette Week*, July 19, 2011, wweek.com/portland/blog-27400-stand_for_children_leader_taking_heat.html.

61. In this section, I draw from two stories by Jennifer Anderson: "Stand for Children Pushes Back against Critics," *Portland Tribune*, July 19, 2011, http://portlandtribune.com/pt/9-news/9784-stand-for-children-pushes-back-against-critics and "Simmering Discontent Puts Stand for Children in Hot Water: Portland Group Hammered by Criticism from Volunteers, Others after Leader Brags about Political Maneuvering," *Portland Tribune*, July 19, 2011, http://www.portlandtribune.net/news/story_2nd.php?story_id=131105508519296400.

62. David Love, "Profiteering and Union-Busting Repackaged as School Reform: The Color of Law," *Black Commentator*, July 28, 2011, http://www.blackcommentator.com/437/437_col_school_reform_printer_friendly.html.

63. Schmidt, "The Union-Busting Billionaires behind Phony 'Grass Roots' Groups."

64. Ibid.

65. Joy Resmovits and Will Guzzardi, "Illinois Education Reform: Gov. Pat Quinn Signs Bill into Law," *Huffington Post*, June 13, 2011, http://www.huffingtonpost.com/2011/06/13/pat-quinn-signs-ed-reform-bill_n_876048.html.

66. Susan Ohanian, "Follow the Bouncing Edelman. . . Josh Edelman—Former Chicago 'New Schools' Chief—Helped Cover Up Michelle Rhee's D.C. Test Cheating Scandal According to Federal Lawsuit and Ongoing Investigations by Reporters," *Substance News*, January 12, 2013, http://www.substancenews.net/articles.php?page=3881.

67. See George N. Schmidt's "Josh Edelman Ousted, Jaime Guzman In as Chief at 'New Schools,'" *Substance News*, September 19, 2009, http://substancenews.net/articles.php?page=894§ion=Article. Read, also, his letter to Jim Horn, quoted in Jim Horn, "Renaissance or Dark Ages in Chicago?," *Schools Matter*, November 12, 2007, http://www.schoolsmatter.info/2007-11/renaiisance-or-dark-ages-in-chicago.html.

68. George N. Schmidt, "Emanuel's Billionaire Donors Also Bankrolling 'Stand for Children,' Pushing Union-Busting Organizations in Illinois," *Substance News*, January 22, 2011, http://www.substancenews.net/articles.php?page=1948.

69. Jerry Seper, "Bank Victims Blame Obama Fundraiser," *Washington Times*, October 29, 2008, http://www.washingtontimes.com/news/2008/oct/29/ex-subprime-bank-executive-finances-obama/?page=all.

70. Liza Dittoe and Lauren Sanders, "The Mind Trust Recruits Leading Education Advocacy Group 'Stand for Children' to Indiana," news release, March 4, 2011, http://www.themindtrust.org/files/documents/0304110908-pr-stand-for-children-final-draft.pdf.

71. Steve Hinnefeld, "Oregon Group Lobbying for Teacher Merit Pay in Indiana," *School Matters*, March 8, 2011, http://inschoolmatters.wordpress.com/tag/the-mind-trust/.

72. See Scott Elliott and Jon Murray, "Ballard Wants 'Welcome Mat' for Charter School Groups," *Indianapolis Star*, September 15, 2011, http://www.indystar.com/article/20110915/LOCAL/109150353/Ballard-wants-welcome-mat-charter-school-groups and J.K. Wall, "Mind Trust to Spawn Chains of Charter Schools," *Indianapolis Business Journal*, October 8, 2011, http://www.ibj.com/article/print?articleId=30006.

Notes

73. Karissa Hulse, Gail Payne, and Kristofer Karol, "IU Health Invests $100K in The Mind Trust's Grow What Works Campaign: Indianapolis Young Professionals Decide How Money Is Spent," news release, http://indyhub.org/iu-health-invests-100k-in-ed-reform-indy-yps-to-decide-how-money-is-spent/.

74. Matt Tully, "Charter-School Debate Needs More like Karega Rausch," *Indianapolis Star*, April 19, 2011, indystar.com/article/20110420/NEWS08/104200330/Tully-Charter-school-debate-needs-more-like-Karega-Rausch.

75. Ryan Grime and Cole Stangler, "Mitt Romney Started Bain Capital with Money from Families Tied to Death Squads," *Huffington Post*, August 8, 2012, huffingtonpost.com/2012/08/08/mitt-romney-death-squads-bain_n_1710133.html.

76. Art Levine, "Dark Side of a Bain Success," *Salon*, July 18, 2012, http://www.salon.com/2012/07/18/dark_side_of_a_bain_success/.

77. This quotation comes from Ron Whitehorne, "Response to Transformation Plan: End to Public Education's Promise," *Notebook: An Independent Voice for Parents, Educators, Students, and Friends of Philadelphia Public Schools*, April 30, 2012, http://thenotebook.org/blog/124772/response-transformation-plan-end-public-education. For my in-depth study on the Boston Consulting Group's corporate school takeover in Philadelphia, see Doug Martin, "In the City of Corporate Love and Beyond: The Boston Consulting Group, Gates, and the Filthy Rich," *Common Errant*, May 18, 2012, http://btownerrant.com/2012/05/18/in-the-city-of-corporate-love-and-beyond-the-boston-consulting-group-gates-and-the-filthy-rich/.

78. Citizens for Public Schools, "Stand for Children's Ballot Initiative: Bad for Teachers, Kids and Schools," n.d., http://www.citizensforpublicschools.org/editions-of-the-backpack/stand-for-childrens-ballot-initiative-bad-for-teachers-kids-and-schools/.

79. Mind Trust, "The Mind Trust Investing $2 Million in First Charter School Incubator Winners," news release, June 23, 2012, http://www.themindtrust.org/news/2012/june/the-mind-trust-investing-2-million-in-first-charter-school-incubator-winners.

80. Patrick Herrel's written comments were part of the Educause Next Generation Learning Challenges Wave IIIa Walkthrough, webinar and chat, November 4, 2011, https://educause.adobeconnect.com/_a729300474/p9tg225um41/?launcher=false&fcsContent=true&pbMode=normal.

81. Gates Foundation's funding information comes from its website. For the Gates Foundation's funding of corporate schooling, see Ken Libby's "A Look at the Education Programs of the Gates Foundation," *National Education Policy Center*, March 2, 2012, http://nepc.colorado.edu/blog/ken-libby-look-education-programs-gates-foundation and "What Shelton's Waiver Tells Us about the Gates Foundation and DOE," *Schools Matter*, August 11, 2010, http://www.schoolsmatter.info/2010/07/what-shelton-waiver-tells-us-about.html. Witness, also, Philip E. Kovacs (editor), *The Gates Foundation and the Future of U.S. "Public" Schools* (New York: Routledge, 2010). For Gates' gift to CEE-Trust, read the Mind Trust news release, "The Mind Trust Lands Gates Funding," *Inside Indiana Business*, October 14, 2011. On Stand for Children's Gates funding, Ken Libby and Adam Sanchez write: "The Bill & Melinda Gates Foundation began by offering a relatively modest two-year grant of $80,000 in 2005. In 2007, Stand for Children received a $682,565 grant. In 2009, the point at which Stand's drastically different political agenda became obvious, Gates awarded a $971,280 grant to support "common policy priorities" and in 2010, a $3,476,300 grant." For Libby and Sanchez's work, read *Rethinking School's* Fall 2011's "For or against Children?: The Problematic History of Stand for Children," http://www.rethinkingschools.org//cmshandler.asp?archive/26_01/26_01_sanchez.shtml. For the history of Gates' money to the University of Indianapolis CELL, go to http://www.cell.uindy.edu/aboutcell/history.php. For Gates' giving to the Com-

Notes

mon Core, see Valerie Strauss, "Gates Gives $150 Million in Grants for Common Core Standards," *The Answer Sheet* (blog), *Washington Post*, May 12, 2013, http://washingtonpost.com/blogs/answer-sheet/wp/2013/05/12/gates-gives-150-million-in-grants-for-common-core-standards/.

82. *Top Corporate Tax Dodgers* (Washington, DC: US Senator Bernard Sanders, I-Vt., n.d.), 6, http://www.sanders.senate.gov/imo/media/doc/102512%20-%20JobDestroyers3.pdf.

83. Charles Kernaghan, "China's Youth Meet Microsoft: KYE Factory in China Produces for Microsoft and Other U.S. Companies," National Labor Committee, April 2010, http://www.globallabourrights.org/admin/reports/files/Chinas_Youth_Meet_Micro.pdf.

84. Steve Brill, *Class Warfare: Inside the Fight to Fix America's Schools* (New York: Simon & Schuster, 2011), 170.

85. Democrats for Education Reform, *President-Elect Barack Obama: Education Transition Memo*, November 7, 2008, 22, http://gothamschools.org/wp-content/uploads/2008/11/education-transition-memo-november-112.pdf.

86. John Martin, "League of Women Voters to Discuss Charter School Bill," *Evansville Courier & Press*, February, 8, 2011, http://www.courierpress.com/news/2011/feb/08/no-headline---08a03charterschools-brf/.

87. Whitney Tilson, "DFER Indiana Update," *Whitney Tilson's School Reform Blog*, February 22, 2011, http://edreform.blogspot.com/2011/02/dfer-indiana-update.html.

88. Ken Libby, "John Walton: DFER Catalyst?," *DFER Watch*, November 27, 2010, http://dferwatch.wordpress.com/2010/11/27/john-walton-dfer-catalyst/.

89. For Tilson's email about McCain, inspect Steve Brill's *Class Warfare*, 217-218.

90. Ken Libby, "Basil's Backers: (Mainly) Charter Supporters and (Some) Real Estate Moguls," *DFER Watch*, August 23, 2010, http://dferwatch.wordpress.com/2010/08/23/basils-backers-mainly-charter-supporters-and-some-real-estate-moguls/.

91. Leonie Haimson, "Tsunami of Pro-Charter Opinion in the Dailies," *NYC Public School Parents* (blog), June 8, 2010, http://nycpublicschoolparents.blogspot.com/2010/06/tsunami-of-pro-charter-opinion-in.html.

92. Joe Williams' pay is highlighted on page 7 of Education Reform Now's 2010 Form 990 at http://www.guidestar.org/FinDocuments/2010/203/687/2010-203687838-07df75ef-9.pdf.

93. Rachel Monahan and Bill Hammond, "Charter School Advocates Hope for Bill to Lift Charter Cap to Get Race to the Top Grants," *New York Daily News*, April 30, 2010, http://www.nydailynews.com/news/charter-school-advocates-hope-bill-lift-charter-cap-race-top-grants-article-1.448516#ixzz2LuJQOb36.

94. Joe Williams has several articles in *From Contracts to Classroom: Covering Teachers Unions: A Primer for Journalists* (New York: Hechinger Institute on Education and the Media, Teachers College, Columbia University, 2007), http://hechinger.tc.columbia.edu/primers/From ContractstoClassroomsPrimer204-2007.pdf.

95. Rotherham's pay can be found on page 7 in Bellwether's September 1, 2010 to August 31, 2011 Form 990 at http://www.guidestar.org/FinDocuments/2011/261/914/2011-261914515-080a0ad5-9.pdf.

96. Marguerite Roza, *Frozen Assets: Rethinking Teacher Contracts Could Free Billions for School Reform* (n.p.: Education Sector, January 2007), 3, http://www.educationsector.org/sites/default/files/publications/FrozenAssets.pdf.

97. Philip E. Kovacs and H.K. Christie, "The Gates' Foundation and the Future of U.S. Public Education: A Call for Scholars to Counter Misinformation Campaigns," *Journal for Critical Education Policy Studies* 6, no. 2 (December 1, 2008), http://www.jceps.com/PDFs/6-2-01.pdf.

Notes

98. For all information on hedge fund managers presented here, see Leo Leopold, "The 6 Economic Facts of Life in America That Allow the Rich to Run Off with Our Wealth," *Alter-Net*, December 5, 2012, http://www.alternet.org/economy/6-economic-facts-life-america-allow-rich-run-our-wealth; Joshua Holland and Les Leopold, "Just What Do Hedge Fund Honchos Do for a Million Bucks an Hour?," *AlterNet,* February 22, 2013, http://www.alternet.org/print/just-what-do-hedge-fund-honchos-do-million-bucks-hour; and Les Leopold, "The Rich Have Gained \$5.6 Trillion in the 'Recovery,' While the Rest of Us Have Lost \$669 Billion," *AlterNet,* May 3, 2013, http://www.alternet.org/economy/rich-have-gained-56-trillion-recovery-while-rest-us-have-lost-669-billion.

99. Jesse Eisinger and Jake Bernstein, "The Magnetar Trade: How One Hedge Fund Helped Keep the Bubble Going," *ProPublica*, April 9, 2010, http://www.propublica.org/article/all-the-magnetar-trade-how-one-hedge-fund-helped-keep-the-housing-bubble.

100. Juan Gonzalez, "Albany Charter Cash Cow: Big Banks Making a Bundle on New Construction as Schools Bear the Cost," *New York Daily News*, May 6, 2010, http://www.ny dailynews.com/new-york/education/albany-charter-cash-big-banks-making-bundle-new-con struction-schools-bear-cost-article-1.448008#ixzz2LA8VinHC.

101. Jeff Faux, "Education Profiteering; Wall Street's Next Big Thing?," *Huffington Post*, September 28, 2012, http://www.huffingtonpost.com/jeff-faux/education-wall-street_b_1919 727.html.

102. Ibid.

2 THE FREE-MARKET JESUS IN THE CLASSROOM

1. The introduction to this chapter draws on Katherine Stewart's *The Good News Club: The Christian Right's Stealth Assault on America's Children* (New York: Public Affairs, 2012), as well as the work of Rachel Tabachnick. The quotation here comes from Stewart, 254.

2. Celia Grundman, "The Soft Bigotry of Low Expectations," *Indiana Daily Student*, September 14, 2010, http://www.idsnews.com/news/story.aspx?id=76880. Visit, also, Karen Francisco's "Mitch Daniels and 'Real Education,'" *Learning Curve* (blog), *Journal Gazette* (Fort Wayne, IN), July 19, 2013, http://www.journalgazette.net/article/20130719/BLOGS13/130719 458, as well as Francisco's "Governor's Education Primer: Daniels Discloses 'The Bell Curve' Author Altered His Views on Schools," *Journal Gazette* (Fort Wayne, IN), July 19, 2013, http://www.journalgazette.net/article/20091011/EDIT05/310119940.

3. For Bradley's grantmaking, I have relied on 990 tax records, annual reports, the group's website, and "P Is for Payoff: Inside the Bradley Foundation's Campaign to Privatize Education in Wisconsin," *One Wisconsin Now/BradleyWatch.org*, April 2013, http://www.onewisconsin now.org/p-is-for-payoff.pdf. Information is also taken from Daniel Bice, Bill Glauber, and Ben Poston, "From Local Roots, Bradley Foundation Builds Conservative Empire," *Milwaukee Journal Sentinel*, November 19, 2011, http://www.jsonline.com/news/milwaukee/from-local-roots-bradley-foundation-builds-conservative-empire-k7337pb-134187368.html.

4. This section and the following one on Bradley's W-2 program pulls from Phil Wilayto, *The Feeding Trough: The Bradley Foundation, 'The Bell Curve' and the Real Story behind W-2, Wisconsin's National Model for Welfare Reform*, A Job Is a Right Campaign. See this link for summaries: http://my.execpc.com/~ajrc/ft.html. You can listen to Phil Wilayto's June 16, 1998 interview on *Democracy Now!* at http://www.democracynow.org/1998/6/16/wisconsin_readies _for_school_voucher_system. For more on Bradley's anti-affirmative action work, also inspect Brendan Fischer, "For Bradley Foundation, Challenging Affirmative Action & Voting Rights Is

Notes

Part of Long-Term Crusade," Center for Media and Democracy's *PR Watch*, June 27, 2013, http://www.prwatch.org/news/2013/06/12142/bradley-foundation-challenging-affirmative-actio n-voting-rights-part-long-term-cr.

5. Ibid.

6. Ibid.

7. Ibid.

8. Ralph G. Neas, Erica Lasdon, and Carol Keys, *Community Voice or Captive of the Right?: A Closer Look at the Black Alliance for Educational Options* (Washington, DC: People for the American Way, December 25, 2001). Updated in July 2003 at http://www.pfaw.org/sites/defaul t/ files/file_237.pdf.

9. Brett Clark and Richard York, "Debunking as Positive Science: Reflections in Honor of the Twenty-Fifth Anniversary of Stephen Jay Gould's *The Mismeasure of Man*," *Monthly Review* 57, no. 9 (February 2006), http://monthlyreview.org/2006/02/01/debunking-as-positive-science. Stephen Jay Gould's book is *The Mismeasure of Man* (New York: Norton, 1996).

10. Phil Wilayto, *The Feeding Trough*. This and the previous paragraph both draw on Wilayto's work.

11. Ibid.

12. Ibid.

13. Alan J. Borsuk and Sarah Carr, "Lessons from the Voucher Schools," *Milwaukee Journal Sentinel*, June 12, 2005, http://epsl.asu.edu/epru/articles/EPRU-0506-125-OWI.pdf.

14. Ibid.

15. Ibid.

16. Ibid.

17. Apart from my own extensive investigation, the section on the Black Alliance for Educational Options uses the research of Glen Ford and People for the American Way's report by Ralph G. Neas, Erica Lasdon, and Carol Keys (*Community Voice or Captive of the Right?*). Howard Fuller's bio is also sketched from *Community Voice or Captive of the Right?*, as is the quotation here.

18. Neas, Lasdon, and Keys, 8.

19. Barato Britt, "Black Alliance Is on the Move," *Heartlander*, September 1, 2001, http://news.heartland.org/newspaper-article/2001/09/01/black-alliance-move.

20. For Edison's lobbying, see *Open Secrets* at http://www.opensecrets.org/ lobby/clientsum. php?id=D000025636&year=2001.

21. Esther Kaplan, "Lights Out for Edison," *PSCcuny News Bulletin*, April 2001, http://archive.psc-cuny.org/lightsOut.htm.

22. Julian Guthrie, "S.F. Schools Vote to End Edison Compact/Academy Expected to Remain Open," *San Francisco Chronicle*, June 29, 2001, http://www.sfgate.com/education/article/ S-F-schools-vote-to-end-Edison-compact-Academy-2904046.php.

23. Martha Woodall, "Of Philadelphia Schools or Edison, Who's Really Rescuing Whom? The Education Firm Loses Money, but Says the District Could Change That," *Philly.com*, August 19, 2001, http://articles.philly.com/2001-08-19/business/25298950_1_peter-j-stokes-edison-schools-edison-reports/3.

24. Jack Miller, "Christel House Hires Edison," *NUVO*, June 9, 2004, reposted at *Susan Ohanian.org* and retitled "Millionaire Hires Edison for Indianapolis Charter," http://www.susanohanian.org/atrocity_fetch.php?id=2556.

25. All information on Flake's time at Wilberforce University is pulled from Isabel Vincent and Melissa Klein, "Rev. Flake 'Looting' Lesson," *New York Post*, October 9, 2011,

Notes

www.n
ypost.com/p/news/local/queens/rev_flake_looting_lesson_yyoLzCOlSsSqxeGdPersnK.

26. Ibid.

27. Ibid.

28. Glen Ford, "Fruit of the Poisoned Tree: The Hard Right's Plan to Capture Newark, NJ," *Black Commentator*, no. 1, April 5, 2002, http://www.blackcommentator.com/poisoned_tree.html.

29. Greg Toppo, "Report: Education Dept. Funds Need Monitoring," *USA Today*, September 3, 2005, http://www.usatoday.com/news/education/2005-09-03-education-funding_x.htm.

30. Michelle R. Davis, "U.S.-Funded Parent Information Centers Questioned on Their Agendas, Efficacy," *Education Week*, June 8, 2005, reposted at http://www.susanohanian.org/show_nclb_outrages.php?id=1392.

31. Don Soifer, "While D.C. Choice Simmers, NCLB Slow to Settle," *Heartlander*, December 1, 2003, http://news.heartland.org/newspaper-article/2003/12/01/while-dc-choice-simmers-nclb-slow-settle.

32. These reports are based on articles that appeared in the *Post Tribune* of Gary and the *Times of Northwest Indiana* (Munster, IN), which are no longer at their websites. Copies of these articles, however, are reposted at *Charter School Scandals* and can be read at http://charterschoolscandals.blogspot.com/2011/04/21st-century-charter-school.html.

33. Carmen McCollum, "Local Charter Schools Cited by Indiana State Board of Accounts," *Times of Northwest Indiana* (Munster, IN), March 31, 2011, http://www.nwitimes.com/news/local/lake/local-charter-schools-cited-by-indiana-state-board-of-accounts/article_c5a344e0-2fe8-5a89-83e7-aa99ba024fdd.html.

34. For the audit, consult John Cutler & Associates' *Pikes Peak Prep: Basic Financial Statements, June 30, 2009*. See, also, Jhon D. Penn, Director of Performance Support, Colorado Department of Education, "Letter to Mark Hyatt, Executive Director of the Charter School Institute," October 20, 2010, http://www.ednewscolorado.org/wp-content/uploads/2010/11/CSIletter.pdf. Read pages 2-4.

35. "Lawsuit against Pikes Peak Prep School, State of Colorado Investigation," *World Law Direct*, July 12, 2010, http://www.worldlawdirect.com/forum/labor-law-matters/40992-lawsuit-against-pikes-peak-prep-school-state-colorado-investigation.html.

36. Teasley's pay is in the Greater Educational Opportunities Foundation's Form 990 for the year starting July 1, 2011 and ending June 30, 2012. You can find it on page 7 at http://www.guidestar.org/FinDocuments/2012/954/406/2012-954406881-0909100b-9.pdf.

37. William Trombley, "Major Fight Looms over Initiative on Vouchers," *Los Angeles Times*, December 15, 1991, http://articles.latimes.com/1991-12-15/news/mn-997_1_public-school-state-scholarship-schools-private-school-voucher-plan.

38. Neas, Lasdon, and Keys, *Community Voice or Captive of the Right?*

39. For the Conseco story, see "Rebuilding Conseco: Epic Stock-Slide Led to Bankruptcy, but the Carmel-Based Insurance Company Survived and Restructured," *Indianapolis Star*, August 13, 2004, http://www2.indystar.com/library/factfiles/business/companies/conseco/2000.html; Francesca Jarosz and Heather Gillers, "Pacers Getting $33.5 Million to Stay," *Indianapolis Star*, July 12, 2010; and Bill W. Hornaday, "SEC Sues Ex-Conseco Execs for $5.6 Million," *Indianapolis Star*, March 12, 2004.

40. For the state chaplain fiasco and Cissell's role, visit Robert King, "State Chaplain's Challenges Multiply: Critics Doubt Program's Legality, Leader's Credentials," *Indianapolis Star*, June 17, 2007. The rest of the story can be surveyed at Freedom from Religion Foundation, "Legal Victory for FFRF Is Final!: Indiana Officially Drops Chaplain Post," *Freethought*

Notes

Today 24, no. 7 (September 2007), http://ffrf.org/outreach/afa/meeting-dates/item/12952-indiana-officially-drops-chaplain-post; and Neela Banerjee, "Indiana, Faced with Suit, Takes Chaplain Off Payroll," *New York Times*, September 28, 2007, http://www.nytimes.com/2007/09/28/us/28indiana.html?_r=0.

41. Kevin P. Chavous, "Why Is the NAACP Fighting African Americans?," *Washington Post*, June 3, 2011, http://articles.washingtonpost.com/2011-06-03/opinions/35234786_1_naacp-leaders-charter-schools-naacp-spokesman. For the Bradley wedge, read Glen Ford, "How the Corporate Right Divided Blacks from Teachers Unions and Each Other," *Black Agenda Report*, reposted at *Common Dreams*, June 15, 2011, https://www.commondreams.org/ view/2011/06/15-10.

42. David Brand, "David Brand of 100 Black Men Comments," *Whitney Tilson's School Reform Blog*, June 8, 2011, http://edreform.blogspot.com/2011/06/david-brand-of-100-black-men-comments.html.

43. Emily Richmond, "Charter School on Thin Ice," *Las Vegas Sun*, June 10, 2008, http://www.lasvegassun.com/news/2008/jun/10/charter-school-thin-ice/.

44. Stephanie Strom, "For School Company, Issues of Money and Control," *New York Times*, April 23, 2010, http://www.nytimes.com/2010/04/24/education/24imagine.html?pagewanted=all&_r=0.

45. Timothy Pratt, "Families Galvanized by Charter School Principal's Suspension," *Las Vegas Sun*, Sept. 11, 2009, http://www.lasvegassun.com/news/2009/sep/11/families-galvanized-principals-suspension/.

46. Strom, "For School Company, Issues of Money and Control."

47. "More Parents Come Forward about North Las Vegas Charter School Investigation," Action 13, March 11, 2010, http://health.ktnv.com/story/12127626/more-parents-come-forward-about-north-las-vegas-charter-school-investigation.

48. Rich Coleman, "Teacher Accused of Starting Fire in School Copier Room," *Las Vegas Sun*, Sept. 8, 2010, http://www.lasvegassun.com/news/2010/sep/08/teacher-accused-starting-fire-school-copier-room/.

49. Richmond, "Charter School on Thin Ice."

50. Mike DeNardo, "Another Guilty Plea in Philadelphia Charter School Fraud Case," CBS Philly, April 3, 2012, http://philadelphia.cbslocal.com/2012/04/03/another-guilty-plea-in-philadelphia-charter-school-fraud-case/.

51. Rachel Tabachnick, "Pro-Voucher Astroturfing: Campaigns across Nation Coordinated by DeVos, Funded by a Few Mega-Donors," *Talk to Action*, April 24, 2011, http://www.talk2action.org/story/2011/4/24/22559/1547.

52. The DeVos speech is transcribed in Rachel Tabachnick's "Strategy for Privatizing Public Schools Spelled Out by Dick DeVos in 2002 Heritage Foundation Speech," *Talk to Action*, May 3, 2011, http://www.talk2action.org/story/2011/5/3/12515/58655. DeVos' almost hour-long speech is at http://www.youtube.com/watch?v=Xt9FmMrvJ3A&feature=related.

53. Tabachnick, "Pro-Voucher Astroturfing."

54. *2010 Election Impact Report: Electing Leaders to Give Kids Hope* (Washington, DC: American Federation for Children, 2010), 12, https://s3.amazonaws.com/AFC/American+Federation+for+Children+Election+Report+2010.pdf.

55. Archdiocese of Indianapolis, "State Education Leader to Be Keynote Speaker at Awards Dinner," *Criterion Online Edition*, October 7, 2011, http://www.archindy.org/criterion/local/2011/10-07/ccsv-sidebar.html.

56. See All Children Matter-Iowa PAC's *Schedule B: Expenditures*, https://webapp.iecdb.iowa.gov/PublicView/statewide/2009/Period_Due_Date_19-Jan/PACs/AllChildrenMatter

Notes

-Iowa_9742/AllChildrenMatter-Iowa_9742_B_Expenditures.pdf. For DeVos, Chavous, and James Bopp Jr.'s influence on the Indiana elections of 2008, as well as the dots that tie DeVos' group to the Iowa branch, look over All Children Matter's 2007-2008 election report at http://brechtheuchan.com/wp-content/uploads/2009/09/2k7-2k8-electionreport.pdf.

57. Associated Press, "School Choice Expanding as Record Fine Languishes," *MLive*, March 28, 2011, http://www.mlive.com/politics/index.ssf/2011/03/school_choice_expanding_as_rec.html.

58. Rachel Tabachnick, "The DeVos Family: Meet the Super-Wealthy Right-Wingers Working with the Religious Right to Kill Public Education," *AlterNet*, May 6, 2011, http://www.alternet.org/story/150868/the_devos_family%3A_meet_the_super-wealthy_right-wingers_working_with_the_religious_right_to_kill_public_education.

59. For Chavous' law firm pay, see page 8 of the Alliance for School Choice's Form 990 at http://www.guidestar.org/FinDocuments/2010/522/111/2010-522111508-0771c0f4-9.pdf. Chavous' secretary salary for this group is on page 7 at http://guidestar.org/FinDocuments/2011/522/111/2011-522111508-08ad946b-9.pdf. Page 8 of the American Federation for Children's 2010 990 gives the pay to Chavous' law firm. You can find it at http://guidestar.org/FinDocuments/2010/330/627/2010-330627955-07791fc1-9O.pdf. Chavous' profit from being secretary for the American Federation for Children is noted on page 7 in the group's 2011 990 at http://www.guidestar.org/FinDocuments/2011/330/627/2011-330627955-08b13f1b-9O.pdf.

60. Rachel Tabachnick, "Pro-Voucher Astroturfing."

61. For the Bradley Foundation's funding to these corporate school groups, see pages 19 and 31 in the group's annual report for 2011 at http://www.bradleyfdn.org/pdfs/Reports2011/2011AnnualReport.pdf.

62. Alan Suderman, "Read Police Records of Kevin B. Chavous' Arrest," *Washington City Paper*, January 3, 2012, http://www.washingtoncitypaper.com/blogs/looselips/2012/01/03/read-police-records-of-kevin-b-chavous-arrest/.

63. To see Chavous and Daniels' complete disrespect for MLK, go to 21st Annual Dr. Martin Luther King Jr. Indiana Holiday Celebration, http://www.youtube.com/watch?v=67I284La5DA.

64. See EAG's 2010 Form 990, page 1, http://www.guidestar.org/FinDocuments/2010/260/877/2010-260877115-07d2014c-9.pdf.

65. For Friedman's money to EAG, see Schedule I, Part II, page 30 (page 25 in PDF box) in the group's 2010 Form 990 at http://www.guidestar.org/FinDocuments/2010/351/978/2010-351978359-0780f469-9.pdf.

66. The Bradley Foundation's funding to EAG is mentioned on page 15 of the group's 2011 annual report, which is cited above.

67. Stewart, *The Good News Club*, 254.

68. On EAG, I have found insights at *EAG Truth*, which exposes the outfit. You can find the site at http://eagtruth.wordpress.com/. For the Claude Lambe Charitable Foundation's funding to Mackinac, see *Sourcewatch* at http://www.sourcewatch.org/index.php/Koch_Family_Foundations. For Lambe's donations to the other groups mentioned above, witness page 26 (in PDF box) of its 2010 Form 990, http://www.guidestar.org/FinDocuments/2010/480/935/2010-480935563-07b96026-F.pdf.

69. David Johnson, "Concern over Republican Embrace of the Ayn Rand Poison," *Campaign for America's Future* (blog), June 10, 2011, http://blog.ourfuture.org/20110610/Concern_Over_Republican_Embrace_Of_The_Ayn_Rand_Poison.

70. For Olson's comments and Fox News clip, examine Fred Klonsky's "EAG's Kyle Olson Exposes Kindergarten Teacher's Use of *Click Clack Moo: Cows That Type* to Indoctrinate

Notes

Students," December 3, 2011, http://preaprez.wordpress.com/2011/12/03/eags-kyle-olson-exposes-kindergarten-teachers-use-of-click-clack-moo-cows-that-type-to-indoctrinate-students/.

71. Michael Malgeri and Michael Schultz, *Johnny Profit: Bedtime Stories about Capitalism* (n.p.: Kids4biz, 2011).

72. The nine-part *Kids Aren't Cars* can be watched on YouTube at http://www.youtube.com/watch?v=nGX1dGgeQF0.

73. "Kids Aren't Cars: How Adult Interests Are Turning Schools into 'Dropout Factories,'" *Nevada News & Views,* n.d., http://nevadanewsandviews.com/archives/8080.

74. Ibid.

75. Charles Anthony Bennett, "The Effects of Just Cause Contract Language on Teacher Dismissals in Indiana between 1999-2004" (EdD diss., Spalding University, 2005), iii-iv.

76. Kim Kilbride, "Scaling Back Contracts: Pending Legislation Would Severely Limit the Items Teachers Could Negotiate," *South Bend Tribune*, April 3, 2011.

77. *Indiana K-12 & School Choice Survey* (Indianapolis: Milton and Rose Friedman Foundation for Educational Choice, January 10, 2011), http://www.edchoice.org/CMSModules/EdC hoice/FileLibrary/664/Indiana-K-12---School-Choice-Survey.pdf.

78. Christopher Lubienski, review of "A Win-Win Solution: The Empirical Evidence on How Vouchers Affect Public Schools," (Boulder, CO: National Education Policy Center, April 2009), http://nepc.colorado.edu/files/NEPC-Win-Win.pdf. See pages 7, 8, 10, and 11 for my summary and Lubienski's quotation.

79. St. Angelo's pay surfaces on page 7 of each of Friedman's 990 tax forms from 2008 to 2010. You can find it at http://www.guidestar.org/FinDocuments/2009/351/978/2009-351978359-0648c621-9.pdf and http://www.guidestar.org/FinDocuments/2010/351/978/2010-351978359-0780f469-9.pdf. Unfortunately, the group's 2008 Form 990 is no longer free online.

80. Enlow's salary is noted in Friedman's 2010 Form 990, page 7, http://www.guidestar.org/FinDocuments/2010/351/978/2010-351978359-0780f469-9.pdf.

81. The following Indiana lawmakers are members of ALEC, just to name a few: Bob Behning, Brian Bosma, Jim Banks, Jim Buck, Luke Kenley, and Carlin Yoder.

82. Ann Babe, "Jensen Officially Leaves Post," *Badger Herald* (Madison, WI), last modified January 23, 2007, http://badgerherald.com/news/2006/03/22/jensen_officially_le.php.

83. Lori Drummer, "School Choice Academy Spurs Legislative Interest," *Heartlander*, November 1, 2005, http://news.heartland.org/newspaper-article/2005/11/01/school-choice-academy-spurs-legislative-interest?quicktabs_4=0.

84. To read the court briefs filed by the Institute for Justice and the other groups, go to http://www.ij.org/arizona-and-national-education-advocates-urge-arizona-supreme-court-to-up-hold-scholarships-for-special-needs-and-foster-children.

85. Atkin's quotation appears at Nate Bailey, "New Study Reveals School Finance Lawsuits Increase Funding Temporarily, Hike Taxes Permanently," *Tax Foundation.org*, July 26, 2007, http://taxfoundation.org/article/new-study-reveals-school-finance-lawsuits-increase-funding-temporarily-hike-taxes-permanently. His study, *Appropriation by Litigation: Estimating the Cost of Judicial Mandates for State and Local Education Spending*, is Tax Foundation's Background Paper, no. 55, July 2007, http://taxfoundation.org/ sites/taxfoundation.org/files/docs/bp55.pdf.

86. Mike Pence recently rehired Chris Atkins to lead the Office of Management and Budget and both played a part in the recent attack on Glenda Ritz, Indiana's new superintendent of public schools. Having moved out of committee but finally killed off by GOP House Speaker Brian Bosma, House Bill 1342 in 2013 sought to strip Ritz and the Department of Education of

Notes

all power to monitor state voucher schools, giving instead, the Koch brothers and ALEC crony Chris Atkins and his Indiana Office of Management and Budget complete control over voucher school funding distribution, oversight, and even voucher school visits.

House Bill 1342 was meant to punish Ritz, who was originally involved in the lawsuit to stop Indiana's school voucher system, and lead to even more lack of oversight. Atkins, however, is not the only Office of Management and Budget employee with ties to school voucher groups. The Friedman Foundation-funded and Tea Party Americans for Prosperity is represented at OMB's Department of Government Efficiency and Financial Planning by Gloria Downham, whose husband Chase heads the Americans for Prosperity's Indiana branch. Chase, a former Mike Pence intern, helped elect Republicans for the Indiana Chamber of Commerce. Chase and Gloria are parishioners at the St. Monica Catholic Church which operates its own Indianapolis school receiving Indiana tax credit scholarships. Former Ice Miller attorney Brian Bailey, OMB's chief of staff and general counsel, is also a Tax Foundation crony. Micah Vincent, at OMB's Department of Local Government Finance, likes to attend Friedman Foundation events, too.

For my entire take on this, see Doug Martin, "Voucher Gospels in Indiana Government," *Schools Matter*, February 22, 2013, http://www.schoolsmatter.info/2013/02/voucher-gospels-in-indiana-government.html.

87. Glen Warchol, "Vouchers Go Down in Crushing Defeat," *Salt Lake Tribune*, November 7, 2007, http://www.sltrib.com/ci_7392263.

88. See page 2, Part IV of Friedman's 2010 Form 990 for its funding to Emmis: http://www.guidestar.org/FinDocuments/2010/351/978/2010-351978359-0780f469-9.pdf.

89. Hiner's 2011 pay from Friedman is noted on page 7 at http://www.guidestar.org/FinDocuments/2011/351/978/2011-351978359-08b4021f-9.pdf.

90. Witness pages 30-35 of Form 990 2010 for Friedman's grants to these and many other anti-public education groups, http://www.guidestar.org/FinDocuments/2010/351/978/2010-351978359-0780f469-9.pdf.

91. Jen McCreight, "This Hilariously Awkward Run-In Made My Reason Rally Trip Worthwhile," March 23, 2012, *Blog Hag*, http://freethoughtblogs.com/blaghag/2012/03/this-hilariously-awkward-run-in-made-my-reason-rally-trip-worthwhile/.

92. "Leading Intelligent Design Think Tank Condemns Passage of Creationism Bill by Indiana Senate as Bad Science and Bad Education," *Discovery Institute.org*, January 31, 2012, http://www.discovery.org/a/18181.

93. Zack Kopplin and Melissa Harris Perry, "Creationism Spreading in Schools, Thanks to Vouchers," NBC News, January 16, 2013, http://nbcnews.com/id/50486507/t/creationism-spreading-schools-thanks-vouchers/.

94. Tiffany Vega, "Liberty Christian Tests Voucher Program," *Andersonian*, September 28, 2011, http://andersonian.com/2011/09/28/liberty-christian-tests-new-school-vouchers/.

95. John Tulenko, "Indiana Crafts Dropout Remedy through Choice of Schools," PBS's *News Hour*, November 9, 2011, http://www.pbs.org/newshour/bb/education/july-dec11/tulenko_11-09.html.

96. Tony Ortega, "Vi Simpson: The Woman Who Punked the Radical Republicans in the Indiana State Senate and Their Creationist Bill," February 1, 2010, *Village Voice*, http://blogs.villagevoice.com/runninscared/2012/02/vi_simpson_the.php.

97. Steve Hinnefeld, "Indiana School Vouchers: Subsidizing Extremism," *School Matters*, August 22, 2011, https://inschoolmatters.wordpress.com/2011/08/22/indiana-school-vouchers-subsidizing-extremism/.

Notes

98. Frances Paterson, *Democracy and Intolerance: Christian School Curricula, School Choice, and Public Policy* (Bloomington, IN: Phi Delta Kappa, 2003).

99. Rachel Tabachnick, "The 'Christian' Dogma Pushed by Religious Schools That Are Supported by Your Tax Dollars," *AlterNet*, May 23, 2011, http://www.alternet.org/story/151 046/the_%27christian%27_dogma_pushed_by_religious_schools_that_are_supported_by_y our_tax_dollars.

100. Rafael Sanchez, "Value of Diplomas Doled Out by Ministry Questioned," RTV6, April 29, 2011, http://www.theindychannel.com/news/education/value-of-diplomas-doled-out-by-ministry-questioned.

101. Ibid.

102. Keith J. Fennimore, *Faith Made Visible: The History of Floyd Starr and His School* (Albion, MI: Starr Commonwealth School, 1988).

103. Kathryn Joyce, "Horror Stories from Tough-Love Teen Homes," *Mother Jones*, July/August 2011, http://www.motherjones.com/politics/2011/08/new-bethany-ifb-teen-homes-abuse?page=4.

104. Kenneth P. Vogel, "Romney Makes Florida Play with Key Fundraiser Hire," *Politico*, March 10, 2011, http://www.politico.com/news/stories/0311/51039.html.

105. Tara Ketola, alumni questionnaire, *The Truth about New Horizons Youth Ministries*, http://nhym-alumni.org/alumni/ketola_tara/.

106. Ibid.

107. Kerri Griffin Santarlasci, alumni questionnaire, *The Truth about New Horizons Youth Ministries*, http://nhym-alumni.org/alumni/griffin_santarlasci_kerri/.

108. This entire section draws from various internet sources and personal interviews with former students, now adults, who went through the horror of these boarding schools.

109. State of Indiana v. Robert D. George, Affidavit for Probable Cause, Sexual Misconduct with a Minor, Class D Felony, No. 27DO2-9408-CF-45, (Grant Superior Ct. II, August 19, 1994), http://nhym-alumni.org/documents/lawsuit_rg.pdf.

110. Julia Scheeres, *Jesus Land: A Memoir*, rev. ed. (Berkeley, CA: Counterpoint, 2012).

111. To witness this scene from *Kidnapped for Christ*, visit http://www.kidnappedforchrist.com/.

112. James D. Payne, Director of Indiana Department of Child Services, email, June 14, 2011, groups.yahoo.com/group/Escuela_Caribe/message/12805. For Payne's resignation, see Tim Evans, "DCS Chief James Payne Fought His Own Agency over Family Matter," *Indianapolis Star*, September 24, 2012.

113. After my research on Lifeline's Crosswinds was picked up by the HEAL watchdog group, officials from Lifeline/Crosswinds revised their website pages to try to conceal things I had pieced together. You can find the original bios of Crosswinds employees still online at the Wayback Archive at http://web.archive.org/web/20120702125121/http://www.crosswindsyouth .org/index.cfm/about/staff/. Much of this info is drawn from that site.

114. You can find HEAL's New Horizons Youth Ministries site at http://www.heal-online.org/nhym2.htm.

115. For proof that Scott and his wife were associated with the Summit Church, see http://www.thesummitchurch.org/test_main/event/932/,http://www.medhelp.org/posts/Child-Behavior/Sexual-thoughts-in-a-6-year-old-child/show/731248. Looks like Summit Church members are now traveling to see kids and Taylor at the Dominican Republic compound.

116. See the National Institute on Money in State Politics's *Follow the Money's* "The Money behind the 2004 Marriage Amendments, Arkansas," http://www.followthemoney.org/press/Rep ortView.phtml?r=236&ext=8.

Notes

117. Robert Lewis, "Raising Sons to Be Godly Men (Part 2 of 2)," Focus on the Family, April 10, 2012, http://www.focusonthefamily.com/radio.aspx?ID={61B3FC1A-19F3-4A72-B3F2-68E66EF5BB14}. Lewis' book with Focus on the Family is entitled *Raising a Modern-Day Knight.*

118. Jon and his wife have worked at the NHYM school since 2005, as this staff bio from the Wayback Machine shows: http://web.archive.org/web/20080110112827/http://www.nhym.org/ec_staff.shtml. For proof of their work at Heartlight Ministries, see http://web.archive.org/web/20000124141309/http://www.heartlightministries.org/leadersh.htm,http://web.archive.org/web/20000124204148/http://www.heartlightministries.org/support.htm.

119. See HEAL's take on Heartlight Ministries at http://www.heal-online.org/heartlight.htm.

120. The picture I refer to can be found at *Sawyers in the Sun* (blog), http://4.bp.blogspot.com/-OmyLLia1CZI/TX4mLfHwsiI/AAAAAAAAa5w/cDM-jZymfPE/s1600/DSC_1037.JPG.

121. Matt in Jarabacoa!, "Answered Prayers and Changes," *Matt in Jarabacoa!* (blog), January 11, 2012, http://mattinjarabacoa.blogspot.com/2012/01/answered-prayers-and-changes.html.

122. The Sawyers mention a Sagemont mission trip in a March 27, 2011 entry on their blog at http://sawyersinthesun.blogspot.com/2011_03_01_archive.html. Rachel says she went to high school with the leaders of Sagemont and they blessed her.

123. Jeremy Hooper, "Video: And This Year's Holy Week Leper Analogy Comes from Houston's Sagemont Church," *Good as You*, April 20, 2011, http://www.goodasyou.org/good_as_you/2011/04/video-and-this-years-holy-week-leper-analogy-comes-from-houstons-sagemont-church.html.

124. Alan Bernstein, "Mom of Drowned Kids Painted as Private, Caring," *Houston Chronicle*, June 23, 2001, http://www.chron.com/news/houston-texas/article/Mom-of-drowned-kids-painted-as-private-caring-2042465.php.

125. Mitch Daniels, too, is well aware of Lifeline. In 2007, while a nonprofit management major at Christ-centered Huntington University, Adam Shoemaker was picked to be the youth member on Indiana's Office of Faith-Based and Community Initiatives (OFBCI) board, a new office started by the governor. In 2010, Daniels selected Shoemaker, while he was employed with Lifeline, to be a commissioner with the Indiana Commission on Service and Volunteerism, a program now in the hands of Indiana's OFBCI. In 2009, OFBCI awarded Lifeline a grant through its Good Works Indiana Initiative. Shoemaker, who now works with the Indiana Youth Institute, was a family consultant for Lifeline from 2008 to May 2011.

126. *Faith-Based Perspectives on the Provision of Community Services, Hearing before the Subcommittee on Criminal Justice, Drug Policy and Human Resources of the Committee on Government Reform*, 108th Cong. (August 25, 2003) (statement of Mark Terrell, Lifeline Youth and Family Services), http://www.gpo.gov/fdsys/pkg/CHRG-108hhrg91692/html/CHRG-108hhrg91692.htm.

127. Maia Szalavitz, "Why Jesus Is Not a Regulator," *American Prospect,* December 19, 2001, http://prospect.org/article/why-jesus-not-regulator.

128. Rob Boston, "Straight Eye for the Queer Guys?: Congressional 'Faith-Based' Panel Hears from 'Ex-Gay' Conversion Ministry," *Americans United.org*, March 2004, https://www.au.org/church-state/march-2004-church-state/featured/straight-eye-for-the-queer-guys.

129. Kayleen Reusser, "Fort Wayne Couple Launches Ministries Aimed at Teens, Motocross Racing World: Couple Feel Called to Evangelize Nationwide from RV," *News-Sentinel* (Fort Wayne, IN), May 18, 2011, http://www.newssentinel.com/apps/pbcs.dll/article?AID=%2F2011

Notes

0518%2FNEWS01%2F105180302.

130. "Goshen The Crossing's Rob Staley Honored with Appleseed Award," *Elkhart Truth*, January 13, 2008, http://www.elkharttruth.com/article/20080113/NEWS01/301139939.

131. See Jesse Davis, "Rep. Souder Tackles Issues of Education, Energy Woes," *Goshen News*, March 29, 2008, http://goshennews.com/local/x395808825/Rep-Souder-tackles-issues-of-education-energy-woes/print and "AAUW Elkhart Branch, Clubs and Organizations: News from Elkhart County Service Clubs and Other Groups, Goshen Rotary Club," *Elkhart Truth*, September 14, 2011, http://ehedit.sx.atl.publicus.com/apps/pbcs.dll/article?AID=/20110914/LIFESTYLE/709139978&template=printart.

132. See page 7 of Crossing's Form 990 for 2010 at http://www.guidestar.org/FinDocuments/2011/260/588/2011-260588186-07e3a0cb-9.pdf.

133. *Innovative Approaches to Preventing Crime and Rehabilitating Youth and Adult Offenders, Hearing before the Subcommittee on Criminal Justice, Drug Policy and Human Resources of the Committee on Government Reform*, 107th Cong. (March 22, 2002) (statement of Mark Terrell, Lifeline Youth and Family Services), http://www.gpo.gov/fdsys/pkg/CHRG-107hhrg85124/html/CHRG-107hhrg85124.htm.

134. For a good overview of Samenow's theories, go to Dr. Cecil E. Greek's Florida State University's criminology page at http://www.criminology.fsu.edu/crimtheory/samenow.htm.

135. Samenow's connection with Reagan is not surprising, given that many troubled-teen programs were spawned out of the Nancy Reagan-supported Straight Inc., started during the anti-drug and anti-gay crusades of the 1980s. Read Maia Szalavitz's frightening book *Help at Any Cost: How the Troubled-Teen Industry Cons Parents and Hurts Kids* (New York: Riverhead, 2006).

136. For the flyer on the event, see http://www.insource.org/pdf/2009_IARCCA.pdf.

137. Kendall Hughes, "USP Leavenworth Chaplain Offers Insight on Lack of Effectiveness in Prison Bible Studies and Observations on Thinking Errors," *Truthought.com*, http://www.truthought.com/learn-more/usp-leavenworth-leaders-offer-insight-into-the-lack-of-effective-prison-bible-studies-and-observations-on-thinking-errors.

138. Stephen T. Hall, "Indiana Implements a Faith and Character-Based Housing Program," American Correctional Chaplains Association, n.d, 65, http://www.correctionalchaplains.org/Hall.pdf.

139. See page 12 in Indiana University School of Social Work and Indiana Department of Child Services, New Family Case Manager Training, Indiana Department of Child Services, Training Overview. in.gov/dcs/files/New_Family_Case__Manager_Training_Overview_0806 10.pdf.

140. Sandra Chapman, "State Continues to See High Turnover of DCS Case Managers," WTHR, April 3, 2012, http://www.wthr.com/story/17324970/state-continues-to-see-high-turnover-of-dcs-case-managers.

141. Joanna Massee, "DCS under Fire for Returning Millions to State: Director Defends Decision to Spend Less," Indy Channel, September 2, 2011, http://www.theindychannel.com/news/dcs-under-fire-for-returning-millions-to-state.

142. Associated Press, "Indiana Child Welfare Supervisor Convicted of Perjury," *Washington Times-Herald*, June 11, 2010, http://washtimesherald.com/statenews/x1358979281/Indiana-child-welfare-supervisor-convicted-of-perjury. See also "Lead Indiana Child Death Investigator Resigns: Says New Law Not in Line with What Experts Nationwide Are Doing," *South Bend Tribune*, March 19, 2012, http://www.southbendtribune.com/news/sbt-lead-indiana-child-death-investigator-resigns-20120319,0,215830.story.

143. You can read Laskey's resignation letter to Mitch Daniels at http://www.indystar.co

Notes

om/assets/pdf/BG186687317.PDF. The study mentioned is discussed at Vanessa Renderman, "Health Commissioner: Indiana Infant Mortality Rate Is 'Horrible,'" *Times of Northwest Indiana* (Munster, IN), August 6, 2013, http://www.nwitimes.com/business/healthcare/health-commiss ioner-indiana-infant-mortality-rate-is-horrible/article_1e6b99d9-e6d8-5ffa-b569-4ff83b613223. html.

144. Eric Bradner, "Legislative Study Committee Reviewing Child Deaths in Indiana," *Evansville Courier & Press*, May 23, 2012, http://www.courierpress.com/news/2012/may/2 3/no-headline---ev_committees/?print=1.

145. Rebecca S. Green, "State Ends Dispute over Child Welfare Testimony," *Journal Gazette* (Fort Wayne, IN), May 25, 2012, http://www.journalgazette.net/article/20120525/LOCAL 03/305259890.

146. Not everyone receiving a degree from a religious institution is an extremist. Actually, Oral Roberts University has its own LGBT organization. I, personally, have met many highly-qualified and professional therapists who have went to faith-based universities. Questions concerning Indiana's DCS, nonetheless, need raised, as does the need to expose how people getting degrees in pseudo-science are "counseling" our children.

147. See pages 7 and 9 in Lifeline's 2010 Form 990, http://www.guidestar.org/FinDocuments/2010/351/167/2010-351167389-07773c0f-9.pdf.

148. *Abuse and Neglect of Children in Institutions, 1979, Hearings before the Senate Subcommittee on Child and Human Development of the Committee on Labor and Human Resources*, 96th Cong. (1979) (statement of Kenneth Wooden, National Coalition for Children's Justice).

3 TRAIN WRECK: THE INDIANA GOVERNMENT-CORPORATE SCHOOL COMPLEX

1. Editorial, "Let Public Vet Takeover Operators," *Indianapolis Star*, June 24, 2011, http://www.indystar.com/article/20110624/OPINION08/106240314/Let-public-vet-takeover-operators.

2. Gerald W. Bracey, *What You Should Know about the War against America's Public Schools* (Boston: Allyn & Bacon, 2002), 104-117. Readers would also highly benefit from the in-depth analysis and history of Edison's antics in DePaul professor Kenneth J. Saltman's *The Edison Schools: Corporate Schooling and the Assault on Public Education* (New York: Routledge, 2005).

3. Dale Mezzacappa, "City Graduation Rate Surprises Expert," *Philly.com*, November 16, 2001, http://articles.philly.com/2001-11-16/news/25320775_1_graduation-rate-edison-schools-three-edison.

4. For media articles on the Edison rape and its aftermath, see http://charterschoolscandal s.blogspot.com/2010/12/stetson-middle-school-edison-managed.html.

5. "Board Denies Renewal of E. Liberty Charter School," *Pittsburgh Post-Gazette*, April 25, 2007, http://www.post-gazette.com/stories/news/education/board-denies-renewal-of-e-liberty-charter-school-482557/.

6. Elisa Crouch, "Confluence Academy Faces Complaint over Suspensions," *St. Louis Post-Dispatch*, July 9, 2010, http://www.stltoday.com/news/local/education/article_21491040-dda2-52b9-a7fe-71a320f35464.html.

7. For several articles on the E2 Project reposted, see *New York Education News's* yahoo group listserv at http://groups.yahoo.com/group/nyceducationnews/message/6181.

Notes

8. To witness several media reports on the Linear Leadership Academy's problems with Edison, go to http://charterschoolscandals.blogspot.com/2010/07/linear-leadership-academy.html.

9. Jessica Williams, "Wilson Charter, Edison Learning Blaming One Another for $400,000 Shortfall," *The Lens*, March 29, 2013, http://thelensnola.org/2013/03/29/andrew-wilson-charter-school-edisonlearning-blame-one-another-for-400000-shortfall/.

10. Ibid.

11. Ibid.

12. David Moberg, "How Edison Survived," *The Nation*, March 15, 2004, reposted at http://www.susanohanian.org/outrage_fetch.php?id=146.

13. Saltman, *The Edison Schools*, 64.

14. Jim Horn, "Bloomberg's Corrupt Headmaster of School Privatization," *Schools Matter*, February 10, 2007, http://www.schoolsmatter.info/2007/02/bloombergs-corrupt-headmaster-of-school.html.

15. Chris Megerian, "Gov. Christie to Unveil Public-Private School Partnership Plan," *NJ.com*, June 9, 2011, http://www.nj.com/news/index.ssf/2011/06/gov_christie_to_unveil_public-.html.

16. See Texans for Public Justice's "Pioneer Profiles: George W. Bush's $100,000 Club," July 2000, http://info.tpj.org/pioneers/j_huizenga.html and "Lawsuit Smokes Out 312 More Bush Pioneer Fundraisers,"n.d., http://info.tpj.org/pioneers/newpioneers/analysis.html. Read, also, Associated Press, "Gore Completes Campaign Fund-Raising," *USA Today*, April 20, 2000, http://usatoday30.usatoday.com/news/e98/e1579.htm.

17. Karen Francisco, "Michigan's Shadowy School Plan," *Learning Curve* (blog), *Journal Gazette* (Fort Wayne, IN), April 19, 2013, http://www.journalgazette.net/article/20130419/BLOGS13/130419440.

18. Editorial, "Questionable Oversight," *Journal Gazette* (Fort Wayne, IN), May 1, 2012, http://www.journalgazette.net/article/20120501/EDIT07/305019996/1147/EDIT07.

19. Ibid.

20. George A. Clowes, "Bringing the Profit Motive and Moral Values to Education: An Interview with J.C. Huizenga," *School Reform News* 9, no. 4 (April 2005): 1, http://heartland.org/sites/default/files/sites/all/modules/custom/heartland_migration/files/pdfs/16689.pdf.

21. *ALEC v. Kids: ALEC's Assault on Public Education*, Alliance for a Better Utah, n.d., 30, http://betterutah.org/wp-content/uploads/2013/06/ALECvKids.pdf.

22. Lisa Rab, "Getting Schooled: Charter Schools Are a Booming Business, and North Carolina Has Opened the Floodgates," *Charlotte Magazine*, October 2012, http://www.charlottemagazine.com/Charlotte-Magazine/October-2012/Getting-Schooled/.

23. City of Indianapolis, "Mayor Grants Full Charter Renewal to School," news release, January 7, 2010, http://www.insideindianabusiness.com/newsitem.asp?id=39489.

24. Kathleen McGrory and Scott Hiaasen, "Charter Schools Enrolling Low Number of Poor Students," *Miami Herald*, December 16, 2011, http://www.miamiherald.com/2011/12/16/2548465_p4/charters-schools-enrolling-low.html.

25. Jeb Bush and T. Willard Fair, *A New Lease on Learning: Florida's First Charter School*, Foundation for Florida's Future, n.d., http://heartland.org/sites/all/modules/custom/heartland_migration/files/pdfs/1880.pdf.

26. Paul A. Moore, "The Death of Florida's First Charter School," March 13, 2008, reposted at *Norm's Notes*, http://normsnotes2.blogspot.com/2008/03/death-of-floridas-first-charter-school.html.

Notes

27. Editorial, "A Charter to Profit," *St. Petersburg Times* (FL), September 22, 2002, http://www.sptimes.com/2002/09/22/Perspective/A_charter_to_profit.shtml.

28. Bill Berkowitz, "Neil Bush's Family Values," *Working for Change.com*, November 22, 2006, reposted at http://www.susanohanian.org/show_nclb_atrocities.php?id=2446.

29. Dan Dimaggio, "The Libyan Dictatorship Partially Owns the Company Scoring Your Kids' Standardized Tests," *Buzzflash*, March 9, 2011, http://www.truthout.org/buzzflash/commentary/item/10561-the-libyan-dictatorship-partially-owns-the-company-scoring-your-kids-standardized-tests.

30. Karen Francisco, "Schoolhouse Junkets," *Learning Curve* (blog), *Journal Gazette* (Fort Wayne, IN), September 19, 2011, http://www.journalgazette.net/article/20110919/blogs13/1109 19512.

31. Ibid.

32. Nicole Belle, "No Bush Left Behind," *Truthout*, reposted at *Crooks and Liars*, October 10, 2006, http://crooksandliars.com/2006/10/11/no-bush-left-behind.

33. William L. Bainbridge, "Bush Ties Prove to Be Lucrative," *Columbus Dispatch* (OH), August 19, 2006, http://schoolmatch.com/articles/cd2006Aug19.cfm.

34. Bill Kaczor, Associated Press, "Senators Ask for Winn Resignation, State Takeover of FCAT Grading," *Florida Times-Union's Jacksonville.com*, June 16, 2006, http://jacksonville.com/apnews/stories/061606/D8I9H3M01.shtml.

35. Information in this paragraph on Charter Schools USA comes from a personal interview with a researcher who wishes to remain unnamed.

36. Doug Martin, "Demetrio Perez Jr. Leading Miami-Dade School Board Race, Despite Not Running," *Common Errant*, December 24, 2011, http://btownerrant.com/2011/12/24/demet rio-perez-jr-leading-miami-dade-school-board-race-despite-not-running/.

37. Kent Fischer, "Public School Inc.," *St. Petersburg Times* (FL), September 15, 2002, http://www.sptimes.com/2002/09/15/State/Public_School_Inc.shtml.

38. Letitia Stein, "Osceola Insiders, Power Players Broker Charter-School Deals," *Orlando Sentinel*, December 22, 2003, http://articles.orlandosentinel.com/2003-12-22/news/0312220038 _1_charter-schools-osceola-building-schools.

39. Joe Follick, "School Changes under Pressure," *The Ledger* (Lakeland, FL), January 10, 2009, http://www.theledger.com/article/20090110/NEWS/901100359.

40. Kathleen Cullinan, "Bonita Charter Tries to Overcome the Turmoil: Education Takes Backseat to Restraining Orders, 911 Calls, Teacher Layoffs, Threats, Rumors," *Naples Daily News* (FL), August 12, 2007, last modified August 13, 2007, http://www.naplesnews.com/news /2007/aug/12/parents_hope_new_year_brings_new_story_bonita_char/?breaking_news.

41. Ibid.

42. Emails released to the media prove that some IDOE officials were very afraid of what was going on at the CS USA charter school in Indiana. Scott Elliott, after the AP email dump, examined more emails and wrote: "Far from minor turbulence, which Bennett and CSUSA suggested publicly at the time, the tone of emails from Bennett's staff suggest deep concern that the takeover at Howe could crash and burn just as it was getting off the ground." In one email, IDOE's director of students services wrote that the for-profit charter school outfit wasn't "'turning around' anything that I can tell," saying, as Elliott writes, that Howe rated "satisfactory on just six of 26 criteria." To see Elliott's story and the emails, go to "More Than a Year after Takeover of Some Failing Indianapolis Schools, Jury Still Out," *Indianapolis Star*, September 8, 2013, http://www.indystar.com/article/20130907/NEWS04/309070016/More-than-year-after-takeover-some-failing-Indianapolis-schools-jury-still-out. For other details I draw from for this section on Charter Schools USA's problems at Howe, see Adrienne Broaddus, "Parents

Notes

Complain about Howe High School," WISH-TV, August 29, 2012, http://www.wishtv.com/dpp/news/local/marion_county/parents-complain-about-howe-high-sch ool; John Tuohy, "Parents Sound Off about Problems with Howe High School: Concerns about Discipline, Teaching Have Mounted since It Became a Charter School This Year," *Indianapolis Star*, September 22, 2012, http://www.indystar.com/article/20120922/NEWS04/209220354/ Parents-sound-off-about-problems-Howe-High-School; and Scott Elliott, "School Takeover Hasn't Quite Taken at Howe," *Indianapolis Star*, September 21, 2012, http:www.indystar.co m/article/20120921/NEWS04/209210355/School-takeover-hasn-t-quite-taken.

43. Scott Elliott, "Star Watch: Concerns Arise on School Contracts: Terms Don't Specify How Much State Money Goes to Profit vs. Classroom," *Indianapolis Star*, August 5, 2012, http://www.indystar.com/article/20120805/NEWS04/208050351/Star-Watch-Concerns-arise-school-contracts.

44. J.K.Wall, "Battle for Students Raises Financial Concern for Turnaround Schools," *Indianapolis Business Journal*, March 8, 2012, http://www.ibj.com/battle-for-students-raises-financial-concern-for-turnaround-schools/PARAMS/article/33089.

45. Kyle Stokes, "Indianapolis Schools Chief: If the Budget's Cut Further, Expect Pain in Classrooms," *State Impact Indiana/NPR*, May 25, 2012, http://stateimpact.npr.org/indian a/2012/05/25/indianapolis-schools-chief-if-the-budgets-cut-further-expect-pain-in-classroo ms/.

46. I was the first one to break the story on Joe Biden's brother Frank's unpaid income taxes. See Doug Martin, "News Flash: VP Biden's Brother Frank Has an IRS Problem," *Common Errant*, December 21, 2011, http://btownerrant.com/2011/12/21/news-flash-vp-bidens-brother-frank-has-an-irs-problem/. In an interview with *Broward/Palm Beach New Times'* Lisa Rab, Frank Biden responded to my article concerning his tax debts. Rab writes the following: "Meanwhile, the vice president's brother also cleared up a mystery about a federal tax lien filed against him in Kentucky. The $32,500 in unpaid income taxes are from 2003 to 2005, a time when Biden says he was still struggling with alcohol addiction. Now, he says, he pays off the debt in monthly installments. 'That will be paid within a year,' he says." See "Frank Biden: 'We're Not Profiting from Our Schools,'" December 30, 2011, http://blogs.browardpalmbeach.com/pulp/2011/12/frank_biden_says_not_profiting_from_mave ricks_high_schools.php.

47. William March, "Jeb Bush's Education Foundation under Fire for Lobbying for Laws That Benefit Corporate Donors," March 3, 2012, *Tampa Tribune*, reposted at huffingtonpost.com/2013/03/03/jeb-bush-education-foundation_n_2802536.html.

48. Joseph B. Hoage, Re: Formal Complaint 12-FC-296; Alleged Violation of the Access to Public Records Act by the Indiana Department of Education, email to Louisa Abada of In the Public Interest, November 2, 2012. My Bennett FOIA story first appeared at *Schools Matter* under my editor Douglas Storm's title "Indiana DOE Stalls FOIA Naming Joel Klein and Jeb Bush and Detailing the Dog and Pony Tony Tour," November 3, 2012, http://www.schoolsmatter.info/2012/11/indiana-doe-stalls-foia-naming-joel.html. On election day, it was carried in the *Washington Post Answer Sheet* in Valerie Strauss's story "The Tangled Webs of Private Influence on Public School Reform," http://www.washingtonpost.com/blogs/answer-sheet/wp/2012/11/06/the-tangled-webs-of-privat e-influence-on-public-school-reform/.

49. Louisa Abada, Re: Formal Complaint, email to Indiana Office of the Public Access Counselor, In the Public Interest, October 3, 2012.

50. For details on Wireless Generation's contract with Indiana, see http://www.amplify.com/pdf/general/EERJanuary14_indiana.pdf.

Notes

51. Karen Francisco, "More Travels with Tony Bennett," *Learning Curve* (blog), *Journal Gazette* (Fort Wayne, IN), January 23, 2012, http://www.journalgazette.net/article/20120123/BLOGS13/120129771/1150.

52. Colin Woodard, "Special Report: The Profit Motive behind Virtual Schools in Maine, Documents Expose the Flow of Money and Influence from Corporations That Stand to Profit from State Leaders' Efforts to Expand and Deregulate Digital Education," *Portland Press Herald,* September 13, 2012, http://www.pressherald.com/news/virtual-schools-in-maine_2012-09-02.html.

53. Eleanor Chute, "Charter Schools Now Big Business Nationwide: Management Firms Bring Money, Clout to Help Operate Them," *Pittsburgh Post-Gazette*, December 30, 2012, http://www.post-gazette.com/stories/news/education/charter-schools-now-big-business-nationwide-668354/.

54. For this data, I cite pages 1 and 3 in David Spring's study *Drawbacks of K12 Inc. Online School Programs in Washington State and Options for Better Alternatives, Spring for Schools.org*, May 15, 2013, http://springforschools.org/.

55. David Safier, "Is AZVA the Only K12 Virtual School Outsourcing Education?," *Blog for Arizona*, August 12, 2008, http://arizona.typepad.com/blog/2008/08/is-azva-the-onl.html.

56. Stephanie Saul, "Profits and Questions at Online Charter Schools," *New York Times*, December 12, 2011, http://www.nytimes.com/2011/12/13/education/online-schools-score-better-on-wall-street-than-in-classrooms.html?_r=1.

57. Ibid.

58. Emma Brown, "Shareholder Lawsuit Accuses K12 Inc. of Misleading Investors," *Virginia Schools Insider* (blog), *Washington Post,* January 31, 2012, http://www.washingtonpost.com/blogs/virginia-schools-insider/post/shareholder-lawsuit-accuses-k12-inc-of-lying-about-student-test-grades/2012/01/31/gIQAGOXRfQ_blog.html.

59. Kristin Rawls, "Who Is Profiting from Charters? The Big Bucks behind Charter School Secrecy, Financial Scandal and Corruption," *AlterNet*, May 8, 2013, http://www.alternet.org/education/who-profiting-charters-big-bucks-behind-charter-school-secrecy-financial-scandal-and.

60. Lyndsey Layton and Emma Brown, "Virtual Schools Are Multiplying, but Some Question Their Educational Value," *Washington Post,* November 26, 2011, http://www.washingtonpost.com/local/education/virtual-schools-are-multiplying-but-some-question-their-educational-value/2011/11/22/gIQANUzkzN_story.html.

61. Lee Fang, "How Online Learning Companies Bought America's Schools," *The Nation*, December 5, 2011, http://www.thenation.com/article/164651/how-online-learning-companies-bought-americas-schools?page=full.

62. Karen Francisco, "Virtual Phys Ed?," *Learning Curve* (blog), *Journal Gazette* (Fort Wayne, IN), August 16, 2012, http://www.journalgazette.net/article/20120816/BLOGS13/120819662. See, too, Kyle Stokes, "Are Online Charter Companies Profiting from Underperforming Indiana Schools?," *State Impact Indiana*/NPR, December 13, 2011, http://stateimpact.npr.org/indiana/2011/12/13/are-online-charter-companies-profiting-from-underperforming-indiana-schools/.

63. You can read the entire Levesque email at *Northeast Friends of Indiana Public Education* (blog), "Florida Privatizer Stumps for Bennett," April 20, 2012, http://neifpe.blogspot.com/2012/04/florida-privatizer-stumps-for-bennett.html.

64. Here is the link to the Send Hub email: https://s3.amazonaws.com/s3.documentcloud.org/documents/559854/itpi-251.pdf. See page 8 in the 2008 990 for Foundation for Excellence in Education, http://www.guidestar.org/FinDocuments/2008/260/615/2008-

Notes

260615175-0575cbcc-9.pdf. Page 8, also, is where you can witness Levesque's payout in the 2009 990 for the Foundation for Florida's Future, http://www.guidestar.org/ FinDocuments/2008/260/615/2008-260615175-0575cbcc-9.pdf

65. Fang, "How Online Learning Companies Bought America's Schools."

66. Steve Hinnefeld, "One-Side Fundraising in the Campaign for Indiana Schools Chief," *School Matters*, April 20, 2012, http://inschoolmatters.wordpress.com/2012/04/20/one-side-fundraising-in-the-campaign-for-indiana-schools-chief/.

67. Karen Francisco, "Campaign Watch," *Learning Curve* (blog), *Journal Gazette* (Fort Wayne, IN), April 11, 2012, http://www.journalgazette.net/article/20120411/BLOGS13/120419 876/-1/blogs13.

68. Joseph B. Hoage, Re: Formal Complaint 12-FC-296.

69. For more on the Daniels and Bakke story, see Jason Vest, "Mitch Daniels: Due Diligence?" *American Prospect*, October 24, 2002, http://prospect.org/article/mitch-daniels-due-diligence and Chris O'Malley and Gargi Chakrabarty, "State Subpoenas 30 Business Elite: Regulators Probe Allegations Insiders 'Dumped' $71 Million in IPALCO Stock," *Indianapolis Star*, May 7, 2003, reposted at http://www.commondreams.org/headlines03/0507-02.htm. My quotation comes from Vest's article.

70. Strom, "For School Company, Issues of Money and Control."

71. Ibid.

72. Brian Louis, "Property Investors Bet on Rising Demand for U.S. Charter Schools," *Bloomberg News*, January 11, 2012, http://www.bloomberg.com/news/2012-01-11/property-investors-bet-on-rising-demand-for-u-s-charter-school-campuses.html.

73. Karen Francisco, "A Taxing Tale," *Journal Gazette* (Fort Wayne, IN), April 17, 2011, http://www.journalgazette.net/article/20110417/EDIT/304179965/1147/EDIT07.

74. This entire paragraph draws on the series of articles by the Fort Wayne *Journal Gazette's* Kelly Soderlund and Dan Stockman entitled "Education Inc." at http://www.journalgazette.net/apps/pbcs.dll/article?AID=/20091102/LOCAL10/311029969. See also Kelly Soderlund's "Imagine's Closed Votes Broke Law, Expert Says: Board Denies Any Secret Dealings on Texas School Plans," *Journal Gazette* (Fort Wayne, IN), December 17, 2009, http://www.journalgazette.net/article/20091217/LOCAL04/312179972/1216/LOCAL1006. In one article, the authors discuss how Bakke sent out a memo to Imagine school officials across the country, reminding them that he (and not the local boards and taxpayers) owns the schools. You can find that piece at http://www.journalgazette.net/article/20091102/LOCAL10/3110299 69/1186/LOCAL1005.

75. Sarah Janssen, "Third Site Denied for Imagine's Bridge Academy," *News-Sentinel* (Fort Wayne, IN), March 18, 2010, http://www.news-sentinel.com/apps/pbcs.dll/article?AID=/SE/ 20100318/NEWS/3180312.

76. Sarah Janssen, "Imagine Continues to Meet Demands: New Board Members Seated as Achievement Report Is Presented," *News-Sentinel* (Fort Wayne, IN), March 16, 2010, http://www.news-sentinel.com/apps/pbcs.dll/article?AID=/SE/20100316/NEWS/3160329.

77. Kelly Soderlund, "Keystone Asks Parents to Pay More: 2 Say Private School Needing $450,000 to Stay Open," *Journal Gazette* (Fort Wayne, IN), February 2, 2010, http://www.journalgazette.net/article/20100202/LOCAL04/302029944.

78. The story on Keystone teachers' walkout was at the Indiana News Center website (http://www.indianasnewscenter.com/news/94743459.html) and has now been removed.

79. Sarah Janssen, "Private Investors to Take Over at Keystone: School Founder Don Willis, Board Members Agree to Step Down," *Fort Wayne.com*, May 25, 2010, http://www.fortwayne.com/apps/pbcs.dll/article?AID=/SE/20100525/NEWS/5250338.

Notes

80. Ashley Smith, "Former Imagine Administrator Files Lawsuit against School," *News-Sentinel* (Fort Wayne, IN), February 17, 2010, http://www.news-sentinel.com/apps/pbcs.dll/art icle?AID=/20100217/NEWS/2170319.

81. Kelly Soderlund and Dan Stockman, "Education Inc.—Part II: It's 'Our School, Not Theirs': Company's Boss Gives Little Authority to Charter Boards," *Journal Gazette* (Fort Wayne, IN), November 2, 2009, http://www.journalgazette.net/article/20091102/LOCAL10/311029969/1216/LOCAL1006.

82. Sylvia A. Smith, "Feds Gave $11 Million to Imagine Schools," *Journal Gazette* (Fort Wayne, IN), November 4, 2009, http://www.journalgazette.net/article/20091104/NEWS03/311049954/-1/NEWS09.

83. Elisa Crouch, "Imagine Schools Executive Named in Contractor's Bank Payments," *St. Louis Post-Dispatch*, October 30, 2011, stltoday.com/news/local/education/article_c1c363e4-b7fb-5d19-8f12-a592e5f7d3d3.html.

84. Niki Kelly, "State School Board Member in Probe Resigns," *Journal Gazette* (Fort Wayne, IN), July 26, 2011, http://www.journalgazette.net/article/20110726/LOCAL04/1107295 90.

85. "Did Indiana State Board of Education Member and Charter School Principal Plagiarize Dissertation at Purdue?," *Plagiaristas* (blog), March 16, 2011, http://plagiaristas.blogspot.com/2011/03/did-indiana-state-board-of-education.html.

86. For comparisons, see G. G. Adell, "African American Female Administrators: Leadership in Context" (PhD diss., Purdue University, 2004), ProQuest (AAI 3166587) and M.L. Amedy, "A Qualitative Study of Female Superintendents: Leadership Behaviors in Context" (PhD diss., Virginia Polytechnic Institute, 1999), CiteSeer (ETD 042699-151803).

87. My letter to Daniels and Purdue officials can be found at Doug Martin, "Purdue Must Investigate Indiana State Board of Education Member Gwendolyn G. Adell for Academic Dishonesty," *MyFiredoglake*, April 12, 2011, http://my.firedoglake.com/dougmartin/2011/04/12/letter-to-mitch-daniels-purdue-university-report-of-academic-dishonesty-by-gwendolyn-g-adell-indiana-state-board-of-education-member/.

88. Karen Franciso, "Plagiarism Charge Dogs Educator," *Journal Gazette* (Fort Wayne, IN), May 1, 2011, http://www.journalgazette.net/article/20110501/EDIT05/305019965/1021/EDIT.

89. Ibid.

90. Tom Matrka, comment on "'Sunlight Is the Best Disinfectant'—Louis Brandeis," *Plagiaristas* (blog), May 15, 2011, http://plagiaristas.blogspot.com/2011/05/sunlight-is-best-disenfectant-louis.html.

91. Rob Earnshaw, "Daniels Addresses Education during Visit to Valpo," *Times of Northwest Indiana* (Munster, IN), April 21, 2011, http://www.nwitimes.com/news/local/porter/valpa raiso/article_97cd474c-d28a-526d-9255-79dcf06e4d38.html.

92. Gwendolyn Adell, "Traditional Public Schools vs. Public Charter Schools," *Times of Northwest Indiana* (Munster, IN), May 8, 2011, http://www.nwitimes.com/news/opinion/guest-commentary/editorial-advisory-board-traditional-public-schools-vs-public-charter-schools/articl e_3d5826a9-cb9b-5866-886f-03a5fe16a97b.html.

93. Curt Dudley-Marling and Diana Baker, "The Effects of Market-Based School Reforms on Students with Disabilities," *Disability Studies Quarterly* 32, no. 2 (2012), http://dsq-sds.org/article/view/3187/3072.

94. Strom, "For School Company, Issues of Money and Control."

95. Doug Martin, "Noble Charter School Network's Taking It to the Bank," *Common Errant*, March 3, 2012, http://btownerrant.com/2012/03/03/noble-charter-school-networks-taking-it-to-the-bank/.

Notes

96. Niki Kelly, "Daniels Awaits Copying Probe: Will Decide Fate of School Official," *Journal Gazette* (Fort Wayne, IN), May 18, 2011, http://www.journalgazette.net/article/20110518/NEWS07/305189953/1067/NEWS07.

97. Karen Francisco, "An Overdue Vacancy," *Learning Curve* (blog), *Journal Gazette* (Fort Wayne, IN), July 27, 2011, http://www.journalgazette.net/article/20110727/BLOGS13/110729540.

98. Ibid.

99. Ibid.

100. Ibid.

101. Before Mitch Daniels headed off to Purdue, he stacked the board of directors at the Indiana School for the Deaf with anti-sign language crusaders and members associated with Hear Indiana, a branch of the Alexander Graham Bell Association for the Deaf and Hard of Hearing, a promoter of cochlear implants for corporations, often futile lip-reading, and the oral-verbal teaching which forces deaf students to stop signing in an attempt to speak English. It is a crude tactic which held sway for one hundred years in the dark ages of our country's linguistic history. The AG Bell group—aligned with cochlear implant companies and the Lilly Endowment—grew out of Bell's outdated, immoral, and dangerous beliefs in eugenics and the inferiority of deaf people. Hear Indiana and medical device companies encourage drilling through the mastoid bone to the inner ear of a deaf infant, risking permanent facial paralysis, bacterial meningitis, and other complications without guaranteeing success. Oticon, MED-EL, and others from the medical industry supporting AG Bell overstate the wonderful results of cochlear implants so they can profit from them. Even the FDA notes that implants do not benefit some children at all to develop spoken language. Recently, IU School of Medicine's Derek Houston claimed that infants with cochlear implants score poorly on recognizing speech years down the road. The earlier the implant is done, IU's Mario Svirsky and Rachael Holt explain, the better the results for language development, but implanting children under the age of one is very risky business and drastically increases the chances for serious health problems. Even implanting infants under the age of one does not seem to guarantee the improvement of the child's speech perception, which is essential for full spoken language comprehension.

One Hear Indiana donor is the Mind Trust/Marian University/Friedman Foundation-funding Ackerman Foundation, whose trustee is John F. Ackerman. Ackerman is now onboard with the Challenge Foundation charter schools. A Teach for America funder and board member of the school voucher-supporting Hoosiers for Economic Growth Network and the Educational Choice Charitable Trust Foundation, Ackerman works at Cardinal Equity Partners, a private equity group which owns a good deal of Angie's List (which Ackerman directed at one point) and Williams Sound (where Ackerman is chairman), a Minnesota manufacturer of assistive listening devices for the deaf and hard of hearing. Scholars believe all deaf children should learn ASL, even if parents do decide to have them equipped with cochlear implants, for there is a window to developing any language, and if this is ignored, children risk growing up with no language whatsoever and no communication avenue, at all, later in life. To eliminate ASL from the ISD curriculum would be a tragedy.

The common-sense argument against having AG Bell/Hear Indiana representatives on the ISD school board is very simple. It is one of human rights—not corporate profit. It should not be left to any governor or special interest group to play God when it comes to language. Daniels ignored protests from the deaf community. Instead of following deaf people's commands of putting deaf people on the board of the school, in early March 2012 the Indiana General Assembly hammered another blow to special needs students when it voted to transfer educational outreach services to deaf kids and families from the Indiana School for the Deaf to a new and

Notes

so-called independent center by July 2013. Republican Cindy Noe, the non-voting member Daniels selected to sit on the Indiana School for the Deaf board, sponsored the House bill. Hear Indiana, the Alexander Graham Bell group, was behind its passage. Scott Rigney, another Hear Indiana-supported person Mitch Daniels handpicked to fill an Indiana School for the Deaf board seat, was a funder to Noe's campaign. Rigney's wife is a board member at Hear Indiana.

Cindy Noe paid the price, though. In November 2013, the deaf community helped kick her out of office. For this history, see Michael Reis, "Guest Voices: An Unusual Political Alliance," *NUVO*, January 18, 2013, http://www.nuvo.net/GuestVoices/archives/2013/01/18/guest-voices-an-unusual-political-alliance#.Ua97WIzD8cA and Michelle Westfall, "Indiana School for the Deaf vs. Hear Indiana," *DeafEcho*, http://www.deafecho.com/2012/01/indiana-school-for-the-deaf-vs-hear-indiana/.

For the above information, see Alexander Graham Bell Association for the Deaf and Hard of Hearing, "Advanced Bionics Renews Circle Alliance Partnership with AG Bell," news release, Washington, DC, February 2, 2006, http://agbell.org//Page.aspx?pid=812. Alexander Graham Bell Association for the Deaf and Hard of Hearing, "Cochlear Americas Renews AG Bell Circle Alliance Partnership," news release, Washington, DC, February 21, 2006, http://agbell.org//Page.aspx?pid=813. US Food and Drug Administration, "Benefits and Risks of Cochlear Implants," http://www.fda.gov/MedicalDevices/ProductsandMedicalProcedures/ImplantsandProsthetics/CochlearImplants/UCM062843; Derek M. Houston, "Deaf Infants' Attention to Speech after Cochlear Implantation," *Acoustical Society of America* 129, no. 4 (2011): 2413-2413, http://asadl.org/jasa/resource/1/jasman/v129/i4/p2413_s3?bypassSSO=1; and Mario Svirsky and Rachael Frush Holt, "The 'Forbidden Experiment' in Language Development." Paper presented at the Joint ASA/CAA Meeting, Vancouver, BC, May 16, 2005, http://www.aip.org/149th/svirsky.html.

102. Gülen's tax money is noted in a protest speech by Sharon Higgins, the person who knows more than anyone about this group's charter school activity. You can find the speech at http://www.youtube.com/watch?v=RM1K12XdOLk.

103. "Turkey's Religious Gülen Community Subject of Latest WikiLeaks," *Hurriyet Daily News*, March 17, 2011, http://www.hurriyetdailynews.com/default.aspx?pageid=438&n=turkish-daily-starts-wikileaks-coverage-with-gulen-community-2011-03-17.

104. Joshua D Hendrick, "Globalization and Marketized Islam in Turkey: The Case of Fethullah Gülen" (PhD diss., University of California, Santa Cruz, 2011), ProQuest (AAT 3367722).

105. As the *Philadelphia Inquirer* noted on March 20, 2011, prosecutors in Scranton, Pennsylvania, were coordinating the investigations which involved hundreds of Gülen charter school members nationwide, but because Gülen is well entrenched in all levels of US government, the FBI has not spoken a word of the investigation since. See Martha Woodall and Claudio Gatti, "U.S. Charter-School Network with Turkish Link Draws Federal Attention," *Philly.com*, March 20, 2011, http://articles.philly.com/2011-03-20/news/29148147_1_gulen-schools-gulen-followers-charter-schools.

106. Mary Taylor, *Horizon Science Academy-Dayton, Montgomery County, Initial Audit for the Period May 1, 2005 through June 30, 2006*, 27, http://www.auditor.state.oh.us/AuditSearch/Reports/2008/Horizon_Science_Academy_Dayton_06-Montgomery.pdf.

107. Ibid., 27.

108. This information comes from the Myvisajobs.com database which draws from a whole host of government records.

Notes

109. Chicago ACTS, "Charter School Agrees to Settlement for Pregnant Teacher Who Was Fired for Organizing Union," news release, April 2011, reposted at http://charterschoolscandals.blogspot.com/2010/08/chicago-math-and-science-academy.html.

110. See Indiana Math and Science Academy's 2007 Form 990, page 10, http://www.guidestar.org/FinDocuments/2008/205/751/2008-205751308-04c999e3-9.pdf.

111. Visit Indiana Math and Science Academy's 2008 Form 990, page 10, http://www.guidestar.org/FinDocuments/2009/205/751/2009-205751308-060710fe-9.pdf.

112. Ibid., 8.

113. See page 46 in Indiana Department of Education's contract with Indiana Math and Science Academy-North, 2010, https/financial.gmis.in.gov/IDOAcontracts/public/59807-000.pdf.

114. For a picture and brief write-up of Bilal's award, see the FBI's website: fbi.gov/about-us/partnerships_and_outreach/community_outreach/dcla/2008/indianapolis08.

115. To witness photos of Tony Bennett and Dick Lugar at the big Gülen event, go to http://www.niagarafoundation.org/indiana/?p=2428.

116. For Mitch posing in front of the cameras with Gülenists, go to http://www.niagarafoundation.org/indiana/?p=2405.

117. "A Day of Remembrance," *Indianapolis Recorder*, April 7, 2011, http://www.indianapolisrecorder.com/news/print_highlights/image_97c03294-612f-11e0-98bc-001cc4c03286.html. Bart Peterson also dropped in on the Niagara Foundation with Dan Burton. See http://www.niagarafoundation.org/indiana/?p=2404.

118. Marc D. Allan, "Building a Bridge: Judy O'Bannon's Foreign Exchange: Turkey Bridge under Construction, November 27 WFYI (Channel 20)," *NUVO*, November 25, 2008, http://www.nuvo.net/indianapolis/building-a-bridge/Content?oid=1263890#.Ug9kxIzD9Ms.

119. Notice, too, that Vernon Smith, an Indiana Democratic lawmaker, is in this photo at http://www.flickr.com/photos/nigaraindiana/5597923869/in/photostream.

120. The award picture can be downloaded at http://www.flickr.com/photos/nigaraindiana/5611672034/.

121. Indiana Resolution 36 for Gülen is posted at http://www.in.gov/legislative/bills/2011/SRESF/SC0036.html.

122. *New Challenges & New Opportunities, Tuskon Proceedings*, Turkic American Alliance, Second Annual Convention, (Washington, DC: Rethink Institute, November 30, 2011), 91, http://rethinkinstitute.org/files/TAA%20Convention%202011.pdf.

123. Edmonds' Gülen testimony segment has been posted on YouTube. You can watch it at http://www.youtube.com/watch?v=OMG35qDzi1E&feature=related. Video tapes of Edmonds' whole deposition are available on *Brad's Blog* at http://www.bradblog.com/?p=7374. Edmonds' story has been mentioned on *60 Minutes* and made into a documentary entitled *Kill the Messenger*. You can study the *60 Minutes* show, "Incompetent Translators at Guantanamo Bay," at http://www.youtube.com/watch?v=aNkXrTWxTrw.

124. Philip Giraldi, "Who's Afraid of Sibel Edmonds?," *American Conservative*, November 1, 2009, http://www.theamericanconservative.com/articles/whos-afraid-of-sibel-edmonds/.

125. Sibel Deniz Edmonds, Before the Ohio Elections Commission, Disposition in the Matter of Jean Schmidt, Plaintiff, v. David Krikorian, Defendant, Case No. 2009E-003 (Washington, DC: National Whistleblower Center, August 8, 2009), 96, http://www.bradblog.com/Docs/SibelEdmondsDeposition_Transcript_080809.pdf.

126. Ibid., 46-47.

127. Ibid., 159.

Notes

128. Although links to all campaign donations mentioned in this book will be online at my website, if you want to easily find the hyperlinks showing the Turkish groups funding Burton's campaign, see my article "Teaching as CIA Cover—Gülen Charter Schools, Dan Burton, and State Secrets," *Common Errant*, May 3, 2012, http://btownerrant.com/2012/05/03/teaching-ascia-cover-gulen-charter-schools-dan-burton-and-state-secrets/.

129. Some of Lincoln McCurdy's bio is drawn from the Sunlight Foundation. See http://reporting.sunlightfoundation.com/2009/defense-contractors-join-turkish-lobbying-effort-in-pursuit-of-/. Visit, also, "Congressman Dan Burton (R-IN) and TCA President Lincoln McCurdy Meet," Turkish Coalition of America, n.d., http://www.tc-america.org/news-events/ev ents/events/past-events/congressman-dan-burton-r-in-and-tca-president-lincoln-mccurdy-meet-19.htm.

130. You can witness a clip of Burton's speech at http://www.youtube.com/watch?v=1uCTHeNi7IM.

131. For details on Baran Cansever's career and this quotation, see his LinkedIn page at http://www.linkedin.com/pub/baran-cansever/45/938/1a.

132. *A Review of the FBI's Actions in Connection with Allegations Raised by Contract Linguist Sibel Edmonds, Unclassified Summary*, US Department of Justice, Office of the Inspector General, Office of Oversight and Review, January 2005, http:www.fas.org/irp/agency/doj/oig/sedmonds.html.

133. Study "FBI Whistleblower Sibel Edmonds: 'I Will Tell All, & Name (New) Names,'" at *Let Sibel Edmonds Speak*, October 29, 2007, http://letsibeledmondsspeak.blogspot.com/2007/10 /10/fbi-whistleblower-sibel-edmonds-i-will.html. See, also, Lauren Johnston, "FBI Whistle-blower Claims Confirmed," CBS *Evening News*, February 11, 2009, http://www.cbsnews.com/ 2100-18563_162-632983.html.

134. For Osman Nuri Gundes' story, read Sibel Edmonds' "Turkish Intel Chief Exposes CIA Operations via Islamic Group in Central Asia," *Boiling Frogs* (blog), January 6, 2011, http://www.boilingfrogspost.com/2011/01/06/turkish-intel-chief-exposes-cia-operations-via-islamic-group-in-central-asia/.

135. Sibel Deniz Edmonds, Before the Ohio Elections Commission, 97.

136. Lesley Stahl, "U.S. Charter Schools Tied to Powerful Turkish Imam," *60 Minutes*, May 13, 2012, http://www.cbsnews.com/8301-18560_162-57433131/u.s-charter-schools-tied-to-powerful-turkish-imam/.

137. "Koch Industries' Secret Meeting," September 24, 2010, posted online by *Think Progress*, page 10, http://images2.americanprogressaction.org/ThinkProgress/secretkochme eting.pdf.

138. "All Receipts Reported by All Children Matter from John Bryan," (Richmond, VA: Virginia Public Access Project, 2007), http://vpap.org/committees/profile/money_in_details/ 97?donor_id=71683.

139. Matt Dixon, "Out-of-State School Choice Cash Winning Votes, Splitting Democrats," *Florida Times-Union (Jacksonville, FL)*, May 23, 2011, http://jacksonville.com/news/florida /2011-05-24/story/out-state-school-choice-cash-winning-votes-splitting-democrats#ixzz2MNsg dXGF.

140. Challenge Foundation, Form 990-PF, Return of Private Foundation. See page 42 for funding to Tindley, page 43 for money for Teach for America, and page 46 for financial gifts to the Institute for Justice and the Friedman Foundation, http://www.docstoc.com/docs/91783718/_Foc-990-PF-Return-of-Private-Foundation.

Notes

141. Sarah Ovaska, "Charter's Conservative Backers Raise Questions," *NC Policy Watch.com*, April 20, 2011, http://www.ncpolicywatch.com/2011/04/20/charters-conservative-backers-raise-questions/.

142. Ibid.

143. This information comes from Team CFA's minutes for a meeting on October 26, 2011, page 7.

144. "New Market Tax Credit Program, Challenge Foundation Academy, Indianapolis, IN, $5,000,000," Charter Schools Development Corporation, http://csdc.org/what-we-do/tax-credit-financing/challenge-foundation-academy.aspx.

145. Challenge Foundation Academy Indy, "Executive Summary," Indianapolis Mayor's Office, page 3, http://www.indy.gov/eGov/Mayor/programs/education/Charter/Documents/PDF / ChallengeProWebsite.pdf.

146. David Harris, "The Mind Trust Announces Second Class of Education Entrepreneur Fellows," news release, December 4, 2008, page 3, www.teachplus.org/uploads/Documents/1296683931_2nd_Cohort_announcement.pdf.

147. For Zink's loan, see page 27 in PDF box in Charles A. Tindley Accelerated School's Form 990 for 2007 at http://www2.guidestar.org/FinDocuments/2008/352/151/2008-352151971-04c05f19-9.pdf.

148. Garcia's paycheck, as well as Phalen's, is noted on page 8 of the Challenge Foundation Academy Indy's 2010 Form 990 at http://www.guidestar.org/FinDocuments/2011/134/289/201 1/134/289/2011-134289579-08409882-9.pdf.

149. Barbara Miner, "Ultimate $uperpower: Supersized Dollars Drive 'Waiting for Super-man' Agenda," *Not Waiting for Superman.org*, October 20, 2010, http://www.notwaitingforsuperman.org/Articles/20101020-MinerUltimateSuperpower.

150. "Warren Buffett: The Man behind the Name," *Indianapolis Star*, September 29, 2011, http://www.indystar.com/article/20110929/BUSINESS/109290356/Warren-Buffett-man-behind -name.

151. Ken Libby, "ERN's Largest Donation," *DFER Watch*, July 26, 2010, http://dferwatch.wordpress.com/2010/07/26/787/.

152. Leonie Haimson, "The Tangled Web of Influence behind Klein's Decision to Allow the Expansion of Girls Prep Charter to Go Forward," *NYC Public School Parents* (blog), August 9, 2010, http://nycpublicschoolparents.blogspot.com/2010/08/tangled-web-of-influence-behind-kleins.html.

153. Amy Hensley, "Tax Credits Enable Strategic Capital Partners to Move Forward with Avondale Meadows Redevelopment," Strategic Capital Partners, news release, July 12, 2010, http://www.strategiccapitalpartners.net/documents/news_documents/2010-05_Tax_Credits.pdf.

154. Kenneth J. Saltman, *Capitalizing on Disaster: Taking and Breaking Public Schools* (Boulder, CO: Paradigm Publishers, 2007), 135-136.

155. Pauline Lipman, "Making Sense of Renaissance 2010 School Policy in Chicago: Race, Class, and the Cultural Politics of Neoliberal Urban Restructuring," Great Cities Institute Publication GCP-09-02, Great Cities Institute Working Paper, January 2009, page 7, http://www.uic.edu/cuppa/gci/publications/workingpaperseries/pdfs/GCP-09-02_Lipman.pdf.

156. Kenneth J. Saltman, *Capitalizing on Disaster*, 135.

157. Shaila Dewan, "Gentrification Changing Face of New Atlanta," *New York Times*, March 11, 2006, nytimes.com/2006/03/11/national/11atlanta.html?pagewanted=all&_r=0.

158. Philippa Strum, "Communities of Hope and Opportunity: The Revitalization of East Lake," *Wilson Center.org*, March 27, 2007, http://www.wilsoncenter.org/event/creating-communities-hope-and-opportunity-the-revitalization-east-lake.

Notes

159. Glen Ford, "The Whitening of Chocolate City," *OpEd News*, January 6, 2011, http://www.opednews.com/articles/2/The-Whitening-of-Chocolate-by-Glen-Ford-110106-286.html.

160. Naomi Spencer, "Atlanta Homeless Shelters Strain under Economic Crisis," *World Socialist Web Site*, October 23, 2009, http://www.wsws.org/en/articles/2009/10/atla-o23.html.

161. Alexandra Rice, "A Community Approach Helps Transform Atlanta Neighborhood: East Lake Went from 'War Zone' to a National Model," *Education Week*, September 14, 2011, http://www.edweek.org/ew/articles/2011/09/14/03community_ep.h31.html.

162. "John Bryan Indy Speech 2011," Team CFA, http://vimeo.com/35720321.

163. Indiana State Board of Accounts, *Examination Report of Challenge Foundation Academy, Marion County, Indiana, October 25, 2005 to June 30, 2007*, filed April 24, 2008, pages 15-16, http://www.in.gov/sboa/WebReports/B31791.pdf.

164. Andy Gammill, "Two Indy Charter Schools Land State Grants: $3.8M Will Help Expand Instruction at Met, Challenge Foundation Academy," *Indianapolis Star*, June 22, 2010, http://www.indystar.com/article/20100622/NEWS04/6220320/1013/NEWS04/2-Indy-charter-schools-land-state-grants.

165. J.K. Wall, "Ball State Gives New Life to Fountain Square Charter," *Indianapolis Business Journal*, April 20, 2012, http://www.ibj.com/ball-state-gives-new-life-to-fountain-square-charter-school/PARAMS/article/33976.

166. David Harris, "Charter Performance Is Strong, but Accountability Is Critical," *Indianapolis Business Journal*, May 5, 2012, http://www.ibj.com/article/shared?userId=41275&key1=mQMvX3iebIQxlTNl5OIeYQpjC7e7AtzT&key2=haxYhiFDpNk%3D.

167. Elle Moxley, "Project School Board Members Tell Mayor New Students Need Time to Catch Up," *State Impact Indiana*/NPR, July 20, 2012, http://stateimpact.npr.org/indiana/2012/07/20/project-school-board-members-tell-mayor-new-students-need-time-to-catch-up/.

168. All quotations in this section, unless otherwise noted, come from personal email communications with interviewees.

169. Shaun Johnson's email can be found online at http://atthechalkface.com/2012/07/19/support-the-project-school-in-indianapolis-as-they-fight-against-closure/.

170. The mayor's December 2011 campaign report can be found at http://www.indy.gov/eGov/County/Clerk/Election/Candidate_Info/MCEBCampaignFinanceArchive/Filings/ballard%2C%20gregory_mayor-indy_2011-12-31_cfa-4-ann.pdf. See pages 21, 31, 41, 50, 54, 65, 78, 93, 109, 110, 111, and 117. These page numbers refer to the pages in the PDF boxes.

171. Scott Elliott, "Meet Jason Kloth, New Deputy Mayor for Education," *Indianapolis Star*, March 14, 2012, http://blogs.indystar.com/education/2012/03/14/meet-jason-kloth-new-deputy-mayor-for-education/.

172. Whitney Tilson, "Teach for America Alumnus, Jason Kloth Named Deputy Mayor of Education in Indianapolis," *Whitney Tilson's School Reform Blog*, March 23, 2012, http://edreform.blogspot.com/2012/03/teach-for-america-alumnus-jason-kloth.html.

173. Indiana State Board of Accounts, *Financial Statement and Federal Single Audit Report of KIPP Lead College Prep Charter School, Lake County, Indiana, July 1, 2009 to June 30, 2011*, filed March 27, 2012. See pages 23-27.

174. Joe Jasinski, "It May Be Do or Die for Indianapolis Charter School," *Indianapolis Business Journal*, November 6, 2010, http://www.ibj.com/it-may-be-do-or-die-for-indianapolis-charter-school/PARAMS/article/23258.

Notes

175. Jim Horn, "KIPP Indianapolis: Dropout and Pushout Factory," *Schools Matter*, August 25, 2011, http://www.schoolsmatter.info/2011/08/kipp-indianapolis-dropout-and-pushout.html. See the original at City of Indianapolis, Office of the Mayor, *Charter School Renewal Report, KIPP Indianapolis*, October 18, 2010, page 6, http://www.indy.gov/OEI/CharterRenewal/Docu ments/KIPP%20Renewal%20Report.pdf.

176. Ibid.

177. Jon Murray, "KIPP Charter School Is Sued in Sexual-Assault Case," *Indianapolis Star*, July 26, 2010, http://www.indystar.com/article/20100726/LOCAL18/7260335.

178. Indiana State Board of Accounts, *Financial Statement and Federal Single Audit Report of KIPP Lead College Prep Charter School*, pages 23-27, http://www.in.gov/sboa/WebReports/B40252.pdf.

179. Jim Horn, "A Former KIPP Teacher Shares Her Story," *Schools Matter*, September 8, 2012, http://www.schoolsmatter.info/2012/09/a-former-kipp-teacher-shares-her-story.html. See, also, Jim Horn, "The Facts about KIPP That Kevin Chavous Ignores," *Schools Matter*, August 6, 2012, http://www.schoolsmatter.info/2012/08/the-facts-about-kipp-that-kevin-chavous.html.

180. Leonie Haimson, "At KIPP, I Would Wake Up Sick, Every Single Day," *NYC Public School Parents* (blog), March 22, 2012, nycpublicschoolparents.blogspot.com/2012/03/at-kipp-i-would-wake-up-sick-every.html.

181. Matthew Tully, "What Glenda Ritz Got from Tony Bennett—A $1.7 Million Boondoggle, *Indianapolis Star*, April 12, 2013, http://www.indystar.com/article/20130412/NEWS08/304120048/Matthew-Tully-What-Glenda-Ritz-got-from-Tony-Bennett-1-7-million-boondoggle. See, also, Editorial, "$1.7 Million Debacle," *Journal Gazette* (Fort Wayne, IN), April 18, 2013, http://www.journalgazette.net/article/20130418/EDIT07/304189995/1021/EDIT.

182. Niki Kelly, "Urban League Employee Must Avoid Charter Process, Ruling Says," *Journal Gazette* (Fort Wayne, IN), November 10, 2011, http://www.journalgazette.net/article/20111110/LOCAL/111119960.

4 CONCLUSION: SAM'S CLUB'S HERO DEFEATED

1. To see Oberndorf's Tony Bennett introduction, go to http://www.youtube.com/watch? v=P1KB6loVMzM. Oberndorf's donations are detailed in Zaid Jilani's "Report: Meet the Billionaires Who Are Trying to Privatize Our Schools and Kill Public Education," *Think Progress*, May 21, 2011, http://thinkprogress.org/politics/2011/05/21/168363/billionaires-privatize-education/.

2. The Walton Family Foundation's donations can be examined at http://www.waltonfamilyfoundation.org/educationreform. For Ballard's gift to his old school, see his news release on May 19, 2011, which is posted at *Inside Indiana Business* under the title "CEOs for New Schools," http://www.insideindianabusiness.com/newsitem.asp?ID=47786.

3. Digby, "American Dynasty: Wal-Mart's Walton Family Has the Wealth of 48.8 Million Families Combined," *AlterNet*, July 19, 2012, http://www.alternet.org/newsandviews/article/1034216/american_dynasty%3A_wal-mart's_walton_famly_has_the_wealth_of_48.8_million_families_combined/. Read, also, Josh Bivens, "Inequality, Exhibit A: Walmart and the Wealth of American Families," *Economic Policy Institute Blog*, July 17, 2012, http://www.epi.org/blog/inequality-exhibit-wal-mart-wealth-american/.

4. Jim Hopkins, "Wal-Mart Heirs Pour Riches into Reforming Education," *USA Today*, March 11, 2004, http://usatoday30.usatoday.com/educate/Entre14walmart.pdf.

Notes

5. Steven Greenhouse, "As Firms Line Up on Factories, Wal-Mart Plans Solo Effort," *New York Times*, May 14, 2013, http://www.nytimes.com/2013/05/15/business/six-retailers-join-bangladesh-factory-pact.html?_r=0.

6. These particulars are highlighted in Robert Greenwald's 2005 Brave New Films movie *Wal-Mart: The High Cost of Low Prices*.

7. David Moberg, "Wal-Mart's Shocking Impact on the Lives of Hundreds of Millions of People," *American Prospect*, April 28, 2011, reposted at alternet.org/story/150781/wal-mart%27s_shocking_impact_on_the_lives_of_hundreds_of_millions_of_people.

8. *Disclosures of Employers Whose Workers and Their Dependents Are Using State Health Insurance Programs* (Washington, DC: Good Jobs First, January 18, 2012), http://www.goodjobsfirst.org/corporate-subsidy-watch/hidden-taxpayer-costs.

9. Ellen E. Schultz and Theo Francis, "Companies Profit on Workers' Deaths through 'Dead Peasants' Insurance," *Wall Street Journal*, April 19, 2002, http://online.wsj.com/public/resources/documents/april_19.htm. For the story of the family who ended up with medical and funeral bills while Walmart got an $80,000 payout, watch Michael Moore's *Capitalism: A Love Story*.

10. David Barstow, Alejandra Xanic von Bertrab, and James C. McKinley Jr., "Wal-Mart Hushed Up a Vast Mexican Bribery Case," *New York Times*, April 21, 2012, http://www.nytimes.com/2012/04/22/business/at-wal-mart-in-mexico-a-bribe-inquiry-silenced.html?pagewanted=all.

11. *Wal-Mart Subsidy Report for Indiana* (Washington, DC: Good Jobs First, n.d.), http://www.walmartsubsidywatch.org/state_detail.html?state=IN.

12. Maureen Groppe, "Gov. Mitch Daniels Claims Teachers Used Illegal Tactics to Defeat GOP State Education Chief Tony Bennett," *Indianapolis Star*, December 1, 2012, http://www.indystar.com/article/20121130/NEWS07/121130014/Gov-Mitch-Daniels-claims-teachers-used-illegal-tactics-defeat-GOP-state-education-chief-Tony-Bennett.

13. Tom LoBianco, Associated Press, "Report: Grade Changed for Republican Donor Christel DeHaan's Charter School," *Indianapolis Star*, July 29, 2013, http://www.indystar.com/viewart/20130729/NEWS05/307290048/Report-Grade-changed-Republican-donor-Christel-DeHaans-charter-school. Bennett's buddy Michael Klentschy also ran into some trouble with his fake statistics, when he was sentenced to time in jail for submitting false test scores for a federal grant. See Karen Francisco, "Blinded by Science," August 28, 2012, *Learning Curve* (blog), *Journal Gazette* (Fort Wayne, IN), http://www.journalgazette.net/article/20120828/BLOGS13/120829507.

14. See page 10 in DeHaan charter school's Forms 990 at http://www.cha.christelhouse.org/includes/CHA990_Current.pdf, http://www.guidestar.org/FinDocuments/2011/020/550/2011-020550824-085750d1-9.pdf, and http://www.guidestar.org/FinDocuments/2012/020/550/2012-020550824-094a6b4a-9.pdf.

15. Visit page 9 of the 2012 Form 990 at http://www.guidestar.org/FinDocuments/2012/020/550/2012-020550824-094a6b4a-9.pdf.

16. You can see the officials in their work hats at http://www.indy.gov/OEI/Media/Pages/MayorBallardHelpsBreakGroundforChristelHouse-WatanabeHighSchool.aspx.

17. "Official Caught Using Escort Service Demanded Anti-Prostitution 'Loyalty Oaths,'" *Think Progress*, April 28, 2007, http://thinkprogress.org/politics/2007/04/28/12368/tobias-prostitution/.

18. DeHaan has a "Donor Honor Roll" posted on the school's website, which can be accessed at http://www.cha.christelhouse.org/includes/AR2006donorlist.pdf.

Notes

19. Steve Hinnefeld, "More on the Money behind the Indiana School-Voucher Law, *School Matters*, July 30, 2012, http://inschoolmatters.wordpress.com/2012/07/30/more-on-the-money-behind-the-indiana-school-voucher-law/.

20. *Program-Related Investments: Social Investments* (Baltimore, MD: Annie E. Casey Foundation, 2006), 9-13, http://www.aecf.org/~/media/Pubs/Other/P/ProgramRelatedInvesti ngandtheIndianapolisChar/accion.pdf.

21. Larry Miller, "JP Morgan Helping Finance Charter Schools," *Larry Miller's Blog*, May 29, 2010, http://millermps.wordpress.com/2010/05/29/jp-morgan-helping-finance-charter-schools/.

22. See page 28 in the Form 990 for Reading Edge Academy at http://www.guidestar.org/FinDocuments/2010/593/455/2010-593455253-068f8c25-9.pdf.

23. Daniels' email can be read at http://hosted.ap.org/specials/interactives/documents/dan iels2.pdf.

24. Editorial, "Daniels Shows His True School Colors," *Journal Gazette* (Fort Wayne, IN), July 19, 2013, journalgazette.net/article/20130719/EDIT07/307199994/1021/EDIT.

25. Christina Wilkie, "Bradley Foundation Awards $250,000 Prizes to Roger Ailes, Mitch Daniels," *Huffington Post*, June 12, 2013, http://www.huffingtonpost.com/2013/06/12/bradley-foundation-awards_n_3430858.html.

26. Daniels' Zinn emails are posted at http://hosted.ap.org/specials/interactives/document s/daniels1.pdf.

27. Matthew Gandal and Chester E. Finn Jr., "Teaching Democracy," Freedom Paper no. 2, Freedom Papers, Info USA (Washington, DC: Department of State, October 1996), http://usinfo.org/enus/media/pressfreedom/freedom2.htm.

28. *Buying a Movement: Right-Wing Foundations and American Politics*, (Washington, DC: People for the American Way, 1996), 9, http://www.pfaw.org/sites/default/files/buyingamovem ent.pdf.

29. Brittany Tyner, "Daniels Gets Extra $58,000 for First Six Months," WLFI, July 22, 2013, http://www.wlfi.com/dpp/news/local/daniels-gets-58000-for-first-six-months.

30. Daniels' original statement can be found at drive.google.com/folderview?id=0B-_vzxuVbPVvQ3hDcm9uMjg4X2s&usp=sharing.

31. David Plotnikoff, "Does Zinn's Alternative History Teach Bad Lessons?," Stanford Graduate School of Education, December 19, 2012, https://ed.stanford.edu/news/does-zinns-alternative-history-teach-bad-lessons.

32. Tom LoBianco, Associated Press, "Mitch Daniels Wanted to Replace Liberal Historian's Teachings in Favor of Bill Bennett's Conservative Review," *Indianapolis Star*, August 18, 2013, http://www.indystar.com/viewart/20130818/NEWS04/308180024/Mitch-Daniels-wanted-replace-liberal-historian-s-teachings-favor-Bill-Bennett-s-conservative-review.

33. "Bennett under Fire for Remarks on Blacks, Crime," CNN, September 30, 2005, http://www.cnn.com/2005/POLITICS/09/30/bennett.comments/.

34. Annual Report 2010, Sagamore Institute, 6, http://mediafiles.sagamoreinstitute.org.s 3.amazonaws.com/uploaded/a/0e1846985_annual-report-2010.pdf.

35. LoBianco, "Mitch Daniels Wanted to Replace."

36. Groppe, "Gov. Mitch Daniels Claims Teachers Used Illegal Tactics."

37. Niki Kelly, "Bennett's Emails Show Dislike for Democratic Opponent," *Journal Gazette* (Fort Wayne, IN), August 8, 2013, http://www.journalgazette.net/article/20130807/LOCAL04/ 130809595/-1/LOCAL11.

38. Douglas Storm, "Coercing Silence," *Schools Matter*, October 16, 2012, http://www.schoolsmatter.info/2012/10/coercing-silence.html.

Notes

39. Tom LoBianco, Associated Press, "Capitol Crossroads: Test Improvements Punctuated with Teacher Layoffs," *News and Tribune* (Jeffersonville, IN), July 15, 2012, newsandtribune.com/local/x941527089/CAPITOL-CROSSROADS-Test-improvements-punctuated-with-teacher-layoffs/print.

40. School Choice Indiana, "Expanded School Voucher Law to Take Effect," news release, June 28, 2013, *Inside Indiana Business*, http://www.insideindianabusiness.com/newsitem.asp?ID=60147.

41. Zack Kopplin, "Creationism Voucher Schools in Indiana: Choice Scholarship Program— 37 Schools," *Say No to Creationist Vouchers*, December 1, 2012, http://creationistvouchers.com/2012/12/01/creationist-voucher-schools-in-indiana/.

42. Megan Erbacher, "School Voucher Supporters Praise Program Expansion That Starts Monday," *Evansville Courier & Press*, June 28, 2013, http://www.courierpress.com/news/2013/jun/28/30pt-hed1-10-hed1-10-inches-p/.

43. Samm Quinn, "Many Vouchers Spent on Low-Rated Schools," *Statehouse File*, April 26, 2013, reposted at http://www.nuvo.net/PerspectivesinEducation/archives/2013/04/26/many-vouchers-spent-on-low-rated-schools#.UY_WmozD_IW.

44. School Choice Indiana gives the 30,000 figure.

45. Steve Hinnefeld, "Charter School Study: 'Tiresome' Questions Remain," *School Matters*, January 10, 2013, http://inschoolmatters.wordpress.com/2013/01/10/charter-school-study-tiresome-questions-remain/.

46. Sarah Janssen, "Imagine Schools to Reopen, Not as Charters," *Journal Gazette* (Fort Wayne, IN), June 8, 2013, http://www.journalgazette.net/article/20130608/LOCAL04/3060899 79/1002/LOCAL.

47. Carmen McCollum, "Gary Charter School to Return Unspent Grant Money," *Times of Northwest Indiana* (Munster, IN), December 11, 2012, http://www.nwitimes.com/news/local/lake/gary/gary-charter-school-to-return-unspent-grant-money/article_61e71333-6403-55 b1-b7e2-6420bee7d9f2.html.

48. Albert Einstein, "Why Socialism?," *Monthly Review,* May 1949, http://monthlyreview.org/2009/05/01/why-socialism.

49. Stewart, *The Good News Club*, 258.

INDEX

ABOUT THE AUTHOR

Awalt Whitman and Language Scholar, poet, and musician, Doug Martin's teaching experience has covered kindergarten through graduate school. While blogging at Bloomington, Indiana's *Common Errant* and *MyFiredoglake*, Martin wrote many exposures of those out to privatize and dismantle public education. Martin's research has been or will soon be used by or featured in the *Washington Post Answer Sheet*, ABC's *Nightline*, the Associated Press, *Diane Ravitch's Blog*, *Parents Across America.org*, *Charter School Scandals*, *Susan Ohanian's Testing Atrocities and Outrages* and *Research That Counts*, *@ The Chalk Face*, the *Rick Smith Show*, *Just Let Me Teach*, *Huntington Teacher*, *Peg with Pen*, NPR/*State Impact Florida*, NPR/*State Impact Indiana*, *The Pulp (Broward-Palm Beach New Times)*, *School Matters*, *A Teacher's Fight*, *Northeast Indiana Friends of Public Education Blog*, HEAL (Human Earth Animal Liberation), *NUVO*, *Advance Indiana*, *Indianapolis Star*, Fort Wayne *Journal Gazette*, Terre Haute's *Tribune Star*, *Times of Northwest Indiana*, and Indiana's *Post-Tribune*, among others.

A native Hoosier, Martin holds an MFA from Bowling Green State University and a PhD in literary prosody and nineteenth-century American literature from Oklahoma State University. His first book, *A Study of Walt Whitman's Mimetic Prosody: Free-Bound and Full-Circle*, was published by Edwin Mellon Press in 2004. He now blogs at *Schools Matter*.